What coaches say about The Basketball Coach

(some coaching positions may have changed)

"I definitely would recommend this to…anyone who wants to teach youngsters the finer points of the game.…I've never read anything more detailed regarding the fundamentals."
Dale Brown, former LSU Coach

"I can say, without question, that this is an excellent tool for teaching the fundamentals.…The great game of basketball is broken down into simple terms. Congratulations on a job well done."
Jim Calhoun, UConn Coach

"This book is not only for the young coach, but it is also appropriate for coaches, experienced or not, at all levels.…Young basketball players will be better trained, if coaches use your methods."
Charlene Curtis, former Temple U Coach

"It is one of the best teachers and guides for beginning coaches of young teams that I've seen."
Jack Mckinney, former NBA Coach

"What a wonderful basic resource.…It gave me the perfect information to coach effectively and with confidence."
John Been, Coach, Prairie duSac, WI

"Your discussions of a planned agenda for every practice has inspired me for two years now and, in a great part, is responsible for my success during this time."
Tom Luker, 7th grade Coach, Hartford, CT

"A coach's dream. A must for a beginning or experienced coach."
Lurline Jones, Univ. City HS Coach, Phila., PA

"Anyone interested in coaching basketball, from volunteer youth coach to high-school coach, should read this book."
Jon Wilson, former PA Director of Biddy Basketball

"Thank you for your efforts in putting this book together. It has proved invaluable…throughout our 7-12 program."
Steve Hartman, Beatrice, Nebraska, Coach

The Basketball Coach's
Phil Jackson, NBA

"People who know basketball, coaches who care about players, say this is the best book on fundamentals they have seen."
Robert Kuiserling, Odessa, MO, Youth Coach

"An outstanding learning tool for all ages. A must read for all coaches."
Stephanie Gaitley, former St. Joseph's Univ. Coach

"[A] splendid job. I wish there was a similar book when I began coaching."
"Speedy" Morris, former LaSalle University Coach

"Great for any level of coaching. Being a fundamentals fanatic, this is the best guide I have seen."
John Cornet, High School Coach, Tenafly, NJ

"Without question it is a very good book about fundamental basketball."
Tom Shirley, Philadelphia U., AD & Coach

"Fantastic! A book like this is long overdue."
Bob Huggins, Kansas State University

"*The Coach's Bible* is a real winner! It offers a thorough insight into the basic foundations of basketball. A truly outstanding book. If you love basketball, you will love *The Coach's Bible*."
Jim Tucker, Englewood High School Coach

"The ideas in this book will be as helpful for you as they were for our team."
Bernie Ivens, former West Philadelphia HS Coach

"My girls really benefited from this great program of individual and group skill development."
Jennifer Lynch, Youth Coach, Edmond, OK

"[Y]our book was a huge help. I highly recommend this book to all coaches, young or experienced."
Scott Whaley, Head Jr. High Coach

"The best books I have seen on the subject. The best money I've spent."
Gregory S Bigg, Coach, Howell, NJ

What sportswriters and reviewers say...

"These two... guides [with *The Basketball Player's Bible*] offer a remarkably detailed, painstaking organized approach to teaching and mastering basketball skills....Goldstein breaks down basketball's many teachable skills (shooting, passing, dribbling, cutting, rebounding, etc.) into their component parts and supplies incrementally more difficult lessons for each task. The lessons themselves...are practical, well presented, and part of a unified whole. Directions are clear, and diagrams accompanying each lesson... are always decipherable.... The need for 'fundamentals' is a rallying cry at every level of competition: these books deliver the goods."
Booklist

"[A] minutely detailed analysis of all of the fundamentals."
Scholastic Coach

"[A] straightforward, well-detailed broad-gauged primer."
The Potomac Reader (Washington, DC)

"[This book] is great! Where was this when I needed it?...some 30 plus years ago..."
Marco Island Eagle (FL)

"Players and coaches can get to the nitty-gritty of basketball with [these books]."
Girard Home News (Philadelphia)

"One of the most comprehensive basketball books available."
Ontario Basketball Association

"This book's secondary title, 'A Comprehensive and Systematic Guide to Coaching,' couldn't be more appropriate."
Winning Hoops

"It is one of the most thorough books on basketball I have read."
National Director of Biddy Basketball

"[A] wonderfully-informative book that lives up to its billing as 'A Comprehensive and Systematic Guide to Coaching.'"
Lompoc (CA) Record

"[C]onsider yourself lucky if Santa left [it] under your Christmas tree....[C]ontains the kind of information anyone needs to develop their hoops understanding....[F]ew [basketball books] are as well done and systematic as Goldstein's."
The Dayton Daily News

"[O]ffers step-by-step lessons to learn and improve as a player or a coach.... [S]martly short on theories and long on exercises."
Denver Post, IN THE SPOTLIGHT

"Worth considering as a gift for the hoops junkie in your family."
Journal Star, Peoria (IL)

"I don't often endorse books or products but a book came across my desk that I feel is of interest to any man or women interested in coaching basketball....The book is sensational!...I highly recommend the book to coaches at any level, from fourth and fifth grade through high school and college."
Oskaloosa (IA) Herald

"If you are looking for a guide to help you coach better, this is the one you're looking for."
The Healdton (OK) Herald

"No aspect of the game is missed as Goldstein walks us through the game step-by-step, from warming up before the contest to warming down afterward to prevent injury."
Chestnut Hill Local (Philadelphia)

"Like basketball? To help you understand what is going on, get a copy....It covers every aspect of the game."
Book Browsing, West Orange Times (NJ)

"[H]olds the potential for wide appeal for a variety of users involved with kids."
Midwest Book Review, The Children's Bookwatch

"[T]he Man Who Could Help Shaq's Shot."
The Christian Science Monitor

WHY THIS BOOK IS UNIQUE

- This book presents a coherent, comprehensive and systematic scheme of lessons that work.

- These lessons not only work, but also yield the maximum improvement for each player.

- This book addresses and answers the most basic questions about learning basketball.

- This is a *do* book. Lessons comprise most of the book. Each one deals with action, not theory.

- This book is about the basics and only the basics. Player and parent or coach start from the beginning. Emphasis is on individual skills, which players readily incorporate into every team skill.

- This book exposes many inappropriate sports mottos and ideas.

- This book redefines the fundamentals, then breaks them down into teachable skills. Each lesson teaches part of a skill, an entire skill, or several skills combined.

- Each lesson highlights vital information needed to better learn each skill.

- This book supplies the know-how to successfully teach all players of all abilities. Learning takes place conspicuously during each practice session. Because of the simplicity and effectiveness of the lessons, players often use them to help each other.

Golden Aura's Nitty-Gritty Basketball Series
by Sidney Goldstein

See the descriptions in the back of this book.

Books

The Basketball Coach's Bible, 2nd Ed.

The Basketball Player's Bible, 2nd Ed.

The Basketball Shooting Guide

The Basketball Scoring Guide

The Basketball Dribbling Guide

The Basketball Defense Guide

The Basketball Pass Cut/Catch Guide

Basketball Fundamentals

Planning Basketball Practice

DVDs

1-4 The Basic Set

5-7 The Shooting Set

8 Dribbling

9-11 Defensive Skills

12-14 Offensive Skills

HOW TO CONTACT THE AUTHOR

The author seeks your comments about this book. Sidney Goldstein is available for consultation and clinics with coaches and players. Contact him at:

mrbasketball.net

800 979 8642 (USA)

215 247-4459 (International)

The Basketball Player's Bible

A Comprehensive and Systematic Guide to Playing
Second Edition

Sidney Goldstein

GOLDEN AURA PUBLISHING

The Nitty-Gritty Basketball Series

Second Edition Copyright © 2008 by Sidney Goldstein

First Edition Copyright © 1994 by Sidney Goldstein

The Basketball Player's Bible

by Sidney Goldstein

GOLDEN AURA PUBLISHING

Published by:

Golden Aura Publishing

Philadelphia, PA

mrbasketball.net

Printed in the U.S.A.

Printing 2nd Edition: 2008

Library Of Congress Cataloging-in-Publication Data

Catalog Card Number: 94-096033

Goldstein, Sidney, 1945

The Basketball Player's Bible: A Comprehensive and Systematic Guide to Playing / Sidney Goldstein.--2nd edition --Philadelphia : Golden Aura Pub., Printings: 2008

352 p. : ill. ; 28cm. -- (The Nitty-Gritty Basketball Series)

Includes index.

ISBN 978-1-884357-00-8

Soft cover

1. Basketball--Coaching--Playing I. Title II. Series: Goldstein, Sidney. Nitty-Gritty Basketball Series.

I dedicate this book to the lovers of basketball—the coaches, volunteers, and parents who spend zillions of hours each year teaching basketball to youngsters.

Sidney Goldstein

BRIEF CONTENTS

CONTENTS

62-65

66-71

72-73

INTRODUCTION

Second Edition

From day one of the publication, over 10 years ago, of *The Basketball Coach's Bible & The Basketball Player's Bible,* I wanted to redo the books. I saw many things that could have been done better. Thankfully, with the continued support of basketballers, I have been able to focus on this project after the completion of our video series. I spent more time on this second edition than on the first, so I hope readers can readily see the improvements.

First, I wanted to improve and simplify the organization of the lessons. Now there are 22 major lesson groups which contain 92 lessons. Each lesson has from 1 to 4 parts. The lessons start with the most basic ones and closely follow the organization of the coaches manual.

Second, I wanted to write more understandable directions, especially for lessons involving the detailed mechanics of movement. Directing players that are right in front of you and writing clear directions when they are not are entirely different tasks. With writing, there is no way to demonstrate, or answer questions, or add directions when players are confused.

Third, I wanted to diagram every lesson so well that coaches and players would be able to understand the lesson even before reading the text. There are well over 400 diagrams in the book including a setup diagram for most lessons.

A fourth goal was to reduce redundancy and clarify the information in Part 1 of the book, the non-lesson part. This section is called Foundations and gives coaches and players a better understanding of the foundations from which the lessons came.

The book is divided into three parts. Part 1, Foundations, has been dramatically changed and improved. The first chapter, Starting, gives essential concepts about playing. The second, The Court, describes the court and many basketball terms. The third, Fundamentals, has been greatly improved with three new smaller flow charts showing the relationships between basketball skills. The fourth, Goals & Keys, lets you know where you are going and how to progress through the lessons. Chapter 5, The Lessons, explains the organization of Part 2, the lesson sections, and features used in the text and diagrams.

The largest part of the book, Part 2, The Lessons, contains 92 numbered lessons organized in a step-by-step progression. The lessons contain between 1 and 4 parts. There are over 160 parts, though many lessons have additional unnumbered parts. The number of cartoons is about 70, nearly double the first edition.

Part 3, The Appendices, contains a cool-down and a table listing every lesson in the book.

Acknowledgements

We all need to give a thanks to Bill Force, a volunteer coach, who went through every page in this edition pointing out omissions and suggesting improvements. Erin Howarth, my editor for the second edition, was incredibly helpful in more than just an editing capacity.

Some other folks deserve a note of thanks and appreciation. Lynn Fleischman, the editor of the first edition, helped shaped this mass of information into something more understandable. Many friends gave me encouragement and ideas including Eddie Brash, Skip Cost, & Dave Bower. Zillions of coaches chipped in formation and ideas. Many gave comments which can be found either in the front of the book or on my website. One group of coaches that are not mentioned elsewhere deserve a lot of credit for my basketball knowledge and interest. These folks coached me in various leagues during my junior and senior high school years. Stephen Kay, Paul Ward, Howie Turnoff, Mr Lieberman, & Bob Mlkvy are some names that I remember. I have great respect for these people.

Inky Lautman circa 1934

Overbrook HS Varsity Basketball

First Edition Introduction
Why I Wrote This Book

My uncle Inky's (Inky Lautman) photograph appears a half dozen times in the Basketball Hall of Fame in Springfield, Massachusetts. In the beginnings of professional basketball in the thirties, he was a player for the Philadelphia SPHAA's. Even though his talent was not transmitted genetically, his interest in the game was. As a kid my only ambition was to play basketball for Overbrook High School in Philadelphia, where Wilt Chamberlain and Walt Hazzard, among other notables, once played. In ninth grade I inscribed Overbrook High School in big black letters on the back of several T-shirts. On others I wrote Hazzard or Jones (for Wally Jones) with a number below. In 10th grade, family problems led me to quit the cadet basketball team. In 11th grade, a chronic foot problem, still a mystery, prevented even a tryout. During my senior year, a sprained ankle just before tryouts doomed my chances. At less than 50% mobility, I played with great pain, only to be cut. I was dazed. My childhood dreams came to an abrupt end. Years of practice, often 3-5 hours a day, culminated without earning a big

O (for Overbrook) or even a fair shake at a tryout. The next day I decided to tell the coach, Paul Ward, about my injured ankle. I asked if I could try out a week later when the ankle was better; I regularly played with the guys on the team, and I felt I was as good as any of them. He gave me the chance. Thirty years later I still have my orange and black warm-up jersey that came with big black letters already printed on it — OVERBROOK HS VARSITY BASKETBALL.

In college my thoughts of basketball lessened even though I continued to play in all my spare moments. Theoretical engineering, my course of study, required over 20 hours of class each week. I always needed a part-time job as well. I played on some independent teams and made the all-star team at the Ogontz campus of Penn State. After college I played on many independent teams, often head-to-head against current college players or professionals-to-be.

Several years after I graduated with a degree in Biophysics, a colleague at Columbia School, a private school in Philadelphia, asked for help with the men's basketball team. After a few practices and games, he saw that I knew what I was doing and let me run the team. After a few more games we won the championship.

My next coaching experience was at a public high school with the girls' junior varsity team. I was not prepared for this situation. The girls had zero skills and very different attitudes than guys. The layup, the dribble, and every other skill seemed too advanced for most of the players.

I didn't have a clue. I wondered, "Where do I start teaching? What and how do I teach?" I thought that you couldn't teach layups and dribbling as well as many other skills. Other coaches only reinforced this idea: kids need to possess some natural talent. My game demeanor was as clueless as my practices. I thought if I yelled loudly enough that players would get the idea. The yelling during my first season helped; it helped the other team. We lost seven of seven close games. My other mistakes are too numerous and embarrassing to mention.

Coaching skilled players is kid's stuff compared to teaching unskilled novices. My learning started abruptly that first day at practice. During the next seven years of coaching, I read everything I could find about basketball. Most books started where I wanted to end up. They assumed players knew the basics or they thought an explanation of the basics, without any methods to accomplish them, was all that was needed. As a gag, a revered men's coach gave me a 20-year-old book about women's basketball. The women on the cover were wearing old-fashioned uniforms with skirts and shoulder straps (tunics I am told). This coach and the other gym teachers watching this presentation didn't expect me to read it, but I did. Even though not detailed nor explanatory, it did give me an idea where the beginning was. I remember best the six or seven types of passes described, most of which we never bother to teach.

I attended many basketball (as well as volleyball and one ice hockey) clinics. Often the top basketball coaches that were invited offered more general information than definite detailed advice. One women's volleyball coach, who at the time seemed old, short, and unathletic, did impress me at one clinic. She had known nothing about volleyball when she started, but quickly learned how to teach the basics. Year after year she beat all the teams in the area. She thought her teams won because her teaching methods were better. The other coaches disliked her, especially the men. She offered free clinics so the other teams could do as well. Few, if any, took her up on it. Her attitude was so refreshing. I even attended an ice hockey clinic hoping to pick up some related tips. The Czech national team practiced three-person fast breaks off ice with a basketball, believe it or not.

I watched the basketball practices of many college, high-school, and other teams as well as talked to many coaches. Each night I often spent hours planning practice. I began to realize that teaching the skills was a puzzle that I could unscramble. To find more effective ways required study, planning, and innovation. I realized that with limited practice time, a coach can only teach the most basic skills. Coaches need to identify and then teach the more dependent individual skills first. Lessons need to focus on one thing at a time, not impart many skills at once. This was both the key to teaching and the biggest impediment to learning. Some skills took years to figure out. Others, like learning that yelling at players during games did no good, took only one season. (Players echo your nervous state, so be calm. The first year I yelled a lot and my team lost every close game. I stayed calm after that season and I remember losing only one close game, when the score was tied in the last minute.)

While I worked on my puzzles, the program developed at our high school, West Philadelphia HS. With the varsity coach, Bernie Ivens, we transformed a women's program that had no respect, no uniforms, and no facility (at first I used the school hallways for part of each practice) or equipment. In five years the result was a public league and city championship as well as a victory over the best of New York's five boroughs in a tournament.

Part 1
Foundations

1. Starting
2. The Court
3. Fundamentals
4. Goals & Keys
5. The Lessons

Chapter One
1

STARTING

This chapter could be called "The Right Stuff," because it will put you on target and make your playing experience more successful and rewarding.

When I was a young player, I loved to play basketball; I loved to run; I wanted to improve; I was happy to do almost anything a coach told me to do. I also had little idea what was most important–what are the priorities in learning; what would allow me to improve the most. I will tell you.

Basketball Is Physical

Conditioning – speed and strength – makes a player of average skills a great player. On the other hand, no matter how skillful you are, a lack of speed and strength will lower your level of play.

Work on cardiovascular conditioning while running full-court, either one-on-one or solo. Start out slowly and gradually increase your time to 30-60 minutes. You can work on many basketball skills as you improve your conditioning. The continuous movement or continuous motion (CM) lessons described in this book give some ideas of the skills to practice while running.

An easy way to improve your strength is to do push-ups. Depending on your condition, you can start out doing as few as one push up, 5 to 10 times each day. Increase the this number by one each day. Weight programs will help even more. Make sure you are guided by a knowledgeable instructor if you use weights. This person should make improvement easy, not painful.

Stretching will also help increase your speed and prevent injury. See the cool down in the appendix for more information. A stretching program like a conditioning or weight program needs to be individualized.

Practice Is About Agility

Improving your ability to play basketball goes hand-in-hand with agility. Practice is the means to improve agility. Each lesson in this book works on agility.

There are 3 different effort levels of practice for the lessons in this book. In a way it is like slow, medium, and fast. The technique level, the first one, is the slow level. These lessons involve the least physical movement, but paradoxically the maximum physical effort because you often need to twist your body into difficult positions. Execute movements slowly; think about what you are doing. Usually, you will need an assistant–a friend, coach, or parent–to assist you. These lessons yield the maximum improvement in agility.

The other two levels of practice are the regular level (level 2), often called the practice level, and the game level (level 3). The regular level is just that: practice at a comfortable level, neither fast nor slow. Most moves are practiced this way. Game level practice involves moving as quickly as possible often against an opponent. Each lesson has a level. You need to know at which level you are working.

Wrist Work

The key to improving all offensive ball skills – shooting, passing, and dribbling – is wrist movement. Because this skill takes much time to learn, start practicing immediately and practice regularly.

Practice & Advance Slowly

Remember that improvement both comes slowly at first and varies based on the skill being practiced. The more complex the skill, the more time is needed. Practice on a regular basis, don't overdo it at any one time. Your body needs time to improve agility. If something is painful, then cut back the time for each session. However, you can work on it more frequently.

Do It Right

You will only improve if you practice properly. Players that practice improperly get into many bad habits that are difficult to change. A player with no habits, can learn faster than a player with bad habits. Proper practice means that you only advance as you improve. Skipping over the most basic and most difficult lessons is self-defeating. The purpose of practice is to improve, not quickly reach the end of the book.

Each Player Needs Every Skill

You need every skill, so you can play each position. So forget about positional play, because it's a thing of the past. Big players need to be able to dribble. Small players need to be able to rebound and post-up an opponent.

Get Help

Get feedback on your progress from a coach, parent, or adult who has read the book or the lesson you are working on. This point is very important—find someone who will read the lesson with you. It does not need to be a former pro player; any one who cares will do. Of course, they must watch you perform to give feedback.

Age-Related Learning

One might think that teaching fundamentals would only yield great improvement with youngsters because they have few skills to start. And that experienced players, like pros, are so skilled that one would rarely see improvement during the season. Not so. Young players have difficulty improving because of their physical limitations. For instance, the shooting improvement of a player with small hands depends more on his/her growth rate than on practice. It might even be better for him/her to practice less.

Pros, on the other hand, do not have these physical limitations. And believe it or not, most pros are not super-skilled players. However, they are individuals with superior physical talent. They can learn physical skills quickly, so they can readily improve their game.

With young small players I highly suggest using a proportionally lower basket, a smaller basketball, and a smaller court. Using a ball that a small player can't handle only causes future problems; it does not prepare them for the future. A 10-foot basket for a 3-foot player only forces the player to throw the ball, rather than shoot. Using a 5-foot-high basket, young players learn technique faster. It's easy to apply learned technique when you later use a higher basket or larger ball. Younger players will also better enjoy the game using a smaller ball and lower basket.

Young & Novice Players

If you are in elementary or junior high school or just starting to play, you can become experienced readily. The lessons in this book will do just that–teach you the stuff needed to play like an experienced player.

You will need a coach, parent, or an older person to assist you. This person does not need to be a fan; mom can do as well, if not better than dad. This book explains things well enough so that anyone can assist. Read through Chapters 1- 5 with them. Make sure they read and even do some lessons with you. A court and/or a ball is not needed to practice some of the most important lessons. You can practice these at home sitting in your living room. Other key lessons can be practiced in any available space inside or outside.

It's okay and even better to learn how to shoot with a smaller ball at a lower basket. Your ease of use determines the smallness and height. Wanting to be like the "big boys" will only get you into life-long bad habits.

To Parents

Being skillful in basketball is not the same as being a great player. As I have said above, physicality is the key to success as a player. I would much rather coach a team of great athletes with few skills, than a group of more skillful, poorer athletes. So, help your child get in shape. Teach him or her important lessons about conditioning that will last and will be of benefit for a lifetime.

Being a great player and having great athletic prowess are not essential criteria for being a teacher or coach. Teachers care predominately about teaching and the people with whom they work, not about exhorting unworkable ideas. So even if you have neither skill nor experience to start, you can do well. Keep in mind that many skills may be too difficult for your child to learn until he/she is older. Don't try to force learning. It can't be done. However, you can prevent him or her from getting into bad habits.

Go slowly, especially when practicing the technique level lessons with your child. Teaching skills to a novice is not an easy job. Remember that you can improve your child's skill level and even improve his/her conditioning. However, you can't make him/her a great player, you can just make them a lot better.

Misconceptions
Drills Do The Teaching

Many coaches believe that finding a bunch of great drills will solve their coaching problems. Unfortunately a drill does not teach anything unless the coach fully understands the drill, then watches players like a hawk. Coaches must do the teaching; a drill only assists.

Fundamentals Are For Little Kids

A widely held attitude by coaches is that fundamentals are for little kids, particularly little girls. These folks should calculate their team's free-throw shooting percentage, then count the number of good dribblers, the number of players that box out, the number that play good defense, the number that pass well, and so on. These numbers won't add up to the number of players on the team or even to the number on the court in a game.

Misconception About Plays

A team's offense needs to react to the other team's defense. A coach can't teach these adjustments by just practicing pre-designed plays. Pre-designed plays actually make teams play worse, because plays teach players to look only in one or two places instead of everywhere. Teaching basic offensive skills enables and empowers players to play off each other as well as opponents. Emphasis needs to be shifted away from plays to basic offensive skills.

Great Players Are Great Teachers

Great players are not necessarily great teachers. Great players are usually great athletes. This physicality does not directly translate into teaching ability. A story to point. Many years ago in a tennis class at my alma mater, Penn State, the instructor used me to demonstrate how to serve. I did not have a clue how to serve. I just threw the ball up and hit it hard. This day the serve went in and I guess it looked good. Did I have a clue how to teach serving? Emphatically no.

Myths & More Bad Ideas
No Pain, No Gain

"No pain, No gain," is another concept that I've been told means something quite different than the wider usage. The common usage for this distorts reality. One distortion is that players are not willing to make the effort. This is hardly the case. The problem is quite the opposite: it's difficult to slow folks down so that they do not injure themselves. The other distortion of reality involves pain. Our bodies are made to react to pain as a warning signal. If a person's hand gets too near the flame, he/she feels pain and moves his/her hand away. A slogan that encourages someone not to listen to his/her own body can readily cause injury.

Practice Makes Perfect

"Practice makes perfect," is another worthless slogan because it assigns blame for poor play to the player. I've heard sports announcers say that to shoot better, the player only had to practice a little more on the free-throw line, "practice makes perfect." Well, what about the zillions of players, including myself, who practiced shooting for hours on end only to get worse?

Actually, the way they (or I) practiced guaranteed failure. Performing a skill improperly hundreds of times only makes one an expert at doing things improperly. Sensible practice yields results. If coaches teach properly, players will improve. No slogan needed.

Winning Is The Only Thing

"Winning is the only thing" is another notorious sports and business motto that is more than worthless. If winning is the only thing, then where do values like fairness, morality, teaching, and so on fit in? In business, where does product quality, customer service, fairness to employees, and so on fit in? We seem to be a "Winning is the only thing" society, where everybody turns out to be losers since so many folks will do anything to win.

How many times have coaches been angry at players who have made a mistake in practice or a game? Winning demands players do things right whether or not they know how. Teaching says that the only limit to a player's ability to learn is the teacher's ability to teach. Face it, most players' mistakes stem from the coaches' inability to teach. Teaching encourages coaches to study basketball and to examine themselves; it is giving of oneself, whereas a philosophy of winning-is-the-only-thing only demands, takes, and uses.

Emotion Is A Big Part Of The Game

Emotion is no part of the game. A coach does not want players any more excited going into a game than a person would want a nuclear technician excited while working on a bomb or a doctor excited while performing surgery.

Going out of the way to excite players or get players up for a game is counterproductive because players are naturally up all the time. It's important to do exactly the opposite—keep players calm, cool and focused. Doing a cheer before the game or even discussing the importance of a game are examples of counterproductive measures.

Playing Street Ball Is Helpful

When I grew up, playing half-court, two-on-two and three-on-three was very common, much more common than full-court games. The basketball experience obtained by playing half-court is useful, especially for developing individual moves, but not nearly as helpful as proper practice.

Street ball is problematic for many reasons. One, there is lack of conditioning because there is often no transition game. Players often just stand around when the ball changes hands. Team play is not encouraged, since a player is always close enough to the basket to score. And, 3-second rules usually never apply in these games, so street-ball offenses do not work in real games.

The Game Is A Great Learning Tool

Many folks who run leagues or various basketball organizations in addition to coaching, think that the game itself is a great teacher. Players in a game oriented-program often have little practice time. In a game there is no timely repetition of any skill, so it's impossible to learn basic basketball skills by simply playing games. Games do have a small role in the learning process, however proper practice that involves basic skills has the major role in learning.

Chapter Two 2

THE COURT

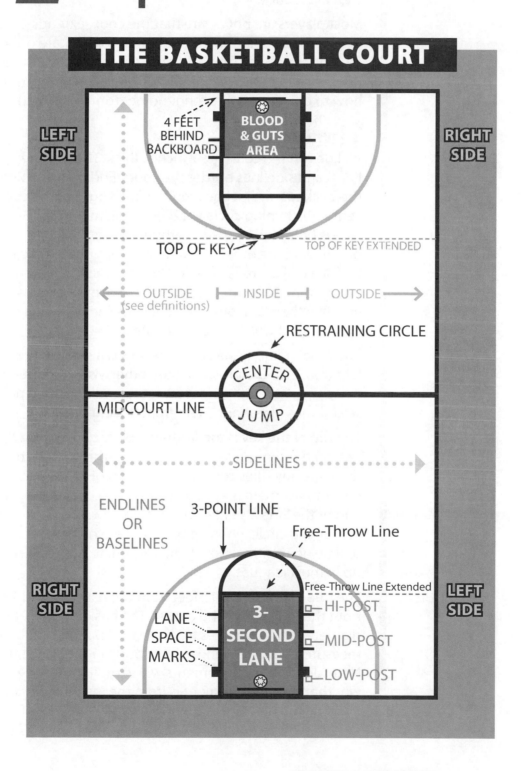

THE BASKETBALL COURT

4 FEET BEHIND BACKBOARD

BLOOD & GUTS AREA

LEFT SIDE

RIGHT SIDE

TOP OF KEY

TOP OF KEY EXTENDED

← OUTSIDE (see definitions) — INSIDE — OUTSIDE →

RESTRAINING CIRCLE

CENTER JUMP

MIDCOURT LINE

← SIDELINES →

ENDLINES OR BASELINES

3-POINT LINE

Free-Throw Line

Free-Throw Line Extended

RIGHT SIDE

LEFT SIDE

HI-POST

LANE SPACE MARKS

3-SECOND LANE

MID-POST

LOW-POST

The Court

If the court were real estate worth $1000, the area around the basket would be worth $999.99. I call this the **blood and guts area**. Games are won and lost here. However, simply stating that this is the most important area on the court is inadequate. Practice each lesson with this in focus. Never ever miss a short shot in practice.

Most players are not aware that the court extends 4 feet behind the backboard. Great rebounders devastate opponents by moving to the ball from this area. Offensive rebounders must use this area to their advantage. Defensive players must learn how to box out players rebounding from this direction.

The Lines

All lines on the court are 2 inches thick. The endlines (or baselines) and sidelines border the court. Endlines run parallel to the backboard. Sidelines run the full length of the court. The center restraining circle is 12 feet in diameter. The 3-second lane is bounded by the free-throw line on one end and the baseline on the other. The midcourt line divides the court in half. If a player steps on a line he/she is **out,** if it is an out-of-bounds line or the midcourt line. A player is **in** if it is any other line. In either case, out or in, the lines can work against you. Players must watch where they step.

The 3-point line, if the court has any, is a semicircle about 20 feet (more for the pros, can vary otherwise) from the basket. Since the basket is 4-6 feet from the endline, the 3-point line straightens out about 5 feet from the endline.

The top of the key is the farthest point, 21 feet from the front rim, on the semicircle behind the free-throw line (I don't think there are any rules concerning the top of the key now. In the distant past there may have been). The semicircle at the court end of the lane also has no function now. It was part of another restraining circle when jump balls were held closest to the actual tie up position. Now teams alternate possessions after a tie up in most leagues.

The free-throw line is 19 feet from the baseline and 13 feet from the front rim of the basket. The basket itself is 18 inches in diameter and is 6 inches from the backboard. Note that these measurements are standard for courts in the U.S. at this time. Note also that measurements will vary slightly depending whether the measurement is from the inside or outside of the line. See the diagram on the next page.

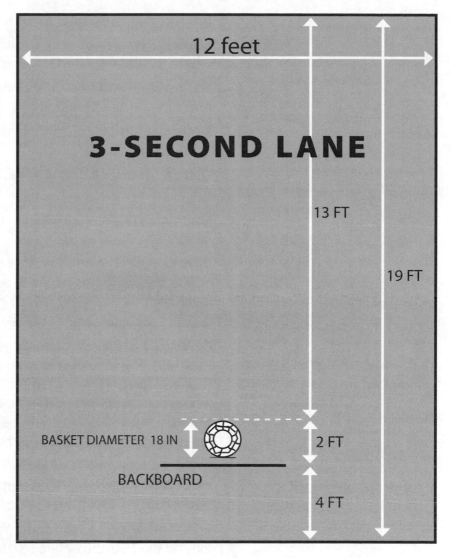

Areas

The 3-second lane contains what I call the **blood and guts area**. Offensive and defensive players line up alternately on the lane for free throws. The defense takes the position on the lane closest to the basket. On offense, players can stay in the lane for a maximum of 3 seconds unless the ball is either shot or loose. The center court jump area is usually only used for the start of the game. More information about play in these areas can be found in the appropriate chapter or section.

Basketball Terms

Most terms are explained in the chapter or section where they are used. Here is a short list of terms.

Backcourt– Away from a team's basket. Backcourt players are guards. A backcourt violation occurs when a player crosses midcourt with the ball and then goes back.

Boards or **Off The Boards**– A rebound.

Corner– The area directly to either side of the basket near where the baseline and sideline meet.

Defensive Position– Is the optimum body position, ready to move in any direction.

Defensive Run– Running while maintaining defensive position.

Discontinuing– A dribbling violation; dribbling for a second time after stopping.

Double-Dribble– A dribbling violation; dribbling with two hands.

Effort Level– The amount of physical effort that is put out in a drill or lesson. The three levels are: level 1 or technique-level; level 2 or practice-level; level 3 or game-level. Many lessons can be run at several different levels.

Forecourt and **Backcourt**– These are not absolute specific locations. The forecourt is where the forwards play on offense. It is fore or closer to the basket than where the guards play. In a full-court press, when the guards take the ball out from the baseline, the forecourt could be near midcourt. In a regular offense the forecourt is around the basket and baseline. Farther away from the basket or back are the guards in the backcourt.

Free-Throw Line– Thirteen feet from the rim, 15 feet from the backboard, 19 feet from the baseline.

Free-Throw Line Extended– With a paint brush a person could extend the free-throw line to the left and right sidelines. These extensions on the left and right sides are considered the free-throw line extended.

Game-Level– Doing a lesson or drill as fast as possible, often with defensive pressure.

Give-And-Go– Passing, then cutting to the basket (or other area) expecting to receive a return pass.

Head-To-Head or **Belly-To-Belly**– Tight one-on-one defense. Also called fronting.

Help-Out– Moving into position to cover and covering another player's offensive assignment.

Inside– Closer to the basket, usually in the lane. The defense usually takes an inside position. The offense always wants to pass inside. Inside can also mean away from the sidelines toward the center of the court.

In– In bounds; inside.

Jab-Step– A short, medium, or long step accompanied by body movement away from the pivot foot.

Jump-Step– The small adjustment steps a player makes on defense.

Man-To-Man– An archaic term for person-to-person defense.

On-Ball/Off-Ball– On-ball refers to defensive coverage on the player with the ball. Off-ball coverage involves the defense on the other four players without the ball.

One-On-One– Person-to-person defensive coverage.

Outside– Farther from the basket. Teams do not want to take too many outside shots. Shorter players usually play outside. Outside can also mean closer to the sidelines than the center part of the court.

Out– Out-Of-Bounds; outside.

Over-And-Back– A game violation called a backcourt violation; when a player crosses half-court with the ball and then goes back.

Paint– The 3-second lane. On most college and professional courts it is painted one color, often a color of the home team.

Palming– A dribbling violation when the palm of the dribbling hand is turned upward (and then downward) to better control the ball. Rarely called.

Pass-Follow – When a player makes a pass to another player at a particular position, then runs to this position. The player catching the pass usually goes somewhere else before the passer arrives.

Pass-Response Fake– When a player fakes a pass to a cutter who is asking for the ball. The response is when the cutter asks for the ball.

Practice-Level– Doing a drill or lesson at a normal pace, neither very fast, nor very slow.

Ready Position– A player's body position when on the court. In general, a position where a player is ready to move in any direction.

Rebound-Ready Position– In the optimum body position to rebound.

Screen or Pick– When a stationary offensive player is used as, or sets up as, a block or impediment on the defensive player assigned to another offensive player. It is a violation if the screen moves to cause contact with the defense.

Shooting Range or **Range**–The maximum distance from which a player can shoot well. Players often shoot from beyond their range.

Slough Off– The defense moves away from their offensive coverage toward an offensive player with the ball.

Strong Side/Weak Side– The area, not necessarily the side, near the ball is called the ball side or strong side of the court. Away from the ball is the weak side of the court. When the ball is in the center of the court, the corner areas are considered the weak side.

Technique-Level– Doing a drill or lesson slowly usually concentrating on body mechanics.

The Lane– The 3-second lane.

3-Second Lane– The lane: the paint. Offensive players can remain in this area for only 3 seconds when their team is in possession of the ball.

Tied Up– When the defense prevents an offensive player from passing or moving the ball. This is a violation if the offense does not move the ball for 5 seconds. If defenders get their hands on the ball, it can be called a jump ball.

Transition or **Transition Game**– Moving from offense to defense or vice-versa. Players need to make quick transitions, especially from offense to defense.

Traveling– See "walking" below.

Violation– Against the rules. The other team is awarded the ball out-of-bounds.

Walking– Traveling; sliding or moving the pivot foot while holding the ball; taking two steps or more after catching the ball; taking 2 steps either before or after dribbling.

Chapter Three 3 | FUNDAMENTALS

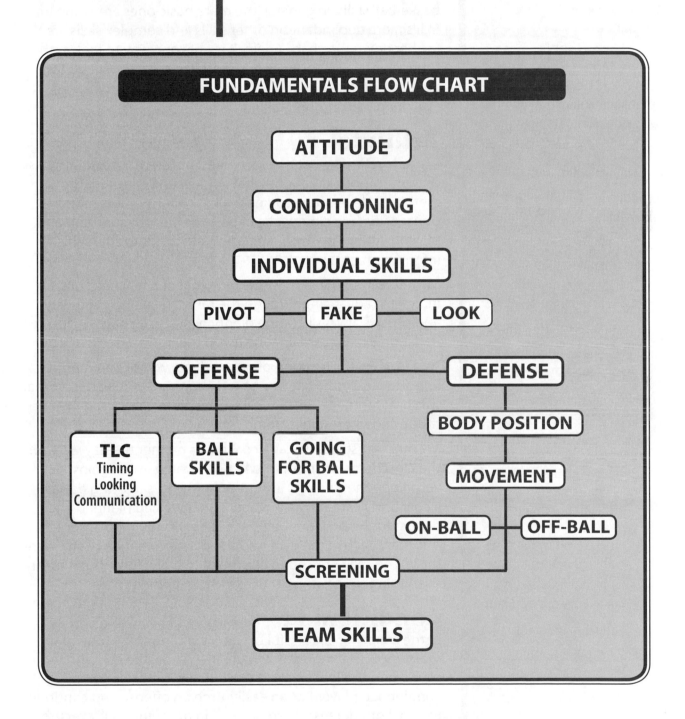

FUNDAMENTALS FLOW CHART

ATTITUDE

CONDITIONING

INDIVIDUAL SKILLS

PIVOT — **FAKE** — **LOOK**

OFFENSE — **DEFENSE**

TLC
Timing
Looking
Communication

BALL SKILLS

GOING FOR BALL SKILLS

BODY POSITION

MOVEMENT

ON-BALL — **OFF-BALL**

SCREENING

TEAM SKILLS

Flow Charts

In this chapter the fundamentals skills are discussed using three flow charts as a guide. The large *Fundamentals Flow Chart* on the chapter page shows an overview of basketball skills. Both the *Offensive Flow Chart* and the *Defensive Flow Chart*, located within the chapter, go into more detail. These flow charts show one way to more readily recognize relationships between basketball skills. In general, the more basic ones are at the top. Skills more dependent on other skills and complex skills are farther down the chart. Again, it is only one way to look at the fundamentals. Words from the chart like pivot, look, and fake are used interchangeably with the same words ending in *ing* - pivoting, looking, and faking.

Attitude

Attitude reflects what a person does, not what a person thinks or says. This book is about what I did when I coached. The methods I developed worked well. I thought others might benefit from my experience in basketball, both coaching and playing. And that it would be a selfish act not to share this information.

My interest in coaching was always that of a teacher. I had no interest in advancing through the ranks. Teaching chemistry and physics always kept me plenty busy. Each coaching job I've had is only because someone asked me.

As a teacher, the learning of my students was of paramount importance. I did what was best for each individual; this is what was best for the team. In the end, my players reflected my attitude and interest in learning.

My most satisfying day as a coach was neither the day we won the city championship, nor when we won games against favored opponents. I was absent on my most satisfying day as a coach. My captain ran a practice that we had planned and discussed the previous day since I knew I would be absent. Another coach in the gym said the players practiced as if I were there. This may not sound like much to many folks, but it means everything to me; my practices are demanding.

Conditioning

In the recipe for successful playing, conditioning is one of the most important ingredients. Late in a game, the conditioned player gets the loose balls; a tired player is much slower. A conditioned player has an easier time on offense and continues to play tight defense; tired players do not think well, execute directions well, play tight defense, or even shoot well. There is no match between a tired and a conditioned player.

A conditioned player is also a better athlete, automatically making them a better player. So the least you can do is work yourself into great shape. Accomplish aerobic or overall conditioning through running and continuous motion (CM) lessons. CM drills keep a player in constant motion for 15-40 minutes while practicing skills at the same time. Older players should also weight train and do pushups.

Individual Skills

A player needs to focus on and spend most practice time on individual skills for several reasons. One, they are the most difficult to learn, and two, a player can't adequately perform team skills without them. Team skills are easy to learn and do not require much time.

Pivot, Fake, & Look

These three disparate skills, pivoting , faking, and looking, are part of every offensive and defensive skill.

Pivot

Pivoting involves balance. Whenever a player has the ball he/she must pivot. Each ball skill—shooting, dribbling, and passing—involves pivoting. Catching, rebounding, and going for loose balls are all affected by pivoting ability. Cuts as well as defensive movement involve pivots to switch direction. Moves, drives, and low-post play also involve pivoting. Improving pivoting ability improves the entire game of a player.

Fake

Faking can make the difference between being an effective or an ineffective player. Faking is something that each player should do just about every second on the court. A big difference between experienced and inexperienced players and teams is faking.

On offense, fakes with the ball and the body are the most obvious types of fakes. However, off-ball players must continuously attempt to misdirect and confuse the defense by faking cuts. There are many lessons on faking throughout the lesson sections.

Defenders fake as well. On-ball defenders regularly fake the offense by forcing them to go one way or the other. Off-ball defenders fake by overplaying aggressively or not depending on the situation. In a two-on-one situation, the lone defender often fakes coverage on one offensive player, then moves to cover the other.

Look

Looking is the most important skill in the game, yet it is rarely recognized as a teachable skill. Every lesson in this guide involves looking skills and a coach needs to supervise players closely to make sure they are looking properly. Poor looking habits often originate from lessons involving dribbling and plays where the coach allows players to dribble with their heads down. Looking in the simplest of drills is quite difficult. Consider one involving two players, 1 yard apart, running downcourt passing back and forth. Each player should be looking forward, seeing the other player out of the corner of the eyes. Even college players have great difficulty executing this properly.

Every instant on the court, whether on offense or defense, a player must follow the ball as well as the position of all other players, both teammates and opponents. Looking properly is difficult because even an instant of improper looking always has negative results. Thousands of problems result from improper looking, so a player must be conscious of where he/she looks every second on the court in games and practice.

Skills Related To Looking

Other offensive skills directly related to looking are *reading the defense*, *decision making*, and *spacing of players*. College coaches especially complain about players' lack of these skills.

To resolve problems related to looking, coaches first need to *teach* players to look at each other, not just tell them to do so. All TLC lessons (timing, looking, and communication), CM lessons, layup drills, and team offensive drills teach proper looking. The actual drills do not teach looking all by themselves; the coach needs to deal with looking in each lesson and then watch players closely. The problem of proper spacing between players disappears once they are in the habit of looking and communicating. Reading the defense is easy once players start to read each other.

Decision making comes from repeatedly experiencing various situations. Learn each situation. Being simply told what to do, does not work. A player should be able to recognise the situation and react appropriately. If a player learns the parts (the skills) they can put things together and/or make the correct decision. Attempting to learn everything all at once never gives a player the opportunity to learn.

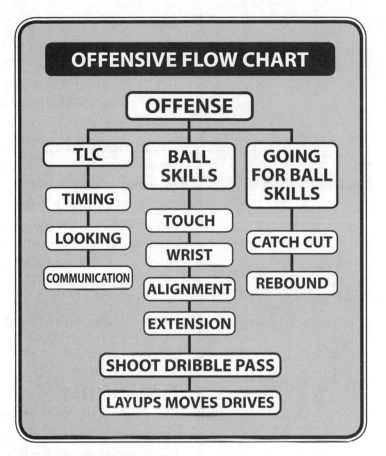

Offensive Skills

There are more than five times as many offensive skills as defensive ones. Learning offensive skills takes lots of time and effort. The big bonus from working on offensive skills is that players automatically incorporate them into the more complex team skills. *See the Offensive Flow Chart.*

TLC

TLC is an abbrevlation for timing, looking, and communication, three of the most difficult offensive skills to teach.

Timing

Timing involves looking, communication, and a lot of experience. One tenth of one second or less is the length of time involved in good timing. That's why as spectators we rarely see good timing in games, but when we do it's a pleasant experience. Timing is the last skill that will come together on offense. Perform each offensive lesson slowly so that timing will develop. To better understand good timing and poor timing, watch video/dvd 14 in our series. In slow motion, we repeat many plays run by high schoolers and some older players. To see the potential of good timing, watch high-level college or pro volleyball.

Looking

Looking, as stated before, means looking around everywhere all the time. The difficulty with looking is that it's easy to look in the wrong direction or not be looking in the right direction at any instant. Instants are what make and break a team's offense or defense.

Communication

Communication usually involves non-verbal signals that a player is going to cut this way or that, dribble this way or that, shoot or not shoot and so on. Offensive players need to be able to read each other all the time. Obvious communication might involve a dribbler directing traffic by pointing with the non-dribbling hand where a player should go. Not so obvious communication involves a back-door play where the cutter fakes away from the basket, then rubs a defender off, on a screen, when cutting to the basket for the ball. Communication is obviously integrally involved with looking and, like looking, involves instants of time.

Ball Skills

The three major ball skills are shooting, dribbling, and passing. Other ball skills involve catching, ball-handling, faking with the ball, moving the ball while in defensive traffic, or grabbing a loose ball or rebound. There are four teaching components for the major ball skills: 1) touch; 2) wrist movement; 3) body alignment; 4) arm extension.

Touch

The three major ball skills have much in common. To control the ball, a player must handle it with the fingerends. Handling a ball with the pads, fingers, or palms does not work. Improving touch is relatively easy and of paramount importance with each ball skill. Touch also helps players called "butterfingers," who try to catch with the palms rather than the fingerends; these players also tend to shut their eyes before catching. To see great examples of touch and other ball-handling skills watch vintage film of Hall of Famers Bob Cousy and/or Pete Maravich.

Wrist Movement

Passes, shots, and dribbles can be thought of as just flicks of the wrist. A tight-wristed player will not be able to improve till he/she, usually he, is able to bend the wrist back close to 90 degrees from the arm. Without the back movement there will be an insufficient flick forward. Tight-wristed players shoot, dribble, and pass using the entire arm. It's impossible to precisely control the ball with the arms. Bad shots, called "bricks," are usually due to players "arming the ball up." Dribblers arm the ball by using lots of arm movement, needing to palm the ball for control. Armed passes are telegraphed passes, allowing the defense a better opportunity to either steal the ball or prepare to defend. Both flexing the wrist back 90 degrees and flicking forward are keys to improving the major ball skills.

Body Alignment

Shooting

Shooting alignment involves squaring-up to the direction of the shot and moving the elbow inward and upward, while keeping the shoulders facing the direction of the shot. The shooting technique section covers this is detail.

Dribbling

Dribbling alignment, in a way, is the opposite of body alignment: the body needs to be twisted in unusual positions. Twisting starts from the half-down or ready position. For example, if a dribbler is dribbling downcourt closely covered, the head needs to be facing downcourt. However, the shoulders and hips face partially forward, partially toward the sideline often in different directions all while moving downcourt. This situation is dynamically changing. Rarely does a covered dribbler dribble the ball in front. Most dribbling is done on the side or even behind the body to protect the ball.

Passing

Passing alignment is more like dribbling alignment than shooting alignment. A passer must twist, turn, and stretch the body in order to pass by a closely covering defensive player. Passing is more difficult than other ball skills because a successful pass must also be properly timed.

Arm Extension

Shooting

Extension on a shot allows a player to more readily shoot over the head of a closely guarding defender as well as to shoot inside under the boards. Nose shooting—releasing the ball at the forehead or nose level—is not just a problem for small players who often start their forward shot motion from the waist. Most female players, and even men 6'5" to 6'10," often release the shot from the nose level. Practicing extension techniques allows the ball to be released 1-3 feet higher.

Dribbling

Keeping the arms extended downward on the dribble makes dribbling easier because the ball is closer to the ground than when the arm is bent. With extended arms, a player must dribble using the wrists. Dribbling properly using the wrists is much more effective than arm dribbling.

Passing

On the pass, extension involves stretching the arms overhead or to one side. Increasing extension, like on the shot, allows the passer to extend past a closely covering defender. Extending the arms (and body) to one side is more difficult to learn than the extension required for shooting.

Shoot, Pass, Dribble

Shoot

Shooting includes the regular shot, the jump shot, the hook and jump hook, underneath shots, the layup, drives and moves. An entire section is devoted to free-throw shooting because it is so problematic.

Pass

Passes include the overhead, side, side back, and bounce passes as well as baseball passes. Chest passes have such limited use that I do not include them. They also teach arm movement, which is undesirable on a short pass. Passing is the most difficult ball skill to learn.

Dribble

Dribbling is easy to teach using the lessons as a guide. Any player can be a good dribbler in a short amount of time. One point about dribbling: it's the worst way to move the ball down the court or anywhere else. If a player must dribble then he/she should be going somewhere quick. I ban dribbling in just about every practice lesson, forcing players to instead work on TLC skills. Making moves like spins and fakes off the dribble are also a waste of time. A good driver can just run by the offense without holding up a game with a bunch of dribbles.

Layups, Moves, Drives

Layups

Approximately 100% of missed layups are due to players, even college and pro ones, not knowing how to correctly perform the layup. Players must be able to perform a strong-handed, usually right-handed, layup on both the left and right sides of the basket. For older players the opposite-hand layup must also be performed on both the left and right side of the basket.

Moves

Most moves involve pivots, jab-steps, and ball fakes along with a shot. The shot could be a regular shot, a jump shot, a hook, jump hook, or an underneath hook. Practicing moves close to the basket is a great way to improve agility as well as shooting technique.

Drives

The four basic drives are important moves that need to be practiced, like the layup, with either hand on both sides of the basket.

Going-For-The-Ball Skills

Cutting, rebounding, and going for loose balls are going-for-the-ball skills. All involve looking, cutting or positioning, then grabbing or catching the ball, and finally pivoting.

Catch Cut

The most difficult part of catching involves cutting full steam to the ball or to the open space, then catching and stopping without walking, all while maintaining balance. Most novices as well as college-level players either have difficulty or cannot catch going full steam. Novices often have trouble catching without walking at any speed. The catching lessons quickly take care of these problems. Teams that catch and cut well can readily beat presses.

Catching becomes quite problematic in tight situations when a player has a favorite landing foot. So make sure to repeat each applicable drill using the other foot as pivot.

Rebound

Rebounding is another going-for-the-ball skill not often taught. The keys to rebounding include watching the shot arc, predicting where the ball will go, and then moving to the best position. Good rebounders even become familiar with how a particular player misses a shot.

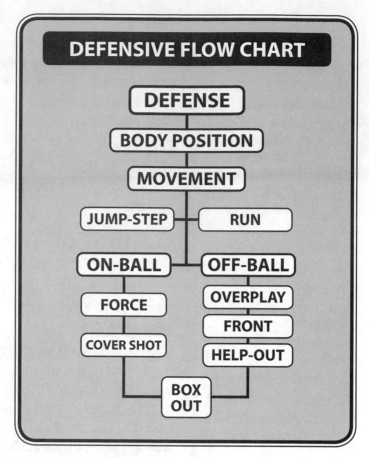

DEFENSIVE FLOW CHART

DEFENSE
BODY POSITION
MOVEMENT
JUMP-STEP — RUN
ON-BALL — OFF-BALL
FORCE — OVERPLAY
COVER SHOT — FRONT
HELP-OUT
BOX OUT

Defensive Skills

Defense is easier to teach than offense because it is mostly physical; it takes less talent to learn. Each skill is less complicated, so players learn them much faster. There are also fewer defensive skills than offensive ones to master. A team's shooting often varies from one game to the next, but the defense should be a constant that one can rely on. *See the Defensive Flow Chart.*

In a zone defense, players must play the offense in their area using person-to-person techniques, rather than just graze in a particular area. So, players must first master person-to-person defense, before playing any zone.

Body Position

The defensive position facilitates quick, fast movements and sprints in any direction.

Movement

There are only two types of movement on defense: jump-steps and runs while in defensive position. Using these in combination allows a defender to sprint or move in any direction at any instant. I often talk about these as being the dance steps for defense. Sliding, walking, and taking long strides do not allow for quick direction changes.

Quite often out-of-shape and/or poorly-trained players like to reach with the arms, rather than move their feet. So, one problem on defense is just getting young players in the habit of moving the feet rather than reaching. Many basic defensive lessons work on this.

Jump-Step

The jump-step is a way to move short distances while staying in defensive position ready to run. Most players use jump-steps in very tight situations without any training. However, to play good defense, players must use jump-steps most of the time. Giving the offense an instant of a head start, because the defense is not ready to move, defeats the defense.

Defensive Run

The other defensive dance step that must be learned is the defensive run. A defensive run involves a sprint where a player starts in defensive position and ends in defensive position. Defensive runs that only involve one or two steps are more difficult to learn than longer runs. In order to effectively cover the offense, defensive players must coordinate jump-steps and runs. Taking a jump-step instead of a run, or vice-versa, often lets the offense get away.

On/Off-Ball Defense

On-ball defensive skills include forcing the dribbler and covering the shot. Only one player is on the ball at any time in a game, four are off-the-ball. So off-ball defense is more important number-wise to team defense than on-ball coverage. Whereas on-ball defenders just cover one player, off-ball defenders have the more difficult task of covering their assignment, watching the ball, and helping-out when needed. The quality of off-ball defensive play measures the quality of a team's defense. Off-ball techniques include overplaying, fronting, and helping-out. Other defensive situations covered in the lesson sections include coverage on a fast break and trapping.

Force

Forcing is the way to cover an offensive player with the ball. Never let the offense go where he/she wants. Force him/her the other way.

Cover Shot

Covering the shooter involves moving the hands properly to alter the shot while not fouling the shooter.

Overplay

Overplaying is the predominant method used to cover off-ball players. Overplaying is much more involved than forcing, because the overplayer must cover the offense, watch the ball, and help-out as needed. Helping-out means moving toward the ball. Overplayers must also learn how to cover low-post players and cutters in the lane area.

Front

Fronting, another technique to cover off-ball players, involves setting up belly-to-belly with the offense, directly between the offense and the ball. Fronters stay belly-to-belly until a pass is thrown. The objective is to deny a short pass to an offensive player, usually in an inbounding situation.

Help-Out

Helping-out means that defenders far away from the ball move toward the ball and away from their coverage. Helping-out is the key to team defense, because one-on-one the offense always has an advantage.

Box Out

Boxing out prevents offensive players from getting rebounds on their own boards. Offensive players who are not covered can more easily get into position to take rebounds from the defense. A smart offensive player can also box out a defender. Boxing out is part of the Rebounding group of lessons.

Screening

The better the defense, the more on and off-ball screening is needed. A screen can free up an offensive player for a cut and/or pass. Setting a screen on the ball often frees a player for a shot. Often a screen leads to a mix-up on defense resulting in an easy score. The screening section covers how to set a screen, how to use a screen, and how to execute the screen and roll, usually called a pick and roll.

Team Skills

Team skills most importantly coordinate the movements of all players. They provide players a court position or platform from which they execute individual skills. However, players need to learn *how* to perform well before they know *where* to do it. That is why team skills take a back seat to the individual ones.

Individual skills make up most of the teachable skills. There are few team skills compared to the individual ones, or at least fewer than most people think.

The team skills include the center jump, the free-throw setup and the transition game, inbounding plays, half-court defense, half-court offense, and full-court pressure defense and offense. The player's manual covers mainly individual skills. However, there are four 2-person play transition lessons.

Center Jump

It's best to use a simple defensive center jump setup with all players setting up on the defensive end of the court for several reasons. One, the center jump is currently used at the start of the game and then rarely afterwards, so don't spend much time on it. Two, a coach needs a defensive setup so the team is not burned. If the opponent retrieves the tap, a team needs to be ready to play defense. Picking up person-to-person coverage is another skill that needs to be worked on at the center jump.

Free Throw & Transition

The free-throw setup is a great place to teach the transition game as well. A transition involves quickly moving from offense to defense or visa versa. Once players learn how to make a transition from the free-throw setup, they will be able to transition just as quickly in other situations. Defenders setting up on the lane learn how to box out a stationary player.

Inbounding

The inbound play is a simple quickly-learned play that can be learned in one day. The keys for this and any play are individual offensive skills, especially the TLC skills. Timing and communication will develop during the season. As with all plays, success requires that players adjust to the defense, so in a game this offense will not look like anything practiced.

Half-Court Defense

Half-court defense is simple: person-to-person with helping-out from the weak side. A zone requires the defense to play an opponent in their area using person-to-person techniques. Zones also involve a zone shift. Believe it or not, most types of defenses—zones, person-to-person, match ups, etc.—when played correctly, look quite similar because defenders should always be in the best position on the court.

Half-Court Offense

Half-court offense involves many offensive skills including passing, cutting, catching, faking, and the TLC skills. Half-court offense develops as long as the coach focuses on offensive skills, instead of working on that ultimate play. Instead of thinking and teaching plays, think and practice patterns of movement. A pattern of movement is a coordinated way for players to move in a half-court offense. A team must learn to coordinate movements in response to how the defense plays. So, even in a game, effective offenses rarely look like any practice pattern.

Pressure Defense

Pressure defense can be as simple as full-court, person-to-person coverage. The full-court trap with most players downcourt leaves a team vulnerable upcourt. A less risky trap is a half-court trap.

A coach uses this and other pressure defenses to wear a team down and/or cause the offense to make a mistake, not for an out-and-out steal. Pressure defenses are more effective when turned on and off, because continual use allows the offense to adjust. However, the constant pressure of a person-to-person defense may be an exception. A coach regularly adjusts the pressure, or tightness of play.

Pressure Offense

The keys to a full-court pressure offense are similar to those for a half-court offense. Do not dribble, and look, look, and look. If players do not have sufficient individual skills, no amount of practice against a press will yield success. On the other hand, when players possess individual skills, no press will be effective.

Chapter Four
4

GOALS & KEYS

Goals

With so many skills to learn, most players, parents, and coaches have great difficulty figuring out what to do first. It's easy to skip over important fundamentals, keeping busy with more advanced topics. This section will give you an idea where you are heading skill-wise and how to advance.

First

Start and work through the Ball Handling Lessons, 1-5, and the Pivoting Lessons, 6-11, because all other skills are dependent on them. No matter what your age, 12 or 22, these skills are the key to all other ones.

Second

The second goal is to make sure a you can catch a pass running full steam. Work on the Catch Cut Lessons, 53-56. Most college players lack these skills.

Third

Work on the Dribbling Lessons, 14-17, as soon as possible because about 100% of players do not know how to dribble.

Fourth

Start and work through the shooting lessons sections, 18-20 & 24-28, before working on the other shooting lessons.

Fifth

Start and work through the Defense Basics Lessons, 74-79, before continuing through the defensive lessons.

Sixth

Fit in the other skills as you can.

Last

The last thing to work on is the Play Transition Lessons, 62-65, because these are the most complex ones.

Keys To Major Skills

One big misconception about learning the basics is that to improve you must practice things millions of times. I've tried it and so has everybody else. It does not work well. Volume of practice does not necessarily bring about improvement; practicing properly insures improvement. The following **principles** tell you what and how to practice. A list of **Counterproductive Beliefs** follows. These often widely held ideas prevent learning because they do not work.

Shooting

1. Shooting improvement starts with technique. See Lessons 18 and 24-28.

2. Technique must be practiced close to the basket. See Lessons 19 and 28.

3. To improve your shooting range start close to the basket and gradually back off. See Lesson 37.

4. To improve game shooting you must shoot in a game-like situation. Do these shooting lessons last. See Lessons 39-43.

5. Every shooting move, as will as every other move to dribble or to pass, starts with a pivot. So, you must be an expert at pivoting. See Lessons 6-10.

Counterproductive Beliefs

1. *Repetition yields improvement.* This is only true to a limited degree. Improvement only follows doing things correctly. Practicing incorrectly yields problems. If you practice correctly, follow the lessons, improvement will come with much less repetition than you initially thought.

2. *Only 7th graders need to practice technique.* Not true. Even Hall of Famers do. Every time you play ball you need to warm up with a few minutes of shooting technique.

3. *Only 7th graders need to practice close to the basket.* No, everybody does for several reasons. One, this is the best way to use and apply technique. And again, without technique improvement, there is no improvement. The other reason is that a great percentage of shots are taken from this area in a game. So, it is most beneficial to practice game level shooting in this area.

4. *You can work on technique as you work on shooting.* Nope. Technique and shooting need to be practiced separately. One, technique improves your shot by changing and focusing on the mechanics (movement) of the shot. You give little thought to the actual shot when working on technique. Conversely or inversely or reciprocally, thinking about technique when in the motion of shooting can only psyche you out. These two things should be practiced, and even more importantly, thought about separately.

5. *If you are a good shooter in practice, then you should be a good game shooter.* No. Shooting rested, under little psychological pressure or physical defensive pressure in practice is not the same as shooting under more adverse game situations. Good shooters are good game shooters.

6. *You need talent to shoot well. Only naturally talented players can shoot well and learn tricky moves.* Not so. Anybody can be a good shooter or dribbler, passer, etc., if they practice properly.

7. *Great shooters are great players.* Not so. Note that many Hall of Famers are not great shooters. Shooting is only one part of the game. If you want to be a great basketball player, you need to be as tall, strong, quick, and fast as possible. Work on being an athlete as well as practicing the skills. All Hall of Famers are great athletes.

Dribbling

1. Dribbling starts with proper hand and arm motion as well as body position. See Lesson 14.

2. Moving and twisting to awkward body positions are keys to dribbling. See Lesson 15.

3. You need to dribble with defensive contact, looking in all directions, even behind, to learn how to protect the ball. Lesson 17 teaches this.

4. Dribbling is never an end unto itself. One major offensive objective is to pass the ball up court to the open player as fast as possible. You must dribble with your head up, constantly looking to pass. All lessons require players to keep their heads up and look while dribbling. Part of Lesson 16 involves both looking and passing while dribbling.

Counterproductive Beliefs

1. *Dribbling can't be taught.* You have to be a natural. This is true if you don't know how to teach dribbling. This inaccurate idea discourages coaches and players alike. Nothing could be further from the truth.

2. *Dribbling between the legs and behind the back are effective methods.* They may look good and be okay to practice, but they do not have much effect in games. Ball and body fakes are more effective.

3. *It is cool to dribble waist high or higher like many of* *the pros.* Dribbling high is much more difficult, and unless you are very quick it will lead to disaster. Bob Cousy dribbled with his elbows nearly straight; the ball was only inches, rather than feet, off the floor.

4. *The more you dribble the better you dribble.* No. Dribbling correctly improves dribbling. Dribbling with the head down, standing straight up, not bothering to look around does the reverse–you learn how to and do dribble incorrectly. So, you need to be aware of how you practice. If you want to improve your dribbling technique stop dribbling improperly, even if it is inadvertent, like the dribbling you do while shooting the ball around. Limit your dribbling to the lessons in this book.

Defense

1. You need to be in a body position than enables you to move quickly as well as maintain this position while moving. See Lesson 74.

2. You need to stay with the offensive player. See Lessons 75-79 for the basics.

3. You always force the offense to one side or the other whether or not they have the ball. See Lessons 80 and 81.

4. You must prevent low post players from moving where they want to go. It is easy to box out if you properly play defense close to the basket. See Lessons 83-86 and 88.

5. Overplaying and helping out are keys to team defense. See Lessons 83-88 on overplaying. Helping out is a team skill easily learned once you can overplay.

6. Hustle is a big part of defense. Lessons 76-79, 83, and 90 as well as several other ones teach this.

Counterproductive Beliefs

1. *Learning* **on-ball** *defense is more important than* **off-ball** *defense.* Nope–both are of nearly equal importance though *off-ball* defense is more difficult. *Off-ball* defense is more important to the team, because four players are off the ball at any moment. One-on-one any good offensive player can usually go around the defense. So, *off-ball* players always need to help out. *Off-ball* players must be in position to rebound as well.

2. *Defense is difficult to learn.* Nope. Defense is much easier to learn than any offensive skill. Less skill is involved. A player can become expert in weeks rather than the months or years it takes for offense.

3. *You can't teach hustle.* Nope. It is one of the easiest, if not the easiest, skill to teach. Every player I have ever coached hustled.

Offensive Skills

These skills include passing, catching, faking, cutting, and the TLC skills.

1. Passing as well as catching involves pivoting. See Lessons 6-7.

2. Passing technique starts with touch and wrist movement as well as arm position. Most passes involve a flick of the wrist with little arm movement. See Lessons 46 and 47.

3. To pass around a closely covering defender, you must use an overhead, side, or bounce pass. See Lessons 47-51 .

4. You need to be able to throw a long baseball pass for fast breaks or to beat a press. See Lesson 52.

5. You need to fake before every cut and just about every second you are on the court. See Lesson 58.

6. Before you can catch a pass running full speed, you need to learn the technique for 3 types of catches. See Lessons 53 and 56.

7. The pass and the catcher meet at a point. A catcher does not slow down until after catching the ball. A catcher does not wait for the ball. The arms are outstretched on all catches. See Lessons 54, 56, and 59.

8. Communication starts with looking and ends with timing.

9. Communication and looking are easy to teach and learn. See Lesson 60.

10. Timing develops only after all other offensive skills develop.

11. You must step in front of your opponent before going for a loose ball. See Lesson 57.

12. You must attempt to catch all passes, even if the pass is off the mark. See Lesson 55.

13. The key to both catching passes and team offense involves faking and cutting to the ball or to an open area. Lessons 47 and 48 cover this.

14. The last part of a cut to the ball is a jump for the ball with arms extended. See Lesson 56.

Counterproductive Beliefs

1. *Good plays are the key to team offense.* Nope. Players need to learn the fundamentals of offense. The greatest play ever concocted cannot work if players do not cut or communicate well. The simplest play ever conceived will work if players know how to cut, pass, and communicate.

2. *Chest passes may have historical significance but they are worthless with defense.* Holding the ball close to the body at waist height is a terrible place to have the ball. You can't pass fake, ball fake or readily reach around the offense. Neither can you fake a shot with the ball in this position. Say good-bye to this pass and use more effective ones.

3. *It is easy to catch a ball.* No—the footwork is quite difficult. The hands also need to be in the proper position. Pros and college players routinely drop passes because their hands are not clawed with fingers spread.

4. *Timing between players just develops.* If you can wait for evolution to take place I bet it will. However, if you practice timing it will develop within recordable time rather than eons.

5. *Passing is an easy skill.* Passing is more difficult to learn than shooting or dribbling. Their are several reasons for this. One, timing between the passer and cutter is involved. Two, flicking passes is not that easy to do. With defense on the passer and catcher, passing is very difficult.

Rebounding

1. Rebounding involves pivoting, so you need to be an expert before you start. See Lessons 6-11.

2. Rebounding involves grabbing and pulling the ball away as well as pivoting. See Lessons 3, 4, and 66.

3. One key to rebounding, which is often skipped, is predicting where the ball will go. You need to watch shot arcs carefully. See Lesson 67.

4. You need to be ready, in the ready position, for errant bounces and loose balls especially in a free throw shooting situation. See Lesson 68.

5. You need to go for offensive and defensive rebounds in a similar way. Positioning and boxing out are keys. See Lessons 69-71.

Counterproductive Beliefs

1. *You need to be tall and have a 4-foot vertical jump to rebound well.* Not necessarily true. These attributes help, but smarts will help just as much. Some players always seem to be around the ball even though they are short or can barely jump. Some of the best rebounders in pro ball history were not great jumpers.

2. *Rebounding involves just going for the ball.* Not so. Good rebounders do the following things:

- •Watch shot arcs and the shooter carefully and then accurately predict where the ball will go.
- •Step in front or get position on the opponent.
- •Rarely get boxed out.
- •Often come from behind the basket.

PART 1: FOUNDATIONS

Chapter Five
5

THE LESSONS

Most of this book, Part 2, contains lessons. Below is information about the structure and features of the lesson sections.

The Lessons, Part 2

There are 92 lessons in 22 major groups. The groups are not numbered. Each lesson has a maximum of 4 parts even though many of the one-part lessons are quite involved.

Major Group Page

Each of the 22 groups of lessons starts with a group page listing which includes a brief description of each lesson.

Lessons

Each lesson that involves individual skills attempts to focus on one aspect of one skill at a time. Lessons that involve both offense and defense always focus on only one, either the offense or defense. Lessons can be quite simple—involving just one type of motion—or complex—involving several related skills. Be aware that each of the last several direction numbers might require that the entire lesson be repeated using the other pivot foot or changing one other aspect of the lesson.

Features Of Each Lesson
Briefs

The Briefs for each part of each lesson are located at the beginning of the lesson. In one sentence the **Briefs** summarize the action and movement.

Player's Corner

The Player's Corner gives pertinent information about each lesson. *See the diagram The Player's Corner on the next page.*

Parts   Each lesson has between 1 and 4 parts.

Type   There are 3 types of lessons in the book. **Core** (CORE) lessons are necessary to learn basic skills and to perform more advanced skills. Whatever your age, spend most of your time on **Core** lessons. **Advanced** (ADV) lessons should be done by high school and older players. **Optional** (OPT) lessons involve applications of a skill already learned.

Indicates the number of Parts in the Lesson. This Lesson has 3 Parts.

A Part can be a core (CORE) or advanced (ADV) or optional (OPT) lesson.

Number of players. Always 1 or 2.

If an assistant is needed, YES, is used. If not, NO.

An icon is used if a ball is needed. An X is used if not.

An icon is used if a court is needed. An X is used if not.

Effort level. Either 1, 2 or 3.

The time in minutes needed for each part.

Player's Corner

Parts	1	2	3
Type	CORE	ADV	OPT
Players	1	2	1
Assist	NO	NO	NO
Ball	X	○	○
Court	🏀	X	🏀
Effort	1	1	2
Time	5	5	5

Players Each lesson involves a maximum of 2 players.

Assistant For many lessons an assistant is necessary for the lesson. The assistant usually passes the ball or receives a pass. For some lessons an assistant is required to watch and correct the movements of a player. The assistant should be familiar with the directions.

Ball Do you need a ball for the lesson?

Court Do you need a court for the lesson?

Effort The effort level indicates the amount of physical energy involved in a lesson, not the difficulty of a lesson. The most difficult lessons are level 1, technique level, lessons because they involve intricate body mechanics, though not much movement. Level one lessons are done slowly. Level two lessons involve movement at a normal pace either walking, shooting, or jogging. Level 3, or game-level lessons, are either full speed lessons or lessons that involve a defender. Sometimes a lesson starts at one level, then advances to the next one as a player gains expertise.

Time This is the estimated time in minutes to perform a lesson. Initially it may take much longer to do a lesson. Eventually you may be able to perform most lessons in as little as 1-2 minutes.

Why Do This

This part explains why this lesson is important and discusses the skills involved.

Directions

These are step-by-step directions usually directed to the player.

Bulleted(•) Information

The bulleted information gives additional information about the lesson that does not fit into a step.

Key Points

This is a brief summary of the directions that need emphasis.

How To Practice

Usually a player practices a lesson till he/she executes it properly. Many lessons need to be practiced every day, some only once.

Features Of The Diagrams
Lines and Arrows

The arrows and lines indicate distance or the movement of a player or the ball. *See the Diagram Legend.*

The wide triangle arrowhead is used when a player passes or runs with the ball. Dribbling is a wide arrowhead with dots, ┄┄▶. Passing is a wide arrowhead with dashes, ┄┄▶. Walking or running with the ball is a wide arrowhead with a solid tinted line, ──▶.

For cutting, a regular triangle arrowhead is used, ──▶. To show walking, jogging, or a path around the court without the ball, often a shaded arrow with the triangle head is used , ──▶.

A combination move, the pass-follow move, which involves passing to a player, then cutting to the position of this player, is indicated by a shaded regular arrow with dashes, ┄┄▶.

All fakes are gray using a simple arrowhead. A pass fake is a simple arrowhead with the pass dashed line, ┄┄➤. The cut fake is a simple gray arrowhead with a solid line, ──➤.

For pivoting with or without the ball a curved arrow is used.

The movement of groups is indicated by a larger arrow with a solid line. Sometimes arrows are shaded in a particular diagram to make the movements more clear.

Distances between players or groups is shown by a double simple wide arrowhead, ◀──▶, or straight lines without an arrowhead, ├──┤. The double simple wide arrowhead is also used to show up-and-back motion.

Diagram Legend

Actions With Ball
┄┄▶ dribble

┄ ┄ ▶ pass

──▶ walk with ball

Movement Without Ball
──▶ cut

──▶ walk, jog, run

Combination Move
┄ ┄ ▶ pass-follow

Fakes
┄ ┄ ➤ pass fake

──➤ cut fake

Pivot
↰ pivot away from pass

↰ pivot with ball

Below is one diagram from an Outside Pattern lesson. **Outside Pass 2** means the second pass in this pattern. **The Outside Pass 2 diagram** is as complicated as a diagram gets.

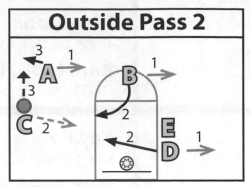

Outside Pass 2

• C starts with the ball.

• A, B, and D fake away as shown by the shaded, simple arrows. The 1 next to the arrows indicates these actions take place first and also at the same time. Numbers next to arrows clarify the sequence of movement.

• The black triangle arrows show the directions that A, B, & D cut after the fake.

• C fakes a pass to B and D when they cut across the lane as indicated by the gray dashed line with the simple arrowhead. The 2 next to the arrow indicates that these actions take place second and also at the same time.

• B & D respond like they are catching the pass (pass-response fake).

• C then passes to A as indicated by the black dashed line with a wide triangle arrowhead. The 3 next to the arrows indicate these actions take place last and also at the same time.

Body Position Of Player

Often it is important to see the direction that a player faces. There are two types of diagrams that show the alignment of a player's body from an overhead view. **See the diagrams to the left.** The line in the diagram **Overhead 1** or the ellipse in the diagram **Overhead 2** represents the shoulders. The feet are directly below the ends of the shoulders so the ends could represent the feet as well. The circle shows the head. The player faces the direction that the head extends from the shoulders.

In the **Squaring-Up diagram**, the body diagram clearly shows the orientation of the body. Player A is directly facing the basket from the side; B is not directly facing the basket; C is facing the backboard. Squaring-up means that a player shoots in the direction that his/her body faces.

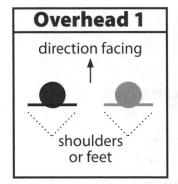

Overhead 1

direction facing

shoulders or feet

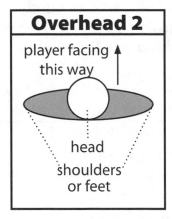

Overhead 2

player facing this way

head

shoulders or feet

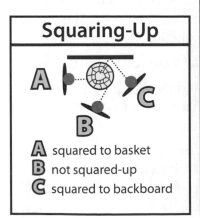

Squaring-Up

A squared to basket
B not squared-up
C squared to backboard

Shading For Different Positions

When a player is shown in two positions in the same diagram, the current position is usually a dark shade. The previous position is usually a very light shade. The movement arrow from the previous position is also very light in some cases. In some places this color scheme is reversed for clarity.

In the diagram Part 3-Right Side, Step 2 shows the light shade as the previous position. The arrow indicates a pivot to the current position where the body is dark. Step 3 shows the previous position as light again with an arrow indicating another pivot to the current position, which is dark.

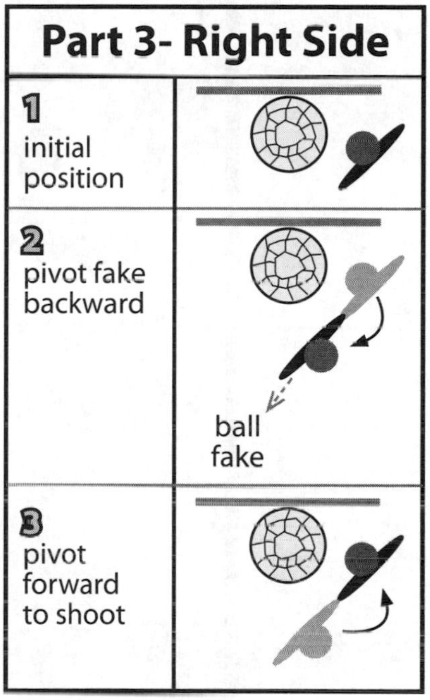

Part 3- Right Side	
1 initial position	
2 pivot fake backward	ball fake
3 pivot forward to shoot	

PART 1: FOUNDATIONS

Part 2
The Lessons

BALL-HANDLING LESSONS

1 Touch
2 Hands Ready
3 Grab
4 Go For Ball
5 Prevent Tie Ups/Fouls

The Ball-Handling lessons involve skills integral to the ball skills: shooting; passing; dribbling; and going-for-the-ball skills including rebounding. These are also prerequisites for faking with the ball. The first lesson, Touch, is a skill necessary to control a shot, pass, or dribble. Hands Ready, Lesson 2, puts the hands in the best position to catch a pass or rebound. Lesson 3, Grab, deals with getting and keeping a rebound and loose ball. Lesson 4, Go For Ball, works on going after a loose ball against an opponent. Prevent Tie Ups/Fouls, Lesson 5, shows how to to keep the ball away from a pressing defender.

1 Touch

Player's Corner

Parts	1
Type	CORE
Players	1
Assist	NO
Ball	◯
Court	X
Effort	1
Time	3

Setup

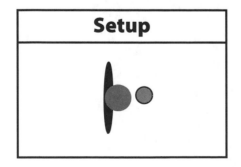

Brief
Hold the ball in an exaggerated position in contact with the fingerends.

Why Do This
Shooting, passing, dribbling, rebounding, and especially catching depend on fingertip ball control. This lesson increases the sensitivity of the fingertips. Sensitivity is another name for touch, a word used in connection with shooting. However, touch is needed just as much for passing, catching, and dribbling.

This lesson also particularly helps a player who routinely drops easy passes, rebounds, and loose balls. Usually these miscues result when a player attempts to catch the ball with the hands, palms, and fingers, rather than the fingerends. Butterfingers involve more than sixth grade players; some pros are butterfingers as well.

Directions
1. Put the ball down. Spread the fingers apart as far as possible. Shape each hand into a claw and growl. The growl must be fierce.

2. Pick up the ball with your claws, so that only the fingerends touch the ball. ***See the diagram Fingertip Control.***

•Long fingernails make this impossible; trim them as soon as possible.

Fingertip Control

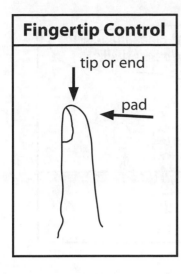

tip or end

pad

3. The palm and other parts of the fingers should not touch the ball.

4. Hold the ball tightly for 30 seconds to one minute.

Key Points

1. Fingers spread apart as far as possible.

2. Fingers clawed, not bent at joints.

3. Hands clawed, not flat.

4. Fingerends only contact the ball.

How To Practice

You can improve your ability to shoot, pass, catch, and dribble without even practicing the actual skill. Work on holding the ball at any time during practice, or at home. You will readily note an improvement in control on shots, passes, and dribbles.

2 Hands Ready

Player's Corner

Parts	1
Type	CORE
Players	1
Assist	NO
Ball	○
Court	X
Effort	1
Time	3

Setup

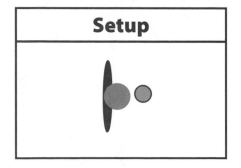

Brief
Jump into the hands ready position.

Why Do This
The hands-ready position involves more than the hands; the entire body must be prepared to rebound, catch a pass, or go for a loose ball. This position is just like the rebounding ready position. Taking an extra instant to get into position gives your opponent an advantage. So, be ready ahead of time.

Directions
1. The ready position insures that you will be able to grab any ball that comes your way, whether it be a rebound, loose ball, or pass.

2. Put the ball down. Bend your knees, extend your arms straight forward with fingers spread apart and hands clawed. Bend the wrists back as far as possible. Bring the elbows toward the body. *See the diagram Hands Ready Position.*

3. The arms are coiled in a sense, ready to spring for the ball.

4. Stand up and when ready jump into the hands ready position again.

5. Then grab the ball with the fingerends.

6. Repeat 5-25 times.

•An assistant can yell, "go", for steps 4 and 5.

Hands Ready Position

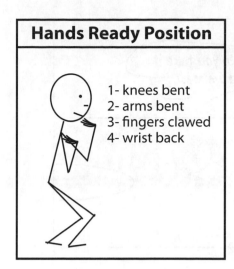

1- knees bent
2- arms bent
3- fingers clawed
4- wrist back

Key Points

1. You should be in a position to move or run.

2. The jump should be quick.

3. The fingers need to be spread apart, hands clawed.

4. The forearms are vertical, up and down.

How To Practice

It is best to practice with an assistant giving cues. This lesson only needs to be repeated 1-3 times.

3 Grab Ball

Player's Corner

Part	1	2	3	4
Type	CORE	CORE	CORE	CORE
Players	2	2	2	2
Assist	NO	NO	NO	NO
Ball	○	○	○	○
Court	X	X	X	X
Effort	2-3	2-3	2-3	2-3
Time	5	5	5	5

Setup

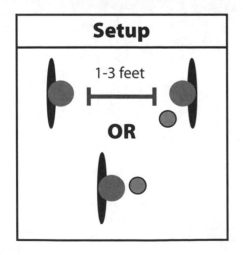

1-3 feet

OR

Briefs

In Part 1, one player holds the ball at waist level, while the other pulls it away.

In Part 2, the ball is held overhead.

In Part 3, the ball is held low.

In Part 4, the grabber pivots away 180 degrees.

Why Do This

In a game, a rebounder does not just wait for the ball to float into his/her hands. The player must grab the ball out of the air and out of the hands of other players, then rip it away to a safer place before the next move. A player going for loose balls on the floor, or even catching a pass in traffic must also go strongly for the ball.

Grabbing is the last step in both catching and rebounding. Initially perform these lessons slowly at the technique level emphasizing fingertip control of the ball. Then add pivoting, increasing the intensity of the drill.

In Parts 1-3 work on turning the body without necessarily pivoting. This is the difficult part of the lesson. Part 4 combines this body turn with a half turn or 180-degree pivot away. Just about all the

Grab Steps

1- hold out ball

2- grab and pull away

Grab Rebound

hold the ball high & out, not overhead

grab a rebound

Grab Loose Ball

grab a loose ball

pivoting in these lessons is forward, the easy direction to pivot. These lessons can be performed individually by one player just tossing the ball high, low, or at waist-height. This may be better for the touch aspects of the lesson, however it is easier to perform the grab and pull away if done in groups of two.

Part 1 Grab Waist High
Directions

1. One player tightly holds the ball at waist-height with the fingertips. *See the Grab Steps diagram.*

2. The grabber sets up in a ready position with arms out, fingers spread apart.

3. Grab the ball with the fingertips, then strongly pull it away, turning the body as you do so. It's okay, though not necessary, to pivot away in this lesson. Just grab the ball like you are angry at this person. Grab it like they stole it from you. It's okay if the momentum from the grab makes you pivot.

4. After one player grabs the ball, the players set up again and the other player grabs it back without changing positions. Continue for 5 minutes.

5. Halfway through the lesson switch grabbing directions; left then right or vice-versa. Better yet, every other grab should be in the other direction.

Key Points

1. Start in the hands ready position.

2. Use fingertip control of ball. No hands touching ball.

3. Grab forcefully with both hands.

4. Turn strongly away with the ball. It's okay to pivot.

How To Practice

Repeat 3--5 times or till you can do this properly.

Part 2 Grab Rebound
Directions

1. Hold the ball high and slightly forward. The rebounder should be able to touch the ball without jumping. Tall players should hold the ball within the reach of shorter players. *See the diagram Grab Rebound.*

2. Grab the ball like you would a rebound. Grab it hard, then turn the body away. Rip the ball away from the opponent.

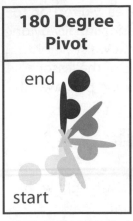

180 Degree Pivot

end

start

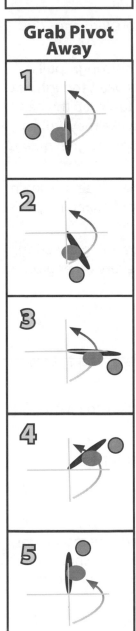

Grab Pivot Away

1

2

3

4

5

3. Halfway through the lesson switch grabbing directions or every other grab is in the other direction.

Key Points

Hold the ball high in front, not overhead.

How To Practice

Repeat 3--5 times or till you can do this properly.

Part 3 Grab Loose Ball
Directions

1. One player places the ball on the floor. *See the diagram Grab Loose Ball.* The other player stretches low for the ball, grabs, and then forcefully pulls the ball away. This is like picking up a loose ball.

2. Place the ball on the floor again, so the other player can grab it back.

3. Halfway through the lesson strongly pull the ball in the other direction or pull in the other direction every other grab.

Key Points

1. This part can easily be done solo.

How To Practice

Repeat 3--5 times or till you can do this properly.

Part 4 Grab Pivot Away
Directions

1. Repeat the first three parts adding a pivot away with the grab. *See the diagrams 180 Degree Pivot and Grab Pivot Away.* It's a good idea to work on basic pivoting, Lesson 6, before doing this part.

2. Start with the left foot pivot first, then switch to the right foot.

3. The only direction change to the first three parts is this: grab the ball, then rip and pivot away in one move. This is very difficult for players at all levels. Rip it away like someone stole it from you and you are assertively taking it back.

4. Initially its okay to go slow with easy grab pivots away. However, the goal is a ferocious rip of the ball with a 180 degree or half-turn pivot.

Key Points

1. Grab forcefully and pivot a half-turn away.

How To Practice

Repeat 3--5 times or till you can do this properly.

4 Go For Ball

Player's Corner

Part	1	2	3
Type	CORE	CORE	CORE
Players	2	2	2
Assist	YES	YES	YES
Ball	◯	◯	◯
Court	X	X	X
Effort	3	3	3
Time	3	3	3

Setup Parts 1-3

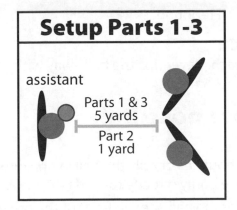

assistant

Parts 1 & 3
5 yards

Part 2
1 yard

Briefs

In Part 1, two players compete for a pass.

In Part 2, two players go for a rebound.

In Part 3, two players go for a loose ball.

Why Do This

In Lesson 4 players apply what was learned in the previous lessons to more realistic situations. Go strongly after any loose ball, rebound, or even a pass, in order to beat an opponent. First get position by stepping in front of the opponent, then grab and rip the ball away. The assistant should toss the ball so that each player ends up with the same number of rips.

Part 1 Go For Ball
Directions

1. Two players set up leaning against each other, facing the assistant who is 5 yards away with the ball.

2. The catchers should be in the hands-ready position.

3. The assistant throws a pass right between the players.

4. Both players go for the ball. The one who catches it should rip it away from the opponent and pivot away.

5. Pass the ball back to the assistant.

6. Switch sides after each pass. Continue for 1-5 minutes.

Key Points

1. Players start side-to-side leaning on each other.

2. The player who gets the ball, rips it away and simultaneously pivots away.

3. Switch sides after each throw.

How To Practice

Practice each part till each player rips the ball away with authority. This may take 2-5 times.

Part 2 Go For Rebound
Directions

1. Two players line up next to each other.

2. The assistant tosses the ball overhead between the players. Do not toss the ball high, just slightly over the head of the shorter player. If the ball is tossed high, the taller player might grab the ball every time. However, if the ball is tossed lower, both players have an equal opportunity to grab it.

3. Both players go for the rebound; the winner rips the ball away and pivots away from the opponent.

4. Pass the ball back to the assistant.

5. Switch sides after each rebound. Continue for 1-5 minutes.

Key Points

1. Players start side-to-side leaning on each other.

2. The toss should only be slightly over the head of the shorter player.

3. Switch sides after each rebound.

How To Practice

Practice each part till each player rips the ball away with authority. This may take 2-5 times.

Part 3 Go For Loose Ball
Directions

1. The assistant slowly bounces or rolls the ball in one direction or another, not necessarily directly towards the players.

2. The two players go for the ball. Step in front of the other player before going for the ball. The winner rips the ball away from the opponent and pivots away.

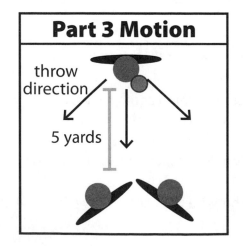

Part 3 Motion

throw direction

5 yards

3. Pass back to the assistant.

4. Switch sides every other time. Continue for 1-5 minutes.

Key Points

1. Step in front of the opponent first.

2. Grab with arms extended and rip the ball away.

3. Pivot away from the opponent.

How To Practice

Practice each part till each player rips the ball away with authority. This may take 2-5 times.

5 Prevent Tie Ups/Fouls

Player's Corner

Part	1	2	3
Type	CORE	OPT	ADV
Players	2	2	2
Assist	NO	NO	YES
Ball	○	○	○
Court	X	X	X
Effort	3	3	3
Time	3-5	3-5	3-5

Setup Parts 1-2

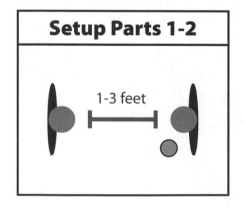

1-3 feet

Briefs

In Part 1, one player quickly moves a ball right in front of another player, who attempts to take it away.

In Part 2, the player with the ball pivots away as well.

In Part 3, the pivoter passes on a signal.

Why Do This

A closely covered offensive player must quickly move the ball to avoid getting tied up. This type of ball movement is also used in fakes and other moves. The defense learns how to tie up the offense without fouling. Young players, in particular, often flail their arms and hands at the offense when going for the ball. This lesson helps to prevent unnecessary fouls and players fouling out.

This is a two-sided drill: you can do this as an offensive, move-ball drill or a defensive, prevent-foul drill. I suggest you first do it as the offensive, move-ball drill. Do it at a later date concentrating on defense. With hackers work on the defensive part immediately. Part 3 introduces the first looking drill.

Move Ball

High and Low

Right and Left

Far and Near

Part 1 Move Ball
Directions

1. Set up 1-3 feet apart facing each other. The closer the better. Do not move your feet once you are set. The objective is to move the ball, not your body.

2. The offense must remain facing the defense. Do not turn away.

3. The defense aggressively goes after the ball without fouling. Flailing the arms without contact is considered a foul. If you foul either by touch or reckless flailing, you stay on defense. The defense loudly counts to 10, then stops.

4. The offense moves the ball quickly up and down, left and right, and/or close to far away from the body in order to keep it away from the defense. *See the diagram Move Ball.* Initially just move the arms. Keep your body facing the defense. Do not turn away; do not bend your knees or turn sideways.

5. The offense calls contact fouls. After a foul, repeat the drill without switching roles. Switch roles if there is no foul.

6. After the defense counts to 10, the offense gives the ball to the defender. Switch roles, not positions, and repeat.

7. A second worthwhile way to perform this lesson is to allow the offense to move the body up and down, rotate hips, and turn away. However, no foot movement, even any swiveling of the feet. Move the ball high, low, left, right, close and far either in the front or on the side of your body.

Key Points

1. Feet do not move, offense or defense.

2. Set up as close as possible, but not so close that the drill can not be properly performed. Too close makes the drill impossible; too far too easy.

3. The offense must face the defense, not turn away. A second way to do the drill involves turning away.

4. No flailing of arms allowed.

5. Offense calls fouls or flailing.

How To Practice
Do this for 5-10 minutes at least 3 times.

Part 2 Pivot And Move
Directions

1. Perform the first several pivoting lessons before doing this part.

2. The player with the ball pivots away from the defense.

3. The defense runs or moves to get the ball. Don't just stand around and reach for the ball. Take off after the ball wherever it is. Try to get in front of the pivoter. Do not stay behind the pivoter.

4. The defense must work hard so the offense gets good practice.

5. Go after the ball for 10 seconds. Offense counts and calls fouls. If no foul is called switch roles.

Key Points

1. This is a move feet and body drill, not like the previous one.

2. The defense must make a great effort so the offense gets practice.

3. Make sure to work on pivoting first.

How To Practice

The offense only needs to practice this drill once or twice. However, the defense may need more practice. There is a very similar defensive drill, Lesson 78.

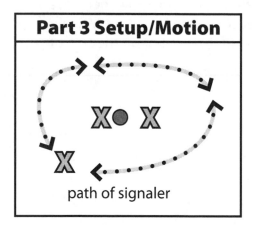

Part 3 Setup/Motion

path of signaler

Part 3 Move, Pivot & Look
Directions

1. This is the same as the previous drill except the pivoter must also look to pass.

2. The assistant walks at a medium pace around the group during the lesson, then signals to the pivoter when to pass. The signal can be just raising an arm.

3. On the signal the pivoter must pass. The pass should be immediate, not 2-3 seconds later.

•Adding a second defender on the ball makes the drill more difficult. This is not for novices. Great for TLC skills.

Key Points

1. The additional skill practiced in this drill is looking.

2. This is very difficult. Most passes will be late.

How To Practice

Practice 5-15 minutes initially. Repeat this as many days as needed until the passer is always watching the signaler.

PIVOTING LESSONS

Just about every movement on the court, whether on offense or defense, involves pivoting. That's because pivoting involves both balance and the ability to change direction. Every player at every level from first grade to pro needs to work through every pivoting lesson. See **About Pivoting** on the next page for more information on pivoting.

Lesson 6, Start Pivoting, involves forward and backward pivots on either pivot foot. Lesson 7, Jab-Step, gives the foundation for driving to the basket, all moves, and all fakes. Lesson 8, Ball Fakes, works on ball fakes with jab steps. Lesson 9, Crossover Step, teaches how to take a crossover step on a drive or pass. Lesson 10, Pivot Routines, involves several routines that can be used against defensive players in a crowd. Lesson 11, Pivot With Defense, adds defensive players to the previous lesson.

purpose of the lesson which is to improve your balance. If you are off balance, then slow down.

5. Swivel on the ball of your pivot foot, the pivot point. Do not slide your foot.

6. Now, go backwards. Go around twice.

7. Now, switch the pivot foot. Put all of your weight on the ball of the other foot. Heel up. Go around twice.

8. Now pivot backwards. Go around twice.

9. Repeat the steps as many times as needed or until you are dizzy. You need to do this till you are very comfortable pivoting.

10. A player can, by the rules, pivot on any part of the body without walking. This includes toes, knees, and your seat. These more unusual pivot points are sometimes employed when a player scrambles on the floor for the ball. However, using the ball of the foot is the most practical and easiest way to pivot.

11. As a check to make sure you do not slide the pivot foot while pivoting, start with your pivot foot, specifically your pivot point, on a marked spot on the floor. This can be where two court lines meet or cross. If your foot is not on the same spot when you complete the lesson, then you are sliding your foot. Sliding is a walking violation.

Key Points

1. A clear pivot point.

2. Heel up.

3. Balance and ease of movement.

4. Head up.

5. Check for sliding of pivot foot.

How To Practice

Repeat this lesson many times each day until you feel comfortable and balanced on each pivot. A practice session can be 100 pivots, 25 each way; forward, then backward, on each foot.

Part 2 Half Turn Pivots
Directions

1. This is the same as the previous lesson except that each pivot is 180 degrees or halfway around.

2. Four pivots equals 2 times around. Pivot 4 times forward, then 4 times backward on each pivot foot.

3. The objective is not to go fast. Slow down so you can improve your balance. Rushing through this lesson off-balance indicates that you need more work on basic pivoting.

4. After you do this several times, repeat holding a ball in an exaggerated position with your fingerends.

Key Points

1. Make sure to keep the heel up.

2. Make sure that you swivel on the pivot point, not slide the foot.

How To Practice

Repeat this lesson several times a day till you feel comfortable pivoting in each direction with each foot. A practice session can be 100 pivots, 25 each way; forward, then backward, on each foot.

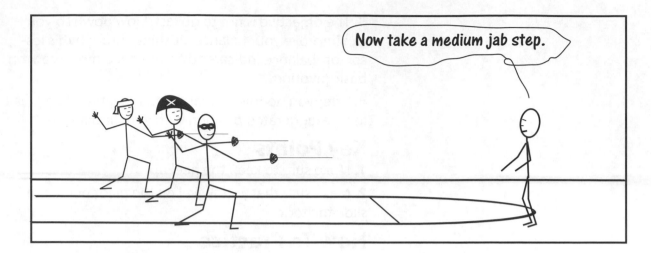

7 Jab Step

Player's Corner

Parts	1	2
Type	CORE	CORE
Players	1	1
Assist	NO	NO
Ball	◯	◯
Court	X	X
Effort	1-2	1-2
Time	3-5	3-5

Setup Parts 1-2

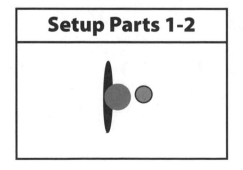

Briefs

In Part 1, take a short jab-step with either foot.

In Part 2, take a long jab-step.

Why Do This

Faking is a major part of the game. Just about every second on the court, whether on offense or defense, you should be faking or misleading the opponent. The jab-step or jab fake involves taking a step in one direction with a shift in weight. You use this type of step virtually each time you control the ball, fake without the ball, and play defense. The jab-step is also the main part of just about every fake a player makes before driving, shooting, or passing.

Part 1 Jab-Step
Directions

•There are three lengths for a jab-step. For a 6-foot player, after the jab-step, the feet are about:

  (a) 2 feet apart on a short jab-step.

  (b) 3 feet for a medium or regular jab-step.

  (c) 4-6 feet for a long jab-step.

For younger, smaller players, the distances are less. So, use stretching to determine the length of the step. A small jab-step involves virtually no

Length Of A Jab-Step
(for a 6-foot player)

Type	Stretch	Diagram
Short	~2 feet	
Regular or Medium	~3 feet	
Long	~4-6 feet	

Jab-Step

Wrong Idea	Right Idea
pivot foot	pivot foot
step with foot only knee points out	body over jab foot knee points to front

stretch; a medium involves a small stretch; a long jab-step involves the maximum amount of stretching possible. *See the diagram Length Of A Jab-Step.*

•Perform medium jab-steps if no length is mentioned.

•The long jab-step is such a long stretch that even college players will readily pull a muscle if they are not careful.

1. Hold the ball at waist-height in an exaggerated position with the fingerends. The feet are shoulder-width apart, with the left foot pivot foot. Make sure the feet are not more than shoulder width apart. Less is okay.

2. Take a step to the right, then return to the starting position. This is called a jab-step.

3. A jab step is actually more than just a step. You want to shift the entire body, including the upper body, in the direction of the jab-step. Initially don't worry about this. *See the diagram Jab-Step.*

4. Repeat this jab-step to the right 10 times.

5. Switch pivot foot and repeat steps 1-4 jab-stepping to the left.

6. If your feet are too far apart when you start, the jab-step does not look like much. Feet should start shoulder-width or less apart.

7. Move the ball to an overhead passing position. Make sure the arms are extended overhead, elbows near straight. Left foot pivot.

8. Now jab-step to the right, leading with the hip instead of the foot. Hip first, then foot. Remember "Get Hip!" This ensures that the jab-step involves the entire body not just the foot. Push the hip right. Don't worry about the foot. This helps keep the body over the foot. Slowly repeat 10 times.

9. Now use the right foot to pivot. Move the hip left before the foot. This is a jab-step left. Repeat 10 times.

Key Points

1. Feet must be shoulder width, or less, apart to start.

2. Move the hip and body on the jab, not just the foot.

How To Practice

Perform 100 jab steps slowly, 50 left, 50 right, till you are clearly moving the body, not just the foot. Perform this routine 5 times or more each day. This may be much more difficult than you think. Just moving the foot without the body is worthless, so take your time and work on this drill.

Part 2 Long Jab-Step
Directions

1. The long jab-step is used to pivot out of trouble, move past a defender when driving to the basket, or passing to the side of an opponent. Most players will not step long enough. The body needs to be over the foot; the long jab-step is more than a step. *See the diagram Long Jab-Step.*

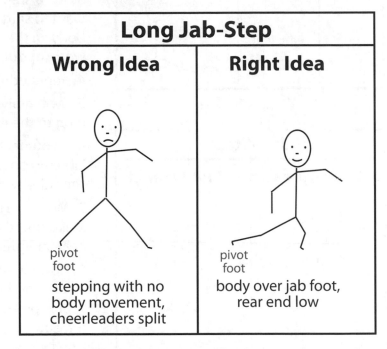

2. Left foot pivot with feet shoulder-width apart. Take a very long step or lunge to the right. The body needs to move with the foot. Hold it. Stretch as far as you can go. Your upper body should be close to the ground. Repeat 10 times. Go at your own pace.

3. This is more than a step, move your entire body in the direction of the jab-step. Stretch to the maximum. Your body should be close to the ground.

4. Switch pivot foot and take a long jab-step or lunge to the left. Repeat 10 times.

5. Initially don't worry about keeping a clear pivot point because your pivot foot may turn to the side and slide on the stretch. Be aware of this and correct the problem when you improve the stretch.

6. Eventually start with the pivot point on a mark on the floor, so you can check of sliding.

Key Points

1. Most of the body weight is on jab foot.

2. Body close to ground.

3. Knee of jab leg pointing forward, not sideways.

4. Body over knee of jab foot.

5. Head up.

6. Eventually, check for sliding of the pivot foot.

7. Eventually, the pivot foot has a clear pivot point.

How To Practice

If you are physically able, do this for 3-5 minutes each day till you can stretch to your maximum without walking. Then work on increasing your jab without walking. This could readily take more than one month.

8 Ball Fakes

Player's Corner

Parts	1	2
Type	CORE	CORE
Players	1	1
Assist	NO	NO
Ball	◯	◯
Court	X	X
Effort	1-2	1-2
Time	3-5	3-5

Setup Parts 1-2

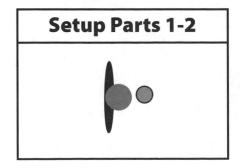

Briefs

In Part 1, add a ball fake to each jab-step.

In Part 2, an overhead pass fake is used with each jab-step.

Why Do This

Parts 1 and 2 involve adding a ball fake to a jab-step. Initially each ball fake will be perfunctory, mechanical in nature and not convincing to a defender. After much practice, the fake can cause a defender to move in the fake direction, shift weight, or freeze.

Fakes, in general, must be slow enough to allow a defender to react, and the fake must be real. A ball fake is only real if the defender thinks he can grab or block the ball. A jab fake or pivot fake is only real if the defender thinks that he can stop the move.

The jab-step with a ball fake is an essential movement for players at every level. Jab-steps and ball fakes will make inexperienced players act like (and be) more experienced ones.

Think of a fake as a simple move rather than as a tricky one. You do not need to be tricky. Just slowly put out a carrot for the defense, then watch the defense like a hawk. When the defense moves for

Foot & Ball Movement

movement
foot - ->   pivot point x   feet (toe / heel)
ball ⟶   ball ●

LESSON	BALL	MOVEMENT
Lesson 7 previous lesson	at waist	
Part 1	at waist	step 1 / 2
Part 2	high	step 1 / 2 / 3

the carrot, you quickly pull it away and move in another direction.

Part 1 Jab Ball Fake
Directions
•This is the same as previous lesson but with ball movement. *See the diagram Foot & Ball Movement.*

1. Left foot pivot. Take a medium jab-step to the right simultaneously pushing the ball right. This is a jab-step with a ball fake. *See Step 1 in Part 1 of the diagram.*

2. Do not perform the move fast. A fake must be slow enough for a defender to react. As you slowly jab-step to the side and slightly forward towards where the defender would be, push the ball out slowly like you want the defense to grab it.

3. In a real situation you must quickly move in the other direction as soon as the defender moves or even just shifts his/her weight towards the ball. In this drill, imagine that a defender reaches for the ball, then immediately pivot away. *See Step 2 in Part 1 of the diagram.* Repeat 10 times. We will spend more time on this pivot away, called a crossover step, in the next lesson.

4. Switch pivot foot. The right foot is now the pivot foot. Jab-step left, pushing the ball left. Repeat 10 times.

Key Points
1. Push the ball slowly to the side and only slightly towards the defense.

2. Simultaneously take a slow jab-step to the side and only slightly towards the defense.

3. When you see the defense move towards the ball, quickly move or pivot away.

How To Practice
Your first attempts at a ball fake will be horrendous. For improvement you will need to work with another player. A proper ball fake is one that causes the defense to react. In a sense, it is not tricky. You need to practice this till the defender goes for the ball.

Part 2 Jab Pass Fake
Directions
1. Start with the ball high overhead. Elbows straight, not bent. Feet shoulder-width apart. Left foot pivot foot.

2. Fake a pass by doing two things: one, look in the direction that you fake; two, fake a pass. *See Step 1 in Part 2 of the diagram Foot & Ball Movement.* Again, the fakes are slow. Really look somewhere at something. The fake pass need only be a flick of the wrist, the arms do not need to move.

3. Now take a short-to-medium jab-step to the right while simultaneously pushing the ball out to the right. *See Step 2 in Part 2 of the diagram.*

4. Pivot away to the left when the imagined defender moves to the ball. *See Step 3 in Part 2 of the diagram.* We will spend more time on this pivot, called a crossover step, in the next lesson.

5. Repeat the jab pass fake 10 times.

6. Switch pivot foot and repeat.

Key Points

1. Hold the ball extended high overhead.

2. The arms move very little on the fake.

3. Look in a particular direction at something, not into the twilight zone.

4. The fake is slow.

How To Practice

Practice this till you can fake out a defender.

9 Crossover Step

Player's Corner

Parts	1	2
Type	CORE	CORE
Players	1	1
Assist	NO	NO
Ball	⬤	⬤
Court	X	X
Effort	1-2	1-2
Time	3-5	3-5

In Part 1, take a long crossover step. In Part 2, perform a long crossover step fake.

Why Do This

The crossover step is used to drive to the basket, dribble past a defender and in many moves close to the basket. You can also perform this starting with an overhead pass fake.

Part 1 Crossover Step

1. Left foot pivot. Feet shoulder-width apart. Ball at waist-height. *See the diagram Part 1 Foot & Ball Movement.*

2. With the right foot take a medium jab-step to the right with a ball fake, pushing the ball out. *Step 1 in diagram.*

3. Then, with the right foot take a step left across your body, then forward. This is a crossover step. Keep the ball low and push it to the far left as you take the step. *Steps 2-3 in diagram.*

4. If you start the crossover step by going almost straight forward, you will bump into the defender. So, the move must be a crossover to the left first, then forward on the same step.

5. Repeat 10 times.

6. Now repeat this again taking a very long crossover step. Your body will be close to the floor after the crossover step.

7. Switch pivot foot and repeat steps 1-6 moving to the right.

Key Points

1. Go across before going forward.

2. After the crossover your body will be stretched close to the floor.

3. Make sure you do not slide the pivot foot. Start with the pivot point on a mark on the floor.

Part 1 Foot & Ball Movement

movement foot - -> ball ⟶	pivot point x ball ⬤	feet ⬭⬭ toe / heel

BALL	MOVEMENT
at waist	step 1 *medium jab first*
	2 *long crossover*
	3 *after crossover step*

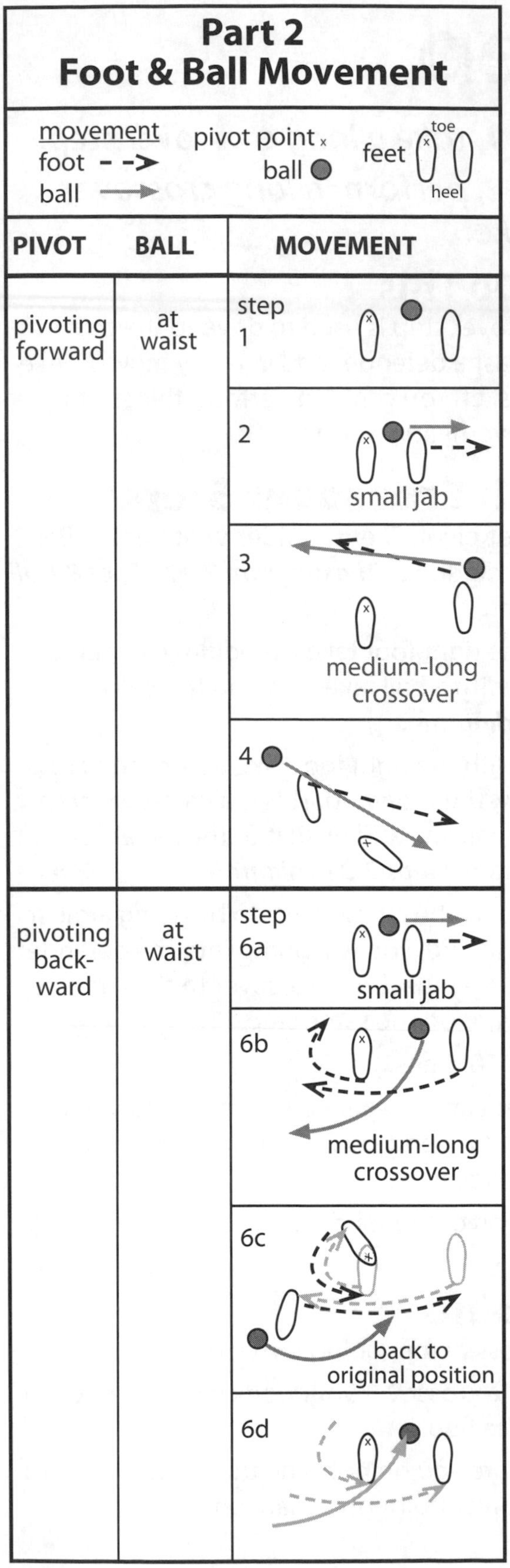

Part 2
Foot & Ball Movement

PIVOT	BALL	MOVEMENT
pivoting forward	at waist	step 1
		2 small jab
		3 medium-long crossover
		4
pivoting back-ward	at waist	step 6a small jab
		6b medium-long crossover
		6c back to original position
		6d

movement
foot - - ->
ball ——>
pivot point x
ball ●
feet (toe / heel)

How To Practice

The first practice goal is to get low, close to the ground on the crossover. The second is to make sure that you are not sliding the pivot foot. Best to have someone watch your movements.

Part 2 Crossover Step Fake
Directions

•This is for more advanced players.

1. Left foot pivot. Feet shoulder-width apart. Ball at waist-height. *See Step 1 in the diagram Part 2 Foot & Ball Movement.*

•You can perform each part of this lesson starting with the overhead pass fake as well.

2. With the right foot take a small jab-step to the right with a slight ball fake. *Step 2 in the diagram.*

3. Then, with the right foot take a step across your body to the left. Pushing the ball to the left and forward. Make sure to extend the arms. This is the crossover step fake. *Step 3 in the diagram.*

4. Step back and move the ball back to the starting position. *Step 4 in the diagram.*

5. Repeat 10 times.

6. Keep the same pivot foot. Repeat the move pivoting backwards. *See the bottom part of the diagram Part 2 Foot & Ball Movement.*

  (a) Take a small jab-step to the right pushing the ball out again with arms extended.

  (b) Pivot around backwards almost a half turn.

  (c) Push the ball outside of the right foot.

  (d) Pivot back to the starting position.

7. Repeat 10 times.

8. Repeat steps 1-7 with the right foot as pivot.

•Part 2 may look just like Part 1 unless it is done properly. In Part 2 the initial jab-step and ball fake are quite small, the crossover is medium-large and the ball is pushed out ahead as a fake, and then there is a back step. In Part 1 the jab-step is medium, the crossover is long and there is no step back to the original position.

Key Points

1. Go slow.

2. Extend on the crossover step.

3. Push the ball out at the end of the crossover pivot.

4. Check for sliding of the pivot foot by starting on a mark.

How To Practice

Remember that all training attempts to improve agility, so Part 2 is at least worthwhile to do once. Part 2 is primarily for more advanced players. Less advanced players will benefit from more basic lessons. It would be worthwhile to have someone watch you do this drill.

10 Pivot Routines

Setup Parts 1-3

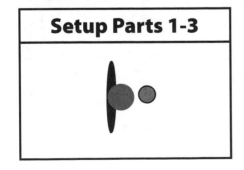

Briefs

In Part 1, perform six drills involving forceful ball movement along with pivoting.

In Part 2, do a high routine, pushing the ball from low to high back down to low on a pivot around.

In Part 3, do a low routine, pushing the ball from high to low back to high on a pivot around.

Why Do This

These lessons are more realistic than the grabbing lessons in the Ball Handling section. Each combines pivoting with ball movement, which helps prevent tie-ups in tight situations. All ball movements need to be strong. *See the Pivot Routine Ball Movement chart to compare movements.*

Part 1 Pivot Rip
Directions

1. These are six rip drills. For each rip drill, jab-step, then forcefully push the ball in the indicated direction. Repeat each rip 5 times.

2. Left foot pivot. Start with ball at waist-height.

  Rip 1-Jab-step right and simultaneously push

Pivot Routine Ball Movement

Routine	Setup To End Of Jab-Step	On Pivot	End
Rip 1	waist to waist	--	--
Rip 2	waist to high	--	--
Rip 3	waist to low	--	--
Rip 4	waist to waist	waist	high
Rip 5	waist to high	high	high
Rip 6	waist to low	low	high
Part 2-3 Routines			
High	waist to low	high	low
Low	high to low	low	high

the ball out waist-high and to the right side.

Rip 2-Jab-step right and simultaneously push the ball out high to the right side.

Rip 3-Jab-step right and simultaneously push the ball out low, close to the ground, to the right.

3. Each of rips 4-6 involve two rips as well as a pivot around. The ball starts at waist-height. On the 180 degree pivot around, make sure to push the ball ahead of the body. Left foot pivot.

Rip 4-Jab-step right and push the ball to the right, waist-high. Then pivot around a half-turn forward, ripping the ball across the body. The ball leads the body around. Bring the ball overhead after pivoting around.

Rip 5-Same as rip 4, but push the ball high first, then keep the ball high as you pivot around. Bring the ball overhead only after pivoting around.

Rip 6-Same as rip 4, but push the ball low first, then keep the ball low as you pivot around. Bring the ball overhead only after pivoting around.

•All ball movement involves forceful rips.

4. Repeat the six rips using the right foot as pivot.

5. It's optional, though worthwhile, to repeat directions 1-4 pivoting backwards.

Key Points

1. The rip and pivot move is difficult.

2. Performed properly, the rip is fast and ferocious.

3. Make sure to do each rip on each pivot foot.

How To Practice

Most players will need work on this. Improve pivoting first.

Part 2 High Routine
Directions

•This routine is called the high routine because you bring the ball across high on the pivot.

•To better understand this routine, practice sev-

Part 2
Ball & Foot Movement

pivot point······ⓧ toe / movement
pivot foot········ / ---> ball ●
heel

STEPS	BALL	MOVEMENT
1	waist to low	
2	low to high	
3	high	
4	high to low	
5	low	

eral times with a defender in front. The defender plays at half speed, going for the ball, but not disrupting the move. You need to know that you are pivoting away from a defender.

1. Hold the ball at waist-height; feet shoulder-width apart. The left foot is the pivot foot. *See the diagram Part 2 Ball & Foot Movement.* The steps in the diagram do not correspond to the direction numbers.

2. Take a long jab-step right pushing the ball low to the ground. Touch the ground with the ball. The ball is to the right of your right foot. This should be a quick powerful move. *Step 1 in diagram.*

3. Start a long 180 degree pivot, pushing the ball high overhead as you pivot. Keep the ball close to and on the right side of your body as you bring it up. This should be a quick powerful move. *Steps 2-3 in diagram.*

4. Near the end of the pivot, bring the ball low again near the ground to the right of your right foot. *Steps 4-5 in diagram.*

5. This should all be one motion. Think of the high routine as starting low, bringing the ball high, then ending low.

6. Repeat the forward pivot 4 times, going around twice.

7. Repeat, pivoting backward with the same pivot foot 4 times. This backward pivot is more difficult.

8. Switch pivot foot and repeat directions 1-7.

Key Points

1. Do this slowly, not as fast as possible.

2. Make sure to complete step 7 pivoting backward and then step 8, which involves repeating the entire lesson using the other pivot foot.

3. Eventually start the pivot point on a mark so you can check for sliding.

How To Practice

Do this lesson till you can perform it while being covered by one or two defenders.

Part 3 Ball & Foot Movement		
pivot point····X toe / pivot foot········ heel		movement / ball ●
STEPS	BALL	MOVEMENT
1	high to low	
2	low	
3	low	
4	low	
5	low to high	
6	high	

Part 3 Low Routine
Directions

•This is called the low routine because you push the ball across low, close to the floor on the pivot around.

•Working with a defender is initially helpful.

1. Hold the ball overhead in a passing position, feet shoulder-width apart. The left foot is the pivot foot. *See the diagram Part 3 Ball & Foot Movement.* Steps do not correspond to direction numbers.

2. Fake a pass with the ball. Then take one long jab-step to the right, pushing the ball low to the far right. The ball should be touching the ground to the right of your right foot. This should be a quick powerful move. *Step 1 in diagram.*

3. Pivot 180 degrees forward, halfway around, keeping the ball low. Push the ball in front as you pivot around. The ball in a sense goes first. Keep the ball close to the body until near the end of the 180 degree pivot. Then move the ball to the right of your right foot. *Steps 2-4 in diagram.*

4. After you pivot around, the ball should be low and to the right of the right foot. Now bring it up high along the right side of your body, not letting the ball come in front. *Steps 5-6 in diagram.*

5. Repeat the forward pivot 4 times total, going around twice.

6. Repeat steps 1-5 pivoting backward.

7. Switch pivot foot and repeat directions 1-6.

Key Points

1. The ball movement is very tricky.

2. Initially it is overhead; next it is outside of the outside foot.

3. On the pivot, the ball is across and in front of the body, close to the ground.

4. Finally the ball is brought up overhead on the side of the body.

5. Start on a mark so you can check for sliding.

How To Practice

Work on this drill till you can perform it while being covered by one or two defenders.

11 Pivot With Defense

Player's Corner

Parts	1	2
Type	ADV	ADV
Players	2	2
Assist	NO	YES
Ball	◯	◯
Court	X	X
Effort	3	3
Time	5	5

Setup Part 1

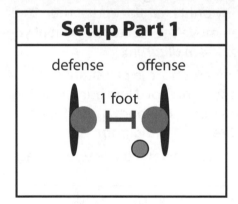

defense   offense

1 foot

Briefs

In Part 1, the defender goes after the ball of the pivoter.

In Part 2, the pivoter must pass on a signal.

Why Do This

These drills work on game-level pivoting, pivoting under pressure. Even a good pivoter will find some of these exercises difficult. Improvement comes from making the attempt. Putting yourself in a situation more difficult than most game situations makes game situations easier.

Each drill is a good defensive lesson as well, however, only concentrate on the offense here. Similar defensive lessons can be found in lessons 69-73. Each defender must put out maximum effort and must not blatantly foul the pivoter.

Part 1 Pivot Move
Directions

1. The offense starts with the left foot as the pivot foot, ball waist-high. *See the diagram Setup Part 1.*

2. The directions for the defense are simple–go after the ball without fouling. Move around the offense for the ball instead of reaching with the arms. Move fast so the offense gets practice. This will wear out the defense if done with the right amount of effort.

3. The offense must continue to pivot and move the ball away from the defense. Call contact fouls. A foul means the defense stays on defense.

4. The defense slowly counts to 10, then stops.

5. Repeat using the other pivot foot.

6. Now switch roles and repeat unless there is a foul.

•If there is an additional player repeat with 2 defenders. This is quite difficult if not impossible.

Key Points

1. The defense must go hard after the ball.

2. The defense must move the feet, not reach for the ball.

3. The defense also times the drill by counting to 10 before stopping.

4. The offense switches pivot foot after each drill.

How To Practice

This only needs to be done 1 to 3 times.

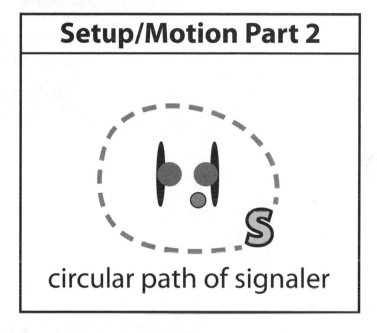

Part 2 Pivot Pass
Directions

1. A signaler, who starts 5-10 yards from the players, is added to the previous lesson. The pivoter must pass the ball to the signaler on cue. *See the diagram Part 2 Motion.*

2. The cue can be a raised arm. The cue must be visual because the pivoter should be looking around while evading the defense.

3. The signaler should walk at a medium pace in a circle around the group. It's okay to frequently change direction in order to stay farther away from the passer. Signal a pass as soon as you see the pivoter is not looking. Time the lesson for 10 seconds.

4. The pivoter passes as soon as he/she sees the signal.

•This part is very difficult because the objective is to pass immediately on cue. Of course, this will be a rarity for several reasons. One, the passer will not be able to look every second, especially when his/her back is turned to the signaler. Two, even if they are looking, passing takes time, maybe even 1-2 seconds, which is eons in a game situation.

5. Repeat, switching pivot foot, then rotate positions.

•If there is an additional player repeat with 2 defenders. This is quite difficult if not impossible.

Key Points

1. The defender must go hard after the ball. No reaching with the arms, move the feet.

2. Switch pivot foot after each try.

How To Practice

This only needs to be repeated 1 or 2 times.

WRIST WORK LESSONS

12 Wrist Work
13 Shoot, Pass, Dribble

After touch, wrist work is the next key to improving shooting, passing, and dribbling. Each player at every level from first grade to pro needs to do wrist work every day of their basketball career.

If you want to see proper wrist work, watch vintage film of a game involving Hall of Famers Pete Maravich or Bob Cousy. If you want to see terrible wrist work, watch any dribbler who nearly palms the ball on every dribble. If you don't flick the wrist on the dribble, then you must dribble with the arm.

Several of the worst free-throw shooters in pro history had stiff wrists. This is not uncommon with very poor shooters, usually men. Instead of flicking the shot, they must arm the ball because their wrists don't bend enough. Practicing hundreds of shots or free throws each day does not help, because arming the ball does not allow a player to precisely control the shot. However, working to loosen the wrists, even without shooting, does help.

Passing, the most difficult ball skill, is all wrist motion. Arming a pass is like telegraphing a pass, allowing a defender a head start to the ball. One reason I don't teach chest passes is that it is an arm pass. A flick-of-the-wrist pass, on the other hand, is nearly impossible to react to ahead of time. The great passes that get fans out of their seats cheering are usually wrist passes.

Working on wrist movement is an incredibly effective way to improve shooting, dribbling, and passing. A player does not even need a ball or court to practice. A player can practice for hours a day at home on the couch. The only impediment is that it is physically difficult to do wrist work for more that 5 minutes at a time. There is also little chance of developing bad habits by just working on the wrists, whereas incorrect practice invariably leads to bad habits.

12 Wrist Work

Setup Parts 1-3

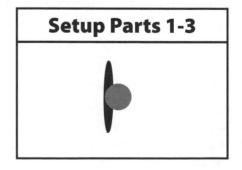

Briefs

In Part 1, loosen up your arms, wrists, hands, and fingers.

In Part 2, flick the wrists upward keeping arms at the sides.

In Part 3, flick one hand while holding the forearm with the other.

Why Do This

The goal of wrist work is to both loosen up the wrists and increase flexibility, so you can improve shooting, passing, or dribbling. Only a small amount of time is needed, but the rewards are great. You can even practice wrist work at home without a ball.

Part 1 Loosen Up
Directions

1. Let your arms loosely hang at your sides. Move the arms and hands like wet noodles. Loosen up. Slightly shake the arms, hands, and fingers.

2. Keep the elbows straight, not bent.

3. Continue for 1-5 minutes.

Key Points

1. Hands and fingers must be loose.

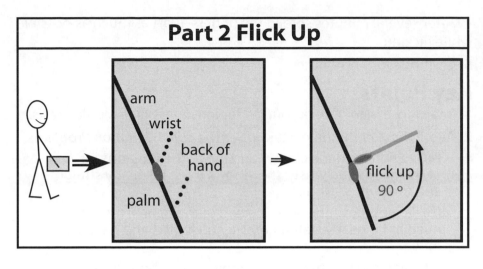

Part 2 Flick Up

arm
wrist
back of hand
palm

flick up
90°

2. Arms should be loose.

3. Shaking the arms and/or forearms indicates these body parts are tight.

How To Practice

Initially work on this ten times a day. You need to make loosening up a regular part of your practice routine. In a game you need to loosen up while running down court, in other free moments, and before shooting free throws.

Part 2 Flick Up
Directions

1. Let your hands hang loosely at your sides again. Turn your arms so that the back of each hand is facing forward; the palms face backward. Let your hands hang loosely. Slightly claw each hand.

2. Keeping the hands slightly clawed, flick your hands forward and upward. Think of the wrist and hand as two different appendages. Let them move back to the original position without using extra effort. ***See the diagram Part 2 Flick Up.*** For clarity the arms are shown forward in the diagram, not at the sides as they should be.

3. The wrists and hands move like a waving, wet noodle. The elbows are straight or only slightly bent. The arms, especially the forearms, do not move. Forearms stay perfectly vertical.

#	**Wrong Motion**	**Should Be**
1	arms moving	stationary
2	elbows bent	extended
3	hand flat	clawed
4	forearms moving	stationary
5	wrists tight	loose

4. After several minutes spread the fingers apart as much as possible while flicking.

5. Continue for 1-5 minutes.

Key Points

1. "Stay loose man". Check yourself for looseness on a regular basis.

2. Avoid these common mistakes. *See the chart Common Problems.*

　　(a) Do not bend the elbows and move the forearms instead of the hands and wrists; the elbows must be nearly straight and the arms vertical.

　　(b) Do not move the arms instead of the hands; the arms need to be nearly stationary, only the wrists and hands move.

　　(c) Using too much muscle to move hands both back and forth rather than letting the hands loosely flick without much effort.

3. This exercise will be difficult for players at all levels. The goal is to flick the wrist back 90 degrees. It often takes months for stiff wrists to loosen up. Older male players have the biggest problem.

How To Practice

Practice this drill along with the previous one.

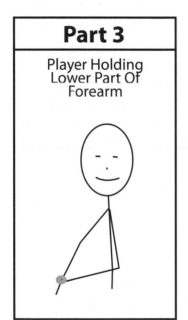

Part 3

Player Holding Lower Part Of Forearm

Part 3 Hold One Hand
Directions

1. Continue the flick-up lesson flicking one hand at a time.

2. With the other hand, grab the lower part of the forearm—close to the wrist of the flicking arm—to prevent the arm from moving. *See the diagram Part 3.*

3. This prevents you from moving the forearm and makes flicking much more difficult, but more effectively corrects the problem for a player with stiff wrists.

4. Continue for 1-5 minutes regularly checking for looseness.

5. Switch flicking hands every 30-60 seconds.

Key Points

1. Continue to check yourself for looseness throughout this lesson.

2. Initially this may be very difficult. Eventually this will be a regular part of any warm-up.

3. Avoid the common problems previously mentioned.

How To Practice

Practice this drill along with the previous one till you are loose enough to practice without holding one arm.

13 Shoot, Pass, Dribble

Player's Corner

Parts	1	2	3
Type	CORE	CORE	CORE
Players	1	1	1
Assist	NO	NO	NO
Ball	X	X	X
Court	X	X	X
Effort	1	1	1
Time	5	5	5

Setup Parts 1-3

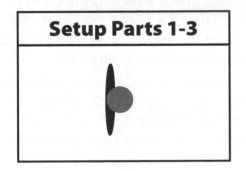

Briefs

In Part 1, flick backward holding the arms overhead.

In Part 2, flick overhead and then with the arms at the sides.

In Part 3, flick with arms at the sides.

Why Do This

Shooting: Shooting involves the body in toto and the wrists for fine tuning. Arm movement throws the shot off. Players often use the arms because they cannot bend their wrist back far enough to get a powerful flick. Unfortunately, it's near impossible to have fine shooting control with the arms. Wrist work can also remedy the occasional tightness that arises in games.

Passing: Most short passes are just flicks of the wrist without arm movement. The more arm movement, the more time the defense has to react. The more wrist movement, the easier it is to pass when closely covered. The arm position and wrist movement needed for a side pass is extremely difficult.

Dribbling: A dribble should be a flick of the wrist, without arm movement. Substituting arm movement for wrist motion yields less control, making dribbling moves more difficult.

Part 1 Flick Shot

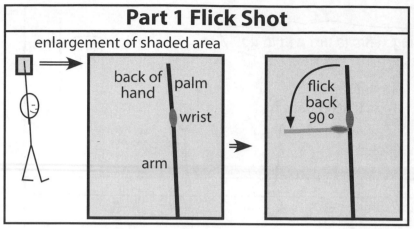

enlargement of shaded area

back of hand · palm

wrist

arm

flick back 90°

Common Problems

#	Wrong Motion	Should Be
1	arms moving	stationary
2	elbows bent	extended
3	hand flat	clawed
4	forearms moving	stationary
5	wrists tight	loose

Moving Through Positions

Up	Half-Down	Full-Down

Arm Extension On Pass

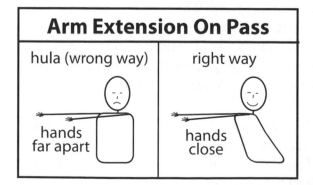

hula (wrong way) · hands far apart

right way · hands close

Part 1 Flick Shot
Directions

1. To simulate shooting and overhead passing, raise your arms directly overhead in a "hands up high" position. The palms face forward, the backs of the hands face backward. Spread the fingers apart and claw the hand.

2. Move the elbows so they are directly over the shoulders.

3. Loosen the wrists and hands and then flick them backward only. Let them come forward without additional effort. *See the diagram Part 1 Flick Shot.*

4. Continue for 1-2 minutes.

Key Points

1. Avoid common problems. *See the chart Common Problems.*

How To Practice

Practice this each day as often as you can for 1-2 minutes.

Part 2 Flick Pass
Directions

1. Start from the flick shot position with arms overhead, hands clawed. Flick back and let the wrists come forward naturally.

2. Continue flicking while bringing the arms down to the left side to about waist-high. In order to keep the hands together, bend the knees and twist the upper torso as you lower the arms. *See the diagram Moving Through Positions.*

3. This may look like a hula dance, especially if the exercise is improperly done. Don't get carried away. Stretch to the side. Keep the arms outstretched. *See the diagram Arm Extension On Pass.*

4. Continue flicking the hands back and forward. The hands should move in the direction of the pass, which is forward. To avoid sideways flicks or flicks at an angle make believe that each flick is a pass to someone.

5. Bring the arms up overhead, then to the other side. Continue for 15 seconds before raising the arms again.

6. Repeat this side to overhead to side motion several times.

Key Points

1. You need to improve your agility in order to throw effective passes. Do this part more slowly than the other flicking parts. Feeling spastic while doing this part means you are attempting to do it correctly.

2. Keep your arms extended. Bending the elbows makes the drill worthless.

3. The hands and wrists need to be loose.

4. Flick the hands backward in one direction only; this lets the hands come forward naturally.

5. Hands should be clawed with fingers far apart, not close together.

6. Remember that you are simulating flicking passes. Visualize that the ball is in your hands. Each flick is a pass.

7. The arm extension to the side is quite difficult, so this may initially look like a hula dance. A player needs to extend both arms and twist the body to the side so the hands are close to each other.

How To Practice

Do this several times a day along with other loosening drills.

Part 3 Flick Dribble
Directions

•This is a continuation of Part 2.

1. Let your hands hang loosely at your sides again. Turn your arms so that the back of each hand is facing forward; the palms face backward. Let your hands hang loosely. Slightly claw each hand.

2. Keeping the hands slightly clawed, flick your wrists forward and upward. Think of the wrist and hand as two different appendages. Let them move back to the original position without using extra effort. *See the diagram Part 3 Flick Dribble.* The arms

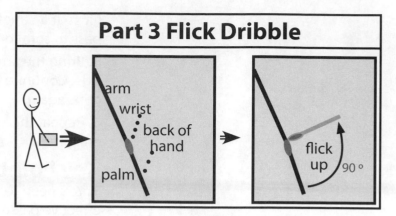

Part 3 Flick Dribble

arm
wrist
back of hand
palm
flick up
90°

are shown slightly forward in the diagram, not at the sides, for clarity.

3. The wrists and hands move like a waving, wet noodle. The elbows are straight or only slightly bent. The arms, especially the forearms, do not move. Forearms stay perfectly vertical.

4. After several minutes spread the fingers apart as much as possible while flicking. Flick your hands like you are actually dribbling the ball.

5. Continue for 1-5 minutes regularly moving between the full up and a half-down dribbling position.

Key Points

1. "Stay loose man". Check yourself for looseness on a regular basis.

2. Avoid these common mistakes. ***See the chart Common Problems.***

    (a) Do not bend the elbows, moving the forearms instead of the hands and wrists; the elbows must be straight and the arms vertical.

    (b) Do not move the arms instead of the hands & wrists; the arms need to be stationary, only the hands move.

    (c) Do not use forearm muscles to flick the hands forward; allow the hands & wrists to fall back naturally without any extra effort.

3. This exercise will be difficult for players at all levels. The goal is to flick the wrist back 90 degrees. It often takes months for stiff wrists to loosen up. Older male players have the biggest problem.

How To Practice

Practice this drill along with the previous one.

DRIBBLING LESSONS

14 Dribble Basics
15 Dribble Twist
16 Dribble Move
17 Protect The Ball

Work on dribbling as soon as possible and become an expert for several reasons. One, 99% of players, including yourself, lack this skill. Two, you will learn quickly with proper instruction. Three, if you continue to dribble poorly, you will have difficulty every time you do a lesson involving dribbling. Four, dribbling position and movement is quite similar to defensive movement, so most dribbling topics help with defense as well.

Lesson 14, Dribble Basics, deals with body position, touch, and wrist work. Lesson 15, Dribble Twist, is the most important lesson actually involving dribbling. In a stationary position, a player twists and turns every part of the body while in dribbling pose. All cues are visual so players must keep their heads up to follow directions. Lesson 16, Dribble Move, involves following a moving leader. Lesson 17, Protect The Ball, is the last aspect of dribbling that needs to be taught. However, it is an essential skill for a player to be expert at dribbling when closely covered or in traffic.

14 Dribble Basics

Player's Corner

Parts	1	2	3
Type	CORE	CORE	CORE
Players	1	1	1
Assist	NO	NO	NO
Ball	X	X	◯
Court	X	X	X
Effort	1	1	1
Time	5	5	5

Setups

Parts 1-2	Part 3

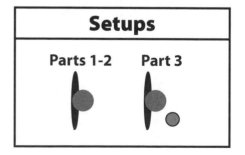

Briefs

In Part 1, work on the body position for dribbling.

In Part 2, work on the wrist movement for dribbling.

In Part 3, dribble using the fingerends and wrists.

Why Do This

It is no coincidence that most good dribblers are also good defensive players. Because the body position for both defense and dribbling are similar, practicing dribbling helps with defense. For both skills, players must be able to move in any direction as quickly as possible. The body is low to the ground with feet slightly greater than shoulder-width apart. The dribbling position is more demanding than the defensive one, since it entails twisting and swiveling the head, shoulders, hips, and legs in different directions. Being able to perform these twisting movements while handling the ball and looking is the key to good dribbling.

Part 1 presents the best body position for dribbling and the best one to use to practice dribbling. Part 2 details how to dribble using the wrist without arm movement. Part 3 forces you to concentrate on controlling the ball with the fingertips and wrists.

Body Positions

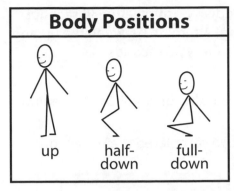

up   half-   full-
            down   down

Half-Down
Ready Position

Common Problems

legs
not
bent
enough

back
bent
too
much

Part 2 Wrist Work

flick up
90°

Part 1 Body Position
Directions

1. Put your feet shoulder-width apart. Keep the trunk straight and bend at the knees. Overdo it by bending down all the way. This is the full-down position.

2. Move halfway up. This is the half-down position which is also called the ready position. The ready position is the best ready-to-run-in-any-direction position. Remain in the half-down position. *See the diagram Body Positions.*

3. Move between the full-down, half-down, and up positions 3 times.

4. Move to the half-down position, which is simply the position you should be in while dribbling on the court. Now tap up and down on the balls of your feet like a football drill.

5. Continue for 1-2 minutes. Every once in a while run one step forward or back, then return immediately to the half-down tapping position.

Key Points

1. If knees are straight and/or backs bent, move into the full-down position for 5-10 seconds before continuing.

2. In the half-down position the legs need to be bent, not straight.

3. Backs need to be nearly straight, not bent.

4. Most players bend the back instead of the legs.

5. *See the diagrams Half-Down Ready Position and Common Problems.*

How To Practice

Practice 3-6 times. You need an assistant to point out common problems.

Part 2 Wrist Work
Directions

1. Let your arms hang straight down at the sides. Loosen up for 10-30 seconds by gently shaking the arms and hands. Think wet noodles.

2. Now with arms at your sides, let the back of your hands face forward, the palms face backward.

3. Flick the wrists upward and let them come back without any additional effort. Keep the arms stationary. *See the diagram Part 2 Wrist Work.*

4. Continue for 1-2 minutes.

5. Move to the full-down position after 30 seconds and continue flicking. Alternate between the up and half-down positions every 30 seconds.

Key Points

1. This is a multiple part lesson involving loosening up and flicking.

2. Make sure you have completed the Wrist Work lessons (12-13).

How To Practice

Practice this multiple times everyday for the rest of your basketball career.

Part 3 Tom Tom
Directions

1. Start in the full-down position with a ball. Shape your hands into claws. Rest your arms on your thighs. *See the diagram Tom Tom Body Position.*

2. Now tap the ball back and forth from hand to hand using the fingerends. Keep the ball low to the ground, around 6 inches.

3. The hand motion and ball motion should be almost up and down rather than side to side. *See the diagram Path of Ball in Tom Tom.*

4. Resting the arms on the thighs removes the arms from the exercise, resulting in more wrist motion.

5. It's okay if you look down during this drill. Focus on how the fingers contact the ball.

Key Points

1. Most players love to do this, however, they rarely do it correctly.

2. The hand and ball motion is up and down, not side to side.

3. Contact the ball with the fingerends, not the pads.

4. The forearms should be stationary.

How To Practice

Do this 5-10 times or more in order to focus on the basics of dribbling.

Tom Tom Body Position

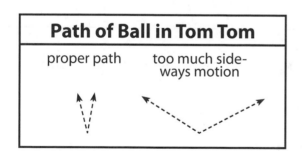

Path of Ball in Tom Tom

proper path   too much side-ways motion

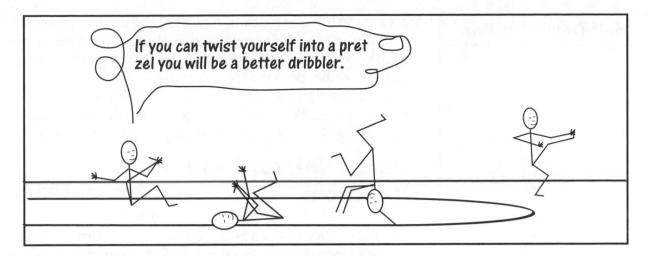

15 Dribble Twist

Player's Corner

Parts	1	2	3	4
Type	CORE	CORE	CORE	OPT
Players	2	2	2	1
Assist	NO	NO	NO	NO
Ball	⚬	⚬	⚬	⚬
Court	X	X	X	X
Effort	2	2	2	2
Time	5	5	5	5

Setup Part 1

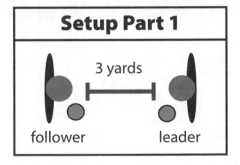

3 yards

follower   leader

Briefs

In Part 1, mirror the dribbling of a stationary leader.

In Part 2, follow a leader facing sideways.

In Part 3, follow a leader who is directly behind.

In Part 4, dribble in place while watching a game.

Why Do This.

After completing Lesson 14, spend most of your dribbling time on this Lesson. The other topics, excluding protecting the ball, are much less important.

The most obvious part of dribbling involves keeping the head up. Players learn to dribble with the head up by forcing them to look up in order to receive directions.

The least obvious part involves dribbling the ball in what might feel like abnormal body positions. The ability to twist and turn the body every which way is a critical part of good dribbling. The inability to twist and turn is the greatest impediment to those attempting to learn.

Half-Down Position

Full-Down Position

Stay in the full-down position most of the time for many reasons. One, in the full-down position, the legs are bent to the maximum. In the half-down position, a player tends to bend the back rather than the legs. Two, in the full-down position, a player dribbles using less arm motion and more wrist motion. Three, it's actually easier to dribble in the full-down position because each dribble is only 6-12 inches high.

Part 1 Mirror Leader
Directions

1. Two dribblers or a dribbler (follower) and an assistant face each other. One leads, the other follows, mirroring the leader's movements. Mirroring means that when one person dribbles with the left hand, the facing dribbler uses the right hand. *See the diagram Setup Part 1.*

2. Start in the full-down position, feet shoulder-width, arms extended straight downward, and elbows only slightly bent. *See the diagrams Half-Down Position and Full-Down Position.*

3. An assistant with old bones is not required to stay in the full-down position (thank God), flick wrists, or even dribble the ball. An assistant can always lead sitting on a chair, just moving his/her hand through the ball positions.

4. The leader slowly dribbles through the 12 ball positions with each hand. *See the diagram Ball Positions.* Initially dribble three times in each position before moving to the next one. Speed up as the follower improves.

Ball Positions

	left front	front center	right front	
corner 6	5	4	3	2 corner
left side 7			1	right side
corner 8	9	10	11	12 corner
	left back	back center	right back	

5. The follower must continuously look up, twisting his/her body to dribble with the ball in the correct position. It's okay for the leader to verbally correct the follower by yelling, "Heads up!," or "I'm dribbling on the side!," or "Use your left (or right) hand!"

Dribbling Directions

steps	hand	ball position
a-b	right	3 → 1 → 7
c-d	left	7 → 1 → 10
e	left	10 → 10
f	right	10 → 10
h-i	right and/or left	around back & through legs either direction

Ball Positions

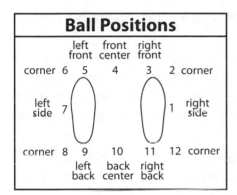

6. Here are some sample directions for the leader. *See the diagram Dribbling Directions.* *Hand* in the diagram means dribbling hand.

(a) Start with the right hand in front position *3*. Move to *2*, then *1*. Initially dribble three times in each position. Wait for the dribbler to catch up. Yell to correct the follower.

(b) Now slowly move your right hand around the circle to *2*, then *3*, *4*, *5*, *6*, and *7*. A player should be twisted a bit. Hold until he/she is dribbling in this position.

(c) Now, switch hands and with the left hand go back toward position *1*. Hold again in this position.

(d) Continue moving the left hand backwards to position *12*, then *11*, then *10*. Wait for the follower to dribble in this position.

(e) Now dribble slowly back to position *1*, then *4*, then *7*, then *10*.

(f) Switch hands and move all the way to the other side from *10* to *7* to *4* to *1* to *10*.

(g) Continue moving the ball in this same way with each hand.

(h) Eventually go all the way around the back switching hands when the ball is in position *10*. You can even try swiveling all the way around and picking up the dribble with the same hand.

(i) To end the lesson go through the legs from position *10* with one hand to *4* with the other. You can even pick up the dribble with the same hand. To make the between-the-legs dribble easier, move one foot or the other forward. Continue the drill with feet in this position.

7. When the follower does well in the full-down position, repeat from the half-down position and with one foot forward. However, do not hesitate to go back to the full-down position if the the dribbler has trouble in the half-down position.

Key Points

1. Back straight up, not bent.

2. Knees bent, not straight.

3. Dribble with hand and wrist movement, little arm movement.

4. The ball stays only 6 inches to 1 foot off floor.

5. Only fingertips touch the ball, no hands.

Ball Positions

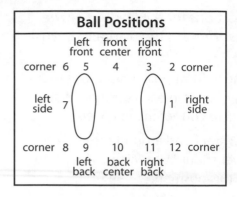

	left front	front center	right front	
corner 6	5	4	3	2 corner
left side 7				1 right side
corner 8	9	10	11	12 corner
	left back	back center	right back	

Setup Part 2

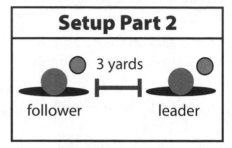

3 yards

follower   leader

Dribbling Directions

steps	hand	ball position
a-b	right	3 → 1 → 7
c-d	left	7 → 1 → 10
e	left	10 → 10
f	right	10 → 10
h-i	right and/or left	around back & through legs either direction

Sideways Feet Positions

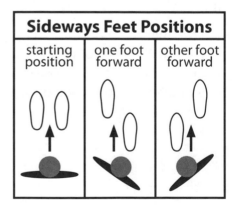

starting position	one foot forward	other foot forward

6. Make sure the follower is actually looking up, not down nor in reverie.

7. The hand is shaped like a claw.

8. The more difficult for the follower, the more beneficial.

How To Practice

Repeat this many times each week working mostly in the full-down position. When you can dribble well when covered in a game, then move to the next lesson. This could take one week or one month or the entire season. If you have not mastered this part, then skipping to the next lesson will not improve your ability to dribble.

Part 2 Look Sideways
Directions

1. Repeat Lesson 1 with players looking sideways. *See the diagram Setup Part 2.*

2. Now the follower does exactly what the leader does, no mirroring. This forces the follower to twist the body more in order to see the leader. Remember the main purpose of practice is to improve the agility of a player, so the more twisting, the better.

3. Start with feet parallel, slightly greater than shoulder-width apart. Follow the dribbling directions from Part 1. *See the diagram Dribbling Directions.* The step letters in the diagram are from Part 1.

4. Repeat with one foot ahead, then the other foot ahead. *See the diagram Sideways Feet Positions.*

5. Repeat steps 3 and 4 with both leader and follower turning around to face the opposite direction. The follower must now look in the other direction to follow the visual cues. *See the diagram Looking.*

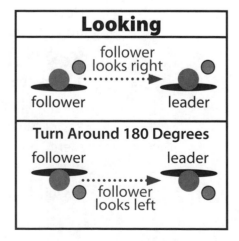

Looking

follower looks right

follower   leader

Turn Around 180 Degrees

follower   leader

follower looks left

Key Points

1. See the key points for the previous part.

2. Leader and follower dribble with the same hand.

How To Practice

Spend less time on this lesson than the previous one. Players learn how to dribble in Part 1.

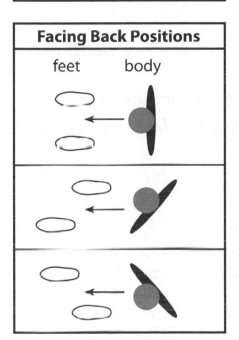

Setup Part 3

3 yards

follower   leader

Facing Back Positions

feet   body

Part 3 Look Back
Directions

1. The follower now faces away from leader. *See the diagram Setup Part 3*.

2. Repeat Part 2 with the follower twisting around to see the leader. *See the diagram Dribbling Directions.* This is great practice looking and dribbling.

3. Repeat the directions changing foot positions. *See the diagram Facing Back Positions.*

4. Make sure the follower does not swivel the feet; the feet always point away from the leader. The follower may only turn the head and/or swivel the body to see the leader.

Key Points

1. See the Key Points for Part 1.

2. The dribbler must not swivel the feet in order to see. Swivel the head and body.

How To Practice

This is a great lesson for improving agility. Work on this several times after mastering Part 1.

Part 4 Watch Game
Directions

1. A lone player dribbles while watching either a game or people warming up. Use the full-down position.

2. Move the ball to every position as well as between the legs as you watch.

3. Actually look at something; do not stare in reverie.

Key Points

1. Same as Part 1.

2. Make sure to stay in the full-down position. Otherwise you may inadvertently bend the back rather than the legs.

How To Practice

Do this anytime you are watching a game in practice or in a gym. You can even do this at home in the garage or driveway or any open space.

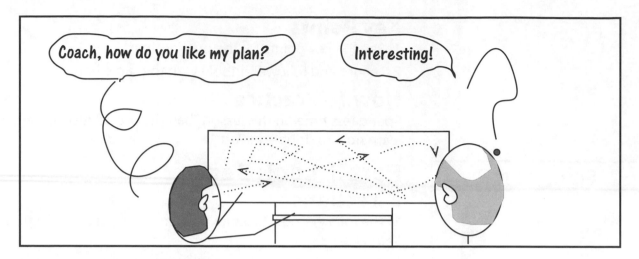

16 Dribble Move

Player's Corner

Parts	1	2	3	4
Type	CORE	OPT	OPT	OPT
Players	2	2	2	2
Assist	NO	NO	NO	NO
Ball	○	○	○	○
Court	X	X	X	X
Effort	2	2	2	2
Time	5	5	5	5

Setup Part 1

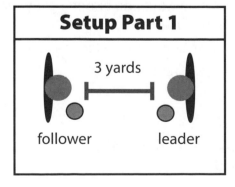

3 yards

follower   leader

Briefs

In Part 1, mirror the movements of a moving leader.

In Part 2, follow a moving leader.

In Part 3, face away from a moving leader.

In Part 4, start 3 yards behind a moving leader.

Why Do This

The dribbling lessons in this topic are a step closer to game-like dribbling. However, the previous topic is more important in the learning process. If you have difficulty dribbling properly in a stationary position, you will do worse while moving.

Dribbling movement involves the same type of jump-steps and runs used on defense. The jump-step is covered more thoroughly in Lesson 75, but the topic needs to be introduced here. The jump-step is a small jump a defender uses to adjust position while remaining in a position ready to run. Sliding instead of jump-stepping is problematic. When sliding, the feet are usually either too close or too far apart to run. Using jump-steps, the feet are always in a position ready to run.

Part 1 Follow Mirror
Directions

1. To practice jump-steps before the dribbling lesson, place the balls 3-4 yards away. Start in the half-down ready position. Take little jump-steps to the right and to the left. Jump-step left 10 times, then right, then one way or the other for 1-2 minutes. Do not slide the feet. Keep the feet slightly more than shoulder-width apart while jump-stepping.

2. When you can adequately move left and right, then jump-step forward and back for a short time.

3. Repeat all movements in steps 2 and 3 with one foot forward and then the other foot forward.

4. Two players, each with a ball, or a player and an assistant line up 3 yards apart facing each other. Either one player is the designated leader or an assistant can point in the direction to jump. *See the diagram Setup Part 1.*

5. With two players, one player leads by jump stepping left and right while dribbling. The other player follows mirroring the movements including the dribbling hand, ball position, and body position. After a minute also move forward and backward. With an assistant and player, the assistant points in the direction of movement with one hand and uses the other hand to show the ball movement.

6. The leader needs to move the ball through most of the 12 positions like in the previous lessons. Positions 8 and 12 in the back corners will be difficult to use. Positions 9-11 in the back are very difficult, if not impossible, to use while moving. *See the diagram Ball Positions.*

7. For sample directions for the leader *see the diagram Sample Directions. Moving* in the diagram means moving direction. *Hand* means the dribbling hand. Moving the ball from position *1* to *7* means to move slowly between these positions, not abruptly from position *1* one second to position *7* the next second.

8. Don't change direction so abruptly that the leader and dribbler are moving in opposite directions.

9. It's okay to move left and dribble with the right hand and/or move right and dribble with the left hand.

10. If a player does poorly, stop the movement, and go to the full-down position. Work stationary before moving again.

Ball Positions

	left front	front center	right front	
corner	6	5	4	3	2 corner

| left side | 7 | | 1 | right side |

| corner | 8 | 9 | 10 | 11 | 12 corner |
| | | left back | back center | right back | |

Sample Directions

moving	hand	ball position
right	right	1→6→1→6
right	left	7→2→7→2
left	right	2→1→4
left	left	4→1→2
right	right	2→6
right	left	6→2
left	right	2→6→1
left	left	1→7→2

11. Repeat or continue this lesson with one foot forward, then the other foot forward. The follower continues to mirror the leader.

•It's okay to switch the leader every 30 seconds.

Key Points

1. Attempt to jump-step left and right as well as forward and back.

2. The dribbler mirrors the leader.

3. The leader should mainly dribble in the side or back positions.

How To Practice

Do this lesson 2-3 times at most.

Part 2 Follow Sideways
Directions

1. This is the same as the previous part except that players line up side by side about 3 yards apart. *See the diagram Setup Part 2.*

2. The follower directly follows the movements of the leader instead of mirroring the motion.

3. The leader starts with one foot ahead of the other, then switches feet position.

4. Jump-step forward and backward as well as taking some running steps. Don't run too much.

5. Repeat this part with leader and follower turning 180 degrees to face the other direction. Now the follower must look in the other direction to follow the leader. *See the diagram Looking.*

6. Most dribbling should be in the side and corner positions. For sample directions for the leader *see the diagram Sample Directions.*

7. Switch the leader every 30-60 seconds.

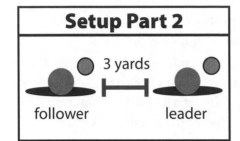

Setup Part 2

3 yards

follower   leader

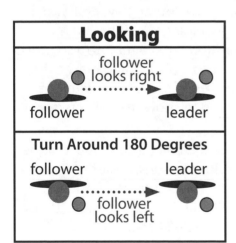

Looking

follower looks right

follower   leader

Turn Around 180 Degrees

follower   leader

follower looks left

Sample Directions

moving	hand	ball position
right	right	1 → 6 → 1 → 6
right	left	7 → 2 → 7 → 2
left	right	2 → 1 → 4
left	left	4 → 1 → 2
right	right	2 → 6
right	left	6 → 2
left	right	2 → 6 → 1
left	left	1 → 7 → 2

Ball Positions

	left front	front center	right front	
corner 6	5	4	3	2 corner
left side 7			1	right side
corner 8	9	10	11	12 corner
	left back	back center	right back	

Key Points

1. The dribbler follows the leader.

2. The leader and follower have one foot or the other forward most of the time.

3. Run and jump-step.

How To Practice

This only needs to be done once.

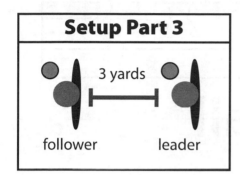

Setup Part 3

3 yards

follower   leader

Part 3 Follow Back
Directions

1. This lesson is the same as the previous lesson except that dribbler faces away from the leader. *See the diagram Setup Lesson 3.*

2. The dribbler follows the exact movements of the leader including the dribbling hand, ball position, and body position.

3. Each player must twist and turn trunk, hips, and head to view the leader. Only jump-step in this lesson, do not run. Do not swivel the feet sideways to better see the leader.

4. For sample directions *see the diagram Sample Directions.*

How To Practice

This only needs to be done once.

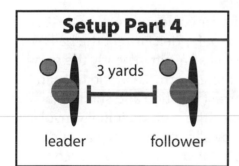

Setup Part 4

3 yards

leader   follower

Part 4 Follow Follow
Directions

1. The leader sets up in front of the dribbler in plain sight. *See the diagram Setup Part 4.*

2. The dribbler follows the leader.

3. The leader can move anywhere on the court and dribble with either hand. Movement can involve twisting around, dribbling between legs, dribbling in circles. Move slow enough so that the follower can perform the same movements.

4. Switch leaders every 20 seconds.

Key Points

1. Players follow the exact movements of the leader, which include the dribbling hand, ball position, and body position.

2. It's okay to run or jump-step or turn around completely. Any type of movement is okay.

How To Practice

This lesson is optional.

17 Protect The Ball

Player's Corner

Parts	1	2
Type	CORE	OPT
Players	2	2
Assist	NO	NO
Ball	○	○
Court	X	X
Effort	3	3
Time	5-10	5-10

Setup Part 1

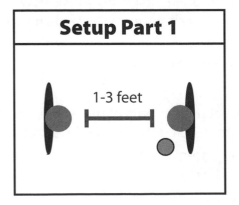

1-3 feet

Briefs

In Part 1, the dribbler protects the ball from an aggressive defensive player.

In Part 2, two dribblers go after each other.

Why Do This

Real-world dribbling involves protecting the ball from an aggressive defender. Protect the ball by keeping the non-ball arm stiff in nearly the same position as the dribbling arm. Learning to keep this arm in the correct position and stiff is relatively easy. However, the method initially involves overdoing things by allowing rough play and fouling. In a few days however, each player becomes expert at protecting the ball.

Part 1 Chase Ball
Directions

1. The dribbler, covered closely by a defender, continuously dribbles in a small area for about 20 seconds. It's okay to just swivel around. The area should be no larger than the lane area of a court. *See the diagram Setup Part 1.*

2. The defender most go aggressively after the ball. Keep moving the feet. When the offense turns, do not stay behind, facing their backs—

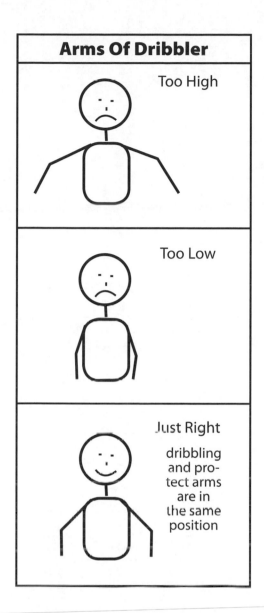

Arms Of Dribbler

Too High

Too Low

Just Right

dribbling and protect arms are in the same position

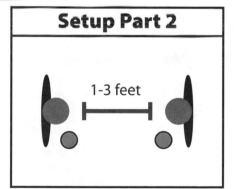

Setup Part 2

1-3 feet

hustle after the ball. Do not reach for the ball from behind. Success in this drill depends entirely on the effort of the defense.

3. Initially it is okay for the defender to foul and lean on the dribbler from the side. This is purposeful.

4. The dribbler must use the non-dribbling arm to protect the ball. Push the defender away. This is a foul, but helps the dribbler learn the correct position for the non-ball arm. Eventually he/she will keep the arm in one stationary position that protects the ball. *See the diagram Arms Of Dribbler.*

Key Points

1. The defense must go aggressively after the ball.

2. The defense must also force the dribbler to push them away.

3. The dribbler must actively push the defense away.

How To Practice

This only needs to be done 1-3 times till the dribbler keeps the non dribbling arm in a position to protect the ball.

Part 2 Dribbler vs. Dribbler
Directions

1. This part is the same as the previous part except that both players have a ball. *See the diagram Setup Part 2.*

2. While dribbling and protecting the ball, each player aggressively goes after the ball of the other dribbler.

3. Start elbow to elbow. Stay in the same small area, no larger than the lane area. Do not run around.

Key Points

1. Each player must dribble, aggressively go after the other dribbler, and protect the ball at the same time.

2. This is not for novices.

How To Practice

This part is optional.

DRIBBLING: LESSONS 14-17

LAYUPS LESSONS

18 No-Step Layup
19 One-Step Layup
20 Speed Layup

Most players, even at the college level, have never developed the ability to properly shoot a layup with each hand on either side of the basket. Most coaches are satisfied with right-handed layups on the right side and left-handed on the left. This short-changes a player and leaves him/her unprepared for real game situations.

Another problem usually not addressed is that most players float or long jump to the basket instead of going straight up for the layup. Approximately 100% of missed layups are due to floating.

Advanced pro and top college players even need to practice going off the wrong foot with either hand on either side, a skill not covered in the lessons. Another skill advanced players need, but is not covered in the lessons, involves shooting high, often off the backboard, against very tall opponents.

Very young or small players may need to practice with a lower basket and a smaller ball initially. After mastering the layup a young player will readily perform it correctly with a larger ball or at a higher basket.

Lesson 18, No-Step Layup, will quickly make a novice an expert, or make an experienced player expert with the opposite hand. Lesson 19, One-Step Layup, adds additional steps and dribbles to what was previously learned. Lesson 20, Speed Layup, is a diagnostic tool for experts.

18 No-Step Layup

Player's Corner

Parts	1	2
Type	CORE	CORE
Players	1	1
Assist	YES	YES
Ball	○	○
Court	X	🏀
Effort	1	1-2
Time	5	5

Setup Part 1

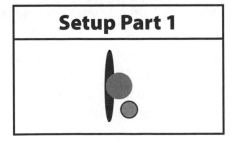

Briefs

In Part 1, practice the shooting motion of the layup.

In Part 2, repeat Part 1 at a basket.

Why Do This

You need to first learn how to perform a layup properly before doing a layup drill, which involves many TLC skills in addition to the layup. An older player can work on opposite-hand layups after a few minutes if he/she performs them properly with the strong hand. With players of all ages, work on strong hand (the right hand in most cases) layups from both the right, center, and left sides before working on weak or opposite-hand layups from right, center, and left.

It's a poor practice to only practice right-handed layups on the right side and left-handed layups on the left side. Players need to develop the dexterity to execute a layup with either hand on either side of the basket. Many players, even at the college level, do not have this skill. The key to both properly learning and performing the layup is how to do the last motion, which is taught in Part 1. Neither a ball nor a court are needed. Fifteen or twenty minutes on this lesson will make any novice become more expert.

No-Step Layup

Step 1   Step 2   Step 3

Layup Cues

1 **Foot Forward**

2 **Turn Ball**

3 **Ball/Back Leg Up**

4 **Shoot**

Part 1 No Step, No Basket
Directions

1. The ball starts at waist-height, feet shoulder-width apart. *See Step 1 in the diagram No-Step Layup.* The steps in the diagram do not correspond to the numbered directions.

2. Righties place the left foot one step forward, lefties the right foot, "not surers" put the left foot forward. You are righties now. *See Step 2 in the diagram.* Twist the ball so that the right hand is on top. Left hand on top for lefties.

3. Move your body forward and shift your weight to, then step on, the forward foot. Simultaneously move the ball up and the knee of the back leg forward and up. You can pretend a string is attached from the shooting arm to the back leg. The thigh of the now forward leg is nearly horizontal. *See Step 3 in the diagram.*

4. Do not bring this foot down for a second or two. Pose like someone is taking a picture.

5. The cues are: foot forward, turn ball, ball & back leg up, shoot. Righties bring up the right foot. Lefties bring up the left foot. *See the diagram Layup Cues.*

6. Repeat 10 to 100 times. On the layup it is okay to shoot the ball one or two feet straight up. However, this takes more time.

7. More experienced players should repeat this part using the other hand.

Key Points

1. Make sure you hold the ball with your fingertips, no palm or finger contact. If you have a problem then go back and work more on Lesson 1, Touch.

2. If you have a basic pivoting problem, then performing layups will be difficult. Go back and work on the pivoting lessons in Lesson 6.

How To Practice

Repeat this as many times as needed till you are comfortable doing it.

Part 2 No-Step Layup
Directions

1. Start about one foot from the basket on the right side.

2. Use the painted rectangle, or any other blemish on the

Setup Part 2

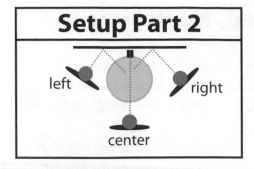

left · center · right

Squaring-Up

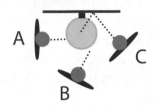

A squared to basket
B not squared-up
C squared to backboard

Who is square?

A _____
B _____
C _____

backboard, as a place to aim. Square-up to the spot at which you aim. *See the diagrams Squaring-Up and Who is square?*

•Squaring-up means that the front of the body and shoulders are lined up to the direction of the shot. If you aim for the backboard, your body should be facing (squared-up to) the backboard, not the basket. If you were shooting over the front rim, then your body would face the rim. The assistant makes sure the player is properly squared-up.

3. Use the cues: foot forward, turn ball, ball & back leg up, shoot. *See the diagram Layup Cues on the previous page.* Righties start with the left foot forward and bring up the right foot. Lefties start with the right foot forward and bring up the left foot.

4. Shoot one shot using the backboard, get your own rebound, and then without dribbling, set up to shoot again. The ball should not touch the floor during this lesson. Dribbling wastes time and can cause a problem. There is no need to rush.

5. If you continue to miss the shot, then repeat the previous lesson shooting the ball 3-4 feet in the air.

6. Shoot 10-20 layups. Repeat from the left side and then the center. Use the same shooting hand and the same footwork. Use the backboard in each case, even the from the center.

7. If you want to work on opposite hand layups then repeat the entire lesson shooting from the right, center, and left.

Key Points

1. Make sure to square-up to the direction that you shoot.

2. Repeat the entire lesson if you want to work on the opposite hand.

How To Practice

Do not advance to the next lesson until you can make 100% of the layups in Part 2 without difficulty.

19 One-Step Layup

Briefs
In Part 1, take one step before shooting a layup.

In Part 2, dribble before shooting a layup.

Why Do This
The last step in a layup is the most important step to learn. If you can do this correctly then you can also properly perform a half-court or full-court layup. On the last step the shooter must go almost straight "up" rather than float forward towards the basket or underneath the backboard. About 100% of missed layups are floaters.

Part 1 One-Step Layup
Directions.
1. Start one step from the basket on the right side. The ball is at waist-height, feet shoulder-width apart.

2. Square-up to the spot on the backboard where you aim.

3. Righties take a step with the left foot, then do the no-step layup. Lefties take a step with the right foot, then do the no-step layup. The step is not long.

4. Use the backboard and rebound your shot. Repeat 10-15 times without dribbling.

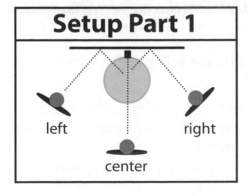

Setup Part 1

left   right

center

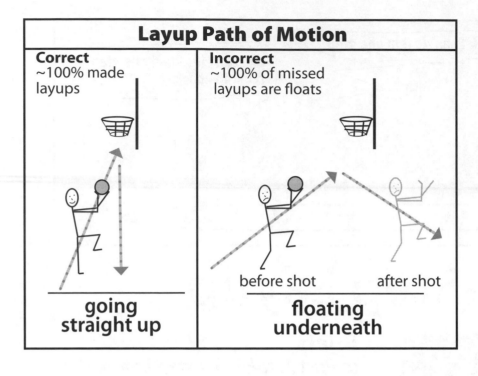

Layup Path of Motion

Correct
~100% made layups

going straight up

Incorrect
~100% of missed layups are floats

before shot   after shot

floating underneath

5. Repeat from the center and then the left side of the basket shooting off the backboard. Make sure to shoot the layup exactly like you did on the right side. If you want to use the other hand, repeat the lesson shooting off the other foot.

6. Repeat steps 1-5 making a conscious effort to go straight "up" on the last step. You may need to start closer to the basket. Taller players should try to release the ball high on the backboard. Shorter ones just release the ball as high as possible. *See the diagram Layup Path of Motion.*

Key Points

1. Motion should be smooth & easy, not jerky.

2. The last step should be short, not long.

3. The knee and ball should move up at the same time.

4. Head should look up at the backboard.

5. The ball should go off the backboard.

6. Go "up", not forward for the layup.

7. Fingertip control of ball.

8. Square-up properly.

How To Practice

Repeat this everyday for at least one week. Continue if you still feel uneasy doing this lesson.

Part 2 Dribble Layup
Directions

1. This is the same as Part 1 with the addition of one step and one dribble. There are actually 4 parts to this part. *See the diagram Setup Part 2.*

2. For the first layup, righties take a step with the right foot and simultaneously take one dribble. Pick up the dribble and take a one-step layup. Go slowly, no need to rush the dribble or shot. Lefties follow the same directions first stepping with the left foot.

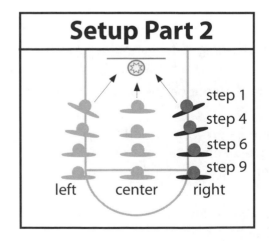

Setup Part 2

step 1
step 4
step 6
step 9

left   center   right

3. Do not look down on the dribble. Dribble with your strong hand all the time, even from the other side of the basket.

4. After repeating 10 times from the right, center, and left move one step back.

5. For the second layup, repeat steps 1-4 taking two steps on the dribble. Righties step with the left foot and then dribble and step with the right foot . Then do a one-step layup. Lefties use the opposite foot and hand.

6. After repeating 10 times from the right, center, and left move back another step.

7. For the third layup take several steps and two dribbles. There are at least 3 ways to give directions for this part. Choose the method that works best.

> **(a.)** Simultaneously take one step with the left foot and one dribble. Then perform the one-dribble layup. (See step 2)

> **(b.)** Simultaneously take one step with the left foot and one dribble. Take another step and another dribble. Pick-up the ball on the 3rd step and perform a layup.

> **(c.)** There Is no need to give specific directions detailing which foot to start, since there are several dribbles and at least three to four steps involved. Players may start with either foot from any position.

8. After repeating from the right, center, and left move back to the free throw line.

9. For the fourth layup take as many dribbles and steps as needed to dribble in for a layup. Do 5-10 layups from the right, center, and left. Make sure to look up, not down at the ball as you dribble to the basket. Go "up" on the last step.

Key Points

1. There are four parts to Part 2.

2. Go slowly.

3. Go "up", not forward, on the last step.

4. Look "up", not at the ball or floor, as you dribble in.

5. Repeat the entire lesson if you want to use the opposite hand.

How To Practice

Do each part as many days as needed till you feel comfortable and you make 100% of the layups.

20 Speed Layup

Player's Corner	
Parts	1
Type	CORE
Players	1
Assist	YES
Ball	◯
Court	🏀
Effort	3
Time	5

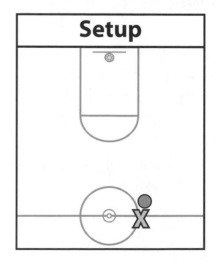

Setup

Brief
Sprint to the basket from midcourt for a layup.

Why Do This
This is a test - one, two, three - and only a test. Sprint to the basket, make the layup and land in front of the backboard. If a player can do this properly, then he/she is ready to advance.

Directions
1. This is a diagnostic tool for a player who thinks he/she is expert.

2. Starting from midcourt sprint, dribbling the ball, as fast as you can towards the basket for a layup. *See the diagram Setup.*

3. Slightly slow down on the last step and go straight up to shoot. Land in front of the backboard. Rebound your shot. Repeat 2 more times.

4. If you miss the layup or end up under the backboard, then go back to Lessons 18-19.

Key Points
1. Sprint hard with the head up.

2. Make the layup.

3. End up in front, not behind the backboard.

How To Practice
This is a test, not practice.

CONTINUOUS MOTION LESSONS

21 Dribble Circuit
22 Pass Circuit
23 Weave Circuit

For older players Continuous Motion (CM) lessons and/or running should be a regular part of your practice regiment. Start running for 15 minutes, working up to 30-40 minutes. The various skills that can be practiced while running are also worthwhile.

The conditioning part of these lessons not only improves aerobic conditioning, but also improves your athleticism, which makes you a better player. The skills involved include basic ball-handling to more complex TLC skills. Unfortunately most players will not initially have the many skills needed to run these lessons. That's okay. Just get going. Eventually go back and zero in on each skill problem, one at a time.

Most CM drills involve a layup or short shot. Make sure you have proper technique and make every shot. An assistant can keep track of misses. Older players need a penalty for each miss such as running 1-10 full-court layups for each one. Youngsters should not do the lesson if they regularly miss shots.

Several other lessons not in this section can be used as a CM lesson. These include parts of the Play Transition Lessons (62-65) and Lesson 38, Practice Shoot.

In Lesson 21, Dribble Circuit, a player just dribbles full-court, or around another circuit, with the head up taking a short shot at each basket. Lesson 22, Pass Circuit, involves running full-court, in groups of two, passing the ball back and forth. For Lesson 23, Weave Circuit, the 3-person Front Weave drill from **The Basketball Coach's Bible** is transformed into a 2-person drill. The Front Weave is one of the most worthwhile timing lessons you can do.

21 Dribble Circuit

Player's Corner	
Parts	1
Type	OPT
Players	1
Assist	NO
Ball	◯
Court	🏀
Effort	2
Time	5-20

Briefs
Dribble in for a layup, then around a circuit.

Why Do This
Use this lesson as a conditioning lesson only after you have worked on the dribbling and layup lessons.

Directions
1. Mark or just run a half-court or full-court circuit where you can shoot a layup at each available basket in the gym. *See the diagrams Half-Court Circuit and Full-Court Circuit.* You can run for 5-20 minutes.

2. Dribble in for a layup at each basket on the circuit. You can change the shot every few minutes. However, you must make 100% of your shots to do this drill.

3. Keep your head up while dribbling. Be looking at something all the time. Often this is a good drill to do on a crowded court because you must look around to navigate through the players.

4. After 5 minutes reverse direction and move around the circuit in the opposite direction.

5. Shoot the layup the same way with the same hand when you go in the reverse direction.

6. If you want to shoot with the opposite hand, then run the entire lesson over using the opposite hand. Again, you must choose a shot that you can make 100% of the time.

Key Points
1. Keep your head up when dribbling.

2. Look at something while you are dribbling. This could be something on the court, the bleachers, the basket, or something on the wall. Do not dribble around in reverie.

3. Make every single shot, 100%.

Half-Court Circuit

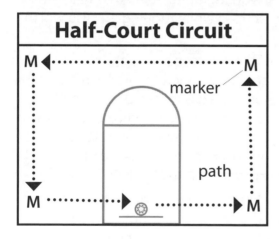

marker

path

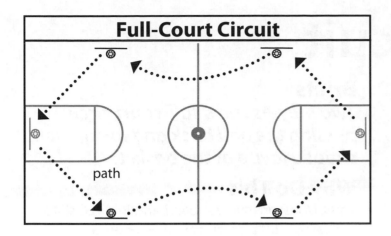

Full-Court Circuit

path

How To Practice

If you don't want to run 3-5 miles a day, then this is great way to practice dribbling and shooting while conditioning. Other continuous motion drills can be added onto this one to extend the session.

22 Pass Circuit

Player's Corner

Parts	1
Type	OPT
Players	2
Assist	NO
Ball	⬤
Court	🏀
Effort	2
Time	5-20

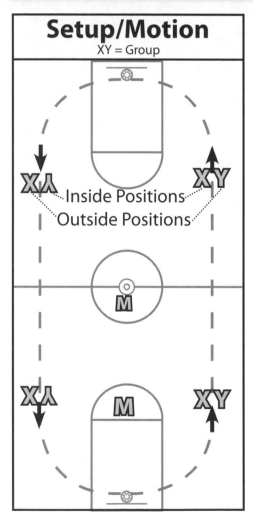

Setup/Motion
XY = Group

Inside Positions

Outside Positions

Briefs

Two players run a full-court circuit passing the ball back and forth, then shoot a layup at the basket.

Why Do This

This CM lesson involves ball-handling, TLC skills, and layups. It's a great way to work on conditioning, though it is quite difficult to properly execute. One big problem involves looking skills. Players running downcourt passing back and forth need to be looking downcourt rather than at each other.

This is the beginning of teaching the most important skill of looking. You will need to work on looking in just about every lesson in the book. Otherwise, you will often look down or in only one place or nowhere.

Directions For Players

1. In a group of two run a circuit (dashed line) on the full-court. *See the diagram Setup/Motion.*

2. You do not need to run at top speed; pace yourself so that you can finish the workout. As you run, pass the ball back and forth without walking.

3. Run down one side of the court. Shoot a layup at the basket, switch inside and outside positions, then run down the other side of the court to the other basket. Alternate shooting the layup. *See the diagram Switch Positions.* The switch is important so that players alternate passing hands.

4. Shoot the layup with your strong hand on either side of the basket. No right hand on right side, left hand on the left side. If shooting with the other hand is important, then shoot layups with the weak hand for part of the lesson.

5. Stay close to each other, 1 foot away, so that the ball does not bounce on the ground. No dribbling. Don't allow rebounds to hit the ground either.

6. Every few minutes stop, turn around and run the circuit in the opposite direction.

Switch Positions
Inside-Outside at Basket

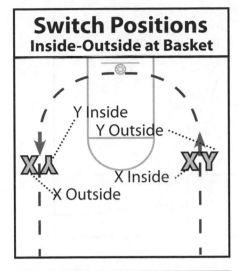

Y Inside
Y Outside
X Inside
X Outside

Short Passes

hand off

lateral

hook

behind back

bounce

7. Each minute change the type of pass. Start out with laterals, which are short underhanded passes that almost look like a hand-off. Either hand or both can be used for a lateral. Use the hand farthest away from your partner to pass the ball. *See the diagram Short Passes.* For clarity In the diagram, players face each other, but during the lesson players face forward. Other types of passes include:

> **(a)** Hand-Off - One player hands the ball to the other.

> **(b)** Grab - One player holds the ball out, the other grabs. This is very difficult while running. It's okay to only do the medium or low grab.

> **(c)** Bounce Pass - A short bounce pass. Bounce the ball slightly ahead and to the side of the catcher.

> **(d)** Behind The Back Pass - When players switch positions they get practice with the other hand.

> **(e)** Hook Pass - Again players get practice passing with the other hand when they switch inside-outside positions. Make sure the hook goes directly overhead, not any higher.

> **(f)** Tricky Pass - Try several tricky passes like behind the back, between the legs, then around the legs behind the back or just make something up. Players might have to walk to perform some of these.

8. If side baskets are available, use them after the first 5 or 10 minutes. Now players can shoot up to six layups each circuit.

9. It's okay if you stop and take a 1-foot shot instead of a layup, especially if you receive a bad pass, or you are too far under the boards to make a layup. It's much better to stop and take the 1-footer, than to miss the layup.

Key Points

1. Look forward while running, not at each other.

2. To continue this lesson, you must make 100% of the shots.

3. Pass the ball back and forth without walking. Don't hold the ball too long.

4. Switch positions, inside to outside, after each layup.

How To Practice

Practice this anytime you want to run with another player. The passing and TLC skills involved make this worthwhile. It's often a good idea to run this on a crowded court because players must look around to navigate through the crowd.

23 Weave Circuit

Player's Corner

Parts	1
Type	CORE
Players	2
Assist	YES
Ball	○
Court	🏀
Effort	2
Time	5-20

Briefs

Two players weave the ball down-court then make a transition.

Why Do This

This continuous motion lesson improves all TLC skills and is probably the number one "must do" lesson when three players weave the ball. With two players the weave is still a worthwhile CM lesson. Adding a transition makes this lesson even better.

Directions For Players

1. Two players start one yard apart at midcourt with a ball. *See the diagram Setup/Motion Half-Court.*

2. Stay close. Lateral the ball back and forth as you run to the basket. Face forward toward the basket, looking at each other out the corner of your eyes.

3. At the basket, slow down to make a layup or a 1-foot shot.

4. The shooter gets his/her own rebound, the other player moves quickly to the sideline for an outlet pass. This is like a outlet pass for a fast break.

5. Rebound without letting the ball hit the floor, pass to the sidelines, then quickly move toward

Setup/Motion Half-Court

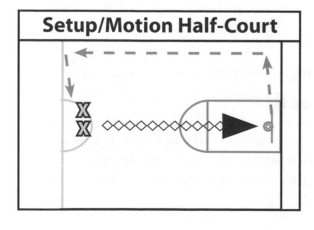

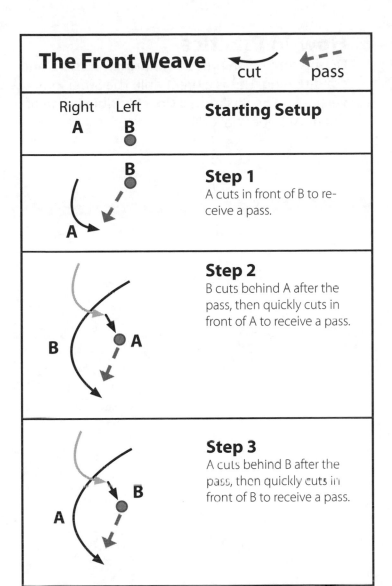

The Front Weave   ⟵ cut   ⟵--- pass

Right **A**	Left **B**	**Starting Setup**
	●	

Step 1
A cuts in front of B to receive a pass.

Step 2
B cuts behind A after the pass, then quickly cuts in front of A to receive a pass.

Step 3
A cuts behind B after the pass, then quickly cuts in front of B to receive a pass.

the sidelines. Do not walk with the ball! You must look at and pass to each other. Do not take more than one step.

6. Continue to pass the ball as you move down the sideline to midcourt, then back to the starting position.

7. Use an assistant to watch for walking. You may not walk at any time during this drill. Only one step is allowed before passing.

8. The second time down court weave the ball to the basket. *See the diagram The Front Weave.*

9. The catcher of the pass in the weave cuts 1 yard in front of the passer. The passer passes ahead, quickly cuts behind the catcher, and then runs one yard in front to receive a pass.

10. This may take a few times to get right. Both players must move quickly and to the right place for a successful weave.

11. At the basket one player shoots the layup and rebounds. The other player breaks to the sideline for the pass.

12. You may need to walk through the weave a few times before jogging.

13. As soon as you can weave properly, go full-court If a full-court is available.

14. Use a bounce pass after several minutes, then alternate between the bounce and non-bounce pass every few minutes. The bounce pass is easier.

Key Points.
1. No walking is allowed at any time. Only one step is allowed before passing. Initially an assistant is needed to make sure players do not walk.

2. Avoid walking by constantly looking at each other.

3. Change the pass to a bounce pass after several minutes.

How To Practice

Do this for 5-20 minutes to improve TLC skills and conditioning. This is a great drill. The 3-person version in **The Basketball Coach's Bible** is one of the most beneficial drills.

SHOOTING TECHNIQUE LESSONS

24 Touch Two
25 Wrist Work
26 Body Alignment
27 Extension
28 1-Foot Shot

Shooting technique is the key to both developing and maintaining shooting ability. These methods work 100% of the time with players of all ages. Every player may not become a great shooter, but every player will improve. Younger players will develop good habits and older players will understand what they need to work on. Good shooters will also be more consistent.

An assistant that has read the material is necessary to help with several lessons, because a player cannot readily adjust technique on his/her own without practicing in front of a mirror. The lessons involved are also quite difficult, especially for a player with shooting problems. Usually each drill needs to be repeated multiple times on a daily basis for months.

A warning: do not adjust your technique when you are actually shooting. Thinking about using more wrists or releasing higher or keeping the elbow in or following through, during a shooting drill only psyches yourself out. You must shoot without thinking—period. Receiving instructions from an assistant that makes you think also destroys technique and concentration, resulting in poor shooting. If an assistant notices a problem, just go back and work on technique-level lessons to correct it.

Lesson 24, Touch Two, shows how to better control the ball. Lesson 25, Wrist Work, is a critical skill usually overlooked. Lesson 26, Body Alignment, twists and turns a player's body into better shooting position. This is related to squaring-up. Lesson 27, Extension, forces a player to release the ball high overhead rather than at the nose or forehead. Lesson 28, 1-Foot Shot, is the best way to practice technique. If you want to shoot with either hand, then repeat the entire lesson with the other hand.

24 Touch Two

Setup

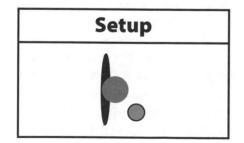

Brief
Hold the ball in an exaggerated position in contact with the fingerends.

Why Do This
A player with poor fingertip ball control will never be able to improve shooting, no matter how much he/she practices. This lesson increases the sensitivity of the fingertips. Sensitivity is another name for touch, a word often used in connection with shooting. This is a repeat of Lesson 1.

Directions
1. Put the ball down. Spread the fingers apart as far as possible. Shape each hand into a claw and growl. The growl must be fierce.

2. Pick up the ball with your claws, so that only the fingerends touch the ball. *See the diagram Fingertip Control.*

3. The palm and fingers should not touch the ball.

4. Hold the ball tightly for one minute.

Key Points
1. Fingers spread apart as far as possible.

2. Fingers clawed, not bent at joints.

3. Hands clawed, not flat.

4. Only fingerends contact the ball.

Fingertip Control

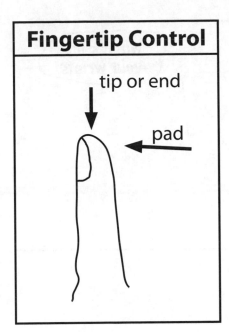

tip or end

pad

How To Practice

Work on holding the ball at any time during practice, or at home. You will readily note an improvement in control on shots, passes and dribbles.

25 Wrist Work

Player's Corner

Parts	1	2	3
Type	CORE	CORE	CORE
Players	1	1	1
Assist	NO	NO	NO
Ball	X	X	X
Court	X	X	X
Effort	1	1	1
Time	3	3	3

Setup Parts 1-3

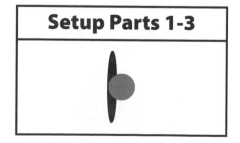

Briefs

In Part 1, loosen up hands and arms.

In Part 2, flick the wrists upward.

In Part 3, flick in the overhead shooting position.

Why Do This

A shot is basically a flick of the wrist with body motion. The arms should not move much on the actual shot. The wrists should be as loose as wet noodles. A player with stiff wrists shoots the ball with the arms, making a shot look more like a shot-put or throw. The result is little control of the shot, a low shooting percentage, and shots that, from the start have little chance of going in.

Think of the wrist as a coiled spring; if the spring is not compressed it cannot expand. Bending the wrist back at least 90 degrees seems to compress the spring enough for a flick. Lesser bending will not allow for a sufficient flick, resulting in the use of the arms and poor shooting. An added result of flicking the ball is a natural backspin, which slows down the ball when it hits the rim and/or backboard. Shots that normally would bang off the rim and go awry often bounce in with backspin.

There are two reasons for what I call stiff wrists:

(a) a player cannot physically bend the wrist back very far.

(b) a player can bend the wrist back, but due to poor habits usually does not.

Wrist work helps both types of players. Flicking the wrist back in the opposite direction of the shooting flick extends the range of motion of the wrist. Making sure the wrists and hands are loose while flicking helps the tight-wristed player.

The importance of wrist motion in improving shooting cannot be overemphasized. Shooting 100, 1000, or a million shots does not necessarily make a player a better shooter. Working on shooting technique, and in particular wrist work, does make a player a better shooter.

Part 1 Loosen Up
Directions

1. With feet shoulder-width apart, arms at sides, relax your hands.

2. Shake your hands and arms back and forth like wet noodles. Loosen up. The arms should not move very much. Continue for 30 seconds to a minute.

Key Point

1. "Stay loose man".

How To Practice

Loosen up before each time you touch a ball.

Part 2 Flick
Directions

1. Now, keep the arms still at the sides; palms face backwards; fingers apart; hands slightly clawed.

2. Flick your hands forward and let them come back naturally. No arm movement. Keep the elbows straight. *See the diagram Flick Up.* The arms should be at the sides. In the diagram the arms are in front of the body for clarity.

3. Continue for as long as you can, usually 1-5 minutes.

Key Points

1. Arms should not move, only wrists move.

2. Elbows should be straight, not bent.

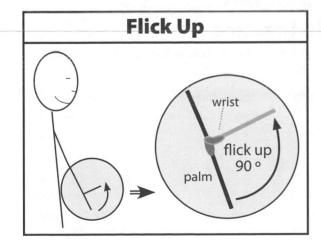

Flick Up

ELBOWS

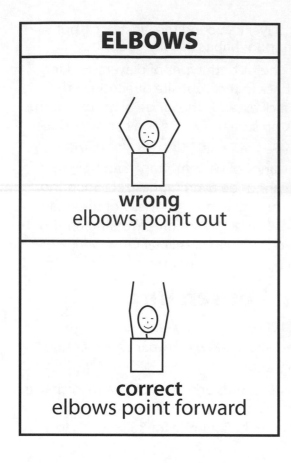

wrong
elbows point out

correct
elbows point forward

Flick Back

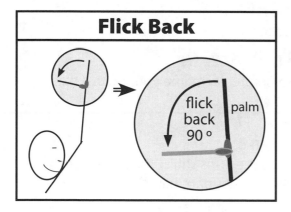

flick back 90°   palm

3. Fingers should be as far apart as possible, not close.

4. Hands should be clawed, not flat.

How To Practice

Work on flicking as much as you can, especially if you are tight. It may take months before you loosen up. However, you will loosen up and improve shooting. Practice flicking before each time you pick up a ball.

Part 3 Flick Overhead
Directions

1. With your feet at shoulder-width, raise your arms straight overhead with the palms facing forward. The elbows point forward, not to the sides. Move the arms closer together if necessary. Straighten the elbows. *See the diagram Elbows.*

2. Flick backwards and let your hands come forward naturally. Keep the hands loose and slightly clawed. The arms do not move. *See the diagram Flick Back.*

Key Points

1. The hands and wrists remain loose.

2. Hand movement is forward and back, not sideways.

3. Elbows point forward, not outward.

4. Fingers are apart and not squeezed together.

5. Hands slightly clawed.

How To Practice

Practice this every day of the season, especially before shooting.

26 Body Alignment

Setup

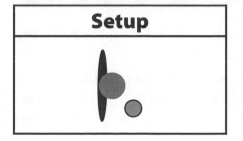

Briefs

Flick the ball directly overhead with the body properly aligned for shooting.

Why Do This

The way you shoot is based on your special body attributes including flexibility, arm length, and strength. However, there are some mechanical movements that are universal to all shooting techniques and, if practiced correctly, will improve the shooting of any player. The wrist flicking lessons involved one of those movements. This lesson involves other important techniques: shoot with the elbow in; ball high overhead; release off the fingerends with a flick of the wrist; body squared-up to the shooting direction.

Older players may take weeks or longer before they can adequately perform these movements. Younger players and poor shooters will need to work on this for months, attempting to do better, improving and changing their shot in small increments.

I often call this lesson the Statue of Liberty drill because players start out with one arm extended overhead like the statue. The instructions "inward" and "outward" in this lesson mean inward and outward from a vertical line going through the

Steps Body Alignment			
Steps	**Directions**	**Side**	**Front**
1	•arm straight •ball overhead		
2	•wrist back •ball on fingertips		
3	•elbow toward nose •pretzel •turn hand		
4	•elbow up •flick ball up 3 inches •catch on fingertips		

Wrong 1	Wrong 2
head moved out instead of elbow in	body twisted at shoulders
x elbow	forward back

belly button (center of the body) or away from the belly button respectively.

Directions

Step 1 Feet shoulder-width apart; shooting arm extended straight overhead; the elbow straight. The elbow remains pointing forward throughout this drill.

•When you repeat this lesson use the cue words in lieu of a more lengthy explanation. All cue words are summarized at the end of the lesson.

•Look very closely at the *diagram Steps Body Alignment,* which shows every little movement of the arms and hands.

•Cue words: Arm straight up.

Step 2 Bend the wrists back as far as possible; claw the hand, separate the fingers. Balance the ball on the fingertips of the shooting hand. Keep the ball on the fingertips throughout this drill.

•Cue words: Wrist back; ball on fingertips.

Step 3a Move the elbow of the shooting arm inward, toward your nose. Keep the elbow as high as possible, don't bring it down to the nose. Just move it inward toward the nose.

•Cue words: Elbow to nose.

•An assistant needs to move the body parts into alignment.

Common problems include:

(a) moving the head toward the elbow, instead of the elbow to the head. *See the diagram Wrong 1.*

(b) turning the body sideways pushing the shooting shoulder forward, the non-shooting shoulder back. *See the diagram Wrong 2.*

Wrong 3

elbow lowered &
moved forward

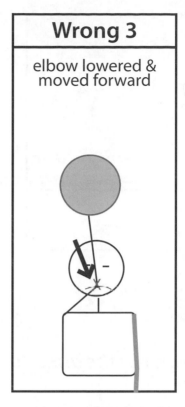

Wrong 4

hand moved more
inward than elbow

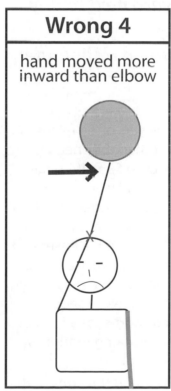

(c) lowering the elbow and moving it forward. The elbow should be above the head. *See the diagram Wrong 3.*

(d) moving the hand more inside than the elbow. *See the diagram Wrong 4.*

Step 3b To combat several problems, reach across the body with the non-shooting arm. Grab and pull the shooting elbow inward. *See the diagram The Pretzel.*

•Cue Words: Pretzel

•Most likely the hand will turn sideways, if it is not sideways already.

Step 3c Slightly rotate the forearm and hand so that the hand is again facing forward.

•Cue words: Turn hand.

Step 4 The shoulders, body, and elbow remain facing forward. The ball is on the fingerends. Make sure the elbow is up. Flick the hand and wrist so that the ball only goes 3 inches straight up, not one foot or two. Catch the ball on the fingertips.

•You will not do this correctly this first time or anytime soon. That's okay, because improvement comes through the attempt. Don't worry about perfection.

Steps Using Cue Words

Step 1 Arm straight up.

Step 2 Wrist back, ball on fingertips.

Step 3 Elbow to nose. Pretzel. Turn hand.

Step 4 Elbow up. Flick.

Key Points

1. You need an assistant watching or you need to perform this lesson in front of a mirror.

2. If your shooting hand gets tired, work with the other hand.

3. Just attempting to do this correctly will improve your technique.

How To Practice

Practice this everyday for at least 5 minutes either in front of a mirror or with an assistant.

The Pretzel

off arm pushes shot
elbow inward

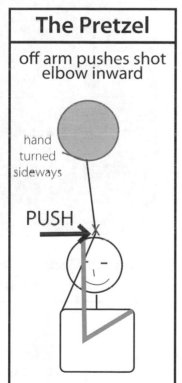

hand
turned
sideways

PUSH

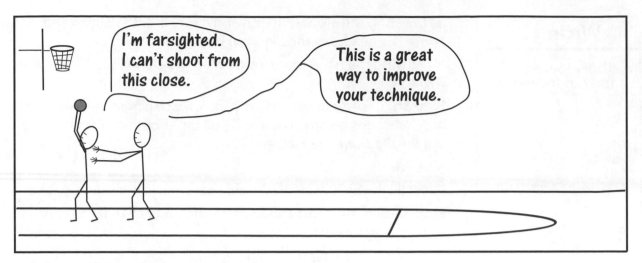

27 Extension

Player's Corner

Parts	1	2	3
Type	CORE	CORE	CORE
Players	1	1	1
Assist	NO	NO	YES
Ball	○	○	○
Court	X	X	🏀|
Effort	1	2	1
Time	3-5	3-5	3-5

Setup Part 1

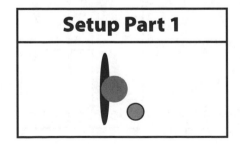

Briefs

In Part 1, use the legs, not the arms, to flick the ball higher.

In Part 2, shoot upward next to any gym wall.

In Part 3, shoot standing right under the basket rim.

Why Do This

Fourth-grade to pro-level players often release the shot from 1-3 feet lower than they need to. *See the diagram Extension On A Shot.* With full extension, *#1 in the diagram,* a player is able to shoot over a closely guarding defender and shoot more easily in traffic. As the shooting-arm elbow bends more, the ball is released from a lower and lower height, *#'s 2 to 4 in the diagram.* Nose shooters, *#4 in the diagram,* cannot shoot over a closely guarding defender nor in traffic. Nose shooters even have difficult shooting short shots, 1-3 feet from the basket, since their shooting motion is forward with the arms instead of up.

These lessons force you to extend the arms to the maximum on the shot. Nose shooters will benefit the most from these lessons. Most started shooting this way before they had the strength to shoot using only wrist motion. The bad habit, like most without correction, just stayed with them.

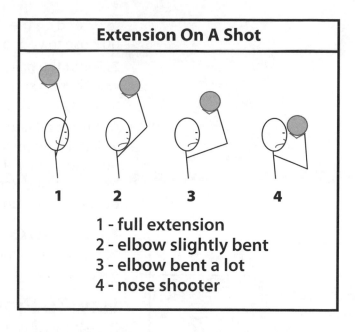

Extension On A Shot

1   2   3   4

1 - full extension
2 - elbow slightly bent
3 - elbow bent a lot
4 - nose shooter

The more players practice extension, the more they naturally extend on the shot without any negative effect on shooting technique. Unfortunately, nose shooting usually returns when players shoot far from the basket. So, nose shooters need to practice close to the basket in all shooting lessons. Extending shooting range while maintaining technique is covered In Lessons 36-38.

Part 1 Shoot Up
Directions
1. Setup in the same position as the previous lesson ready to flick the ball.

2. Flick the ball as high as you can using the wrists and the legs, no arms.

Key Points
1. No arms.

2. Shoot with the arms extended to the maximum.

How To Practice
This only needs to be practiced once or twice.

Part 2 Wall Shot
Directions
1. Start with the ball at waist height rather than overhead.

2. Stay as close to the wall as possible with the ball in front. *See the diagram Setup Part 2.* The ball should almost hit the wall and body as it is brought up. Besides forcing you

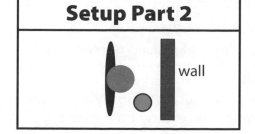

Setup Part 2

wall

to extend on the shot, this part forces you to bring the ball up close to your body.

3. Shoot the ball straight up as high as possible. The key word here is straight up, not to the side or behind. Repeat for a few minutes.

4. A more advanced lesson involves starting so close to the wall that you must bring the ball up from either the left or right side. Bring the ball up 5 times from the left, then 5 from the right. Repeat 3-5 times. Make sure your head is up during this lesson.

Key Points

1. Stay close to the wall.

2. Shoot the ball straight up.

How To Practice

Repeat this lesson 1-3 times.

Part 3 1-Inch Shot
Directions

1. Set up right under the rim with the ball overhead. The forehead should be under the rim. **_See the diagrams 1-Inch Shot 1 & 2._** It best to mark the spot for placement of the heels. Otherwise you will back up, making the lesson less worthwhile. An assistant needs to make sure you are directly under the rim.

2. Square-up to the basket, then attempt to shoot the ball over the rim into the basket. No backboard shots allowed.

3. Since the ball starts overhead, just flick the shot.

4. It is important that the forehead starts directly under the rim.

5. It's okay if the ball just hits the underside of the rim. You are only interested in extension, not making the shot. You succeed if you extend to the maximum, not if you make the shot.

Key Points

1. Line up directly under the rim.

2. Don't cheat by moving backwards.

3. Success involves extending, not making the shot.

How To Practice

Practice this part only once because it is mostly a diagnostic tool indicating how much you extend on the shot.

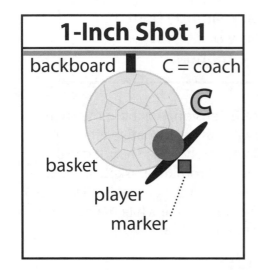

1-Inch Shot 1

backboard   C = coach

basket

player

marker

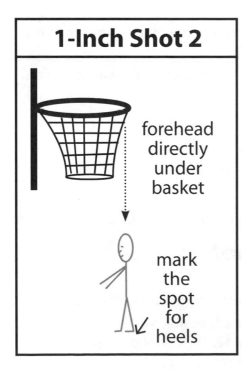

1-Inch Shot 2

forehead directly under basket

mark the spot for heels

28 1-Foot Shot

Player's Corner

Parts	1	2	3
Type	CORE	CORE	OPT
Players	1	1	1
Assist	NO	NO	NO
Ball	○	○	○
Court	🏀	🏀	🏀
Effort	1	2	2
Time	5	5	5

Setup Parts 1-3

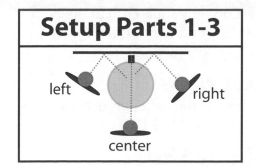

left   right

center

Briefs

In Part 1, square-up properly, then shoot a 1-foot shot off the backboard.

In Part 2, shoot a 1-foot shot at normal speed.

In Part 3, shoot a 1-foot jump shot.

Why Do This

The 1-foot shot should be the mainstay of any practice program because practicing at this distance always improves technique (the 1-foot shot has nothing to do with standing on one foot unless you want to be a clown). Make sure it is a 1-foot shot, not a 3-foot shot. The difference is important. The 1-foot shot, like the 1-inch shot, forces you to extend. Since the shot is short, there is also no physical need to arm the ball to the basket, thus preserving technique.

The first 1-foot shot lesson is a technique-level lesson where you take time to set up, then shoot. Make sure to square-up to the shooting direction, which in this case is the backboard. Squaring-up means that the shoulders and front of the body face the exact direction of the shot. The second lesson involves just shooting. In reality it may be hard to distinguish one part from the other. However, take time to set up properly in the first one.

In the second lesson work at a normal practice pace; there is no need to rush.

In the last lesson, the jump shot is introduced. The best way to practice and shoot a jump shot is to jump and shoot on the way up. Shooting at the height of the jump or purposefully jumping high throws off the shot. These variations should be reserved for shots under the basket and more experienced players. Fadaways and lean-tos are also variations that should only be practiced by more experienced high-school and above players. The best way to shoot a jump shot in traffic is to release early on the way up, before the defense is ready. The quick release beats power most of the time with most players. The quick release is also easy to do.

Part 1 1-Foot Shot Slow
Directions

1. Mark the 1-foot line with masking tape or a cone on the right, center, and left of the basket.

2. Take your time, set up on the mark, square-up properly to the backboard, then shoot flicking the wrist. *See the diagrams Squaring-Up and Squared-Up Properly?*

3. Shoot 10 shots from the right, then center, and then the left. Repeating with the other hand is optional.

4. Use the backboard. Rebound the ball. Do not let the ball hit the ground between shots.

5. Nose shooters will want to back up to 2 or 3 feet because they are not in the habit of extending on the shot. If you are a nose shooter, make sure you stay close to the basket.

Key Points

1. Take your time. Correctly square-up to the backboard. See Lesson 18 for more on squaring-up.

2. Shoot from 1 foot, not 2 or 3 feet.

How To Practice

Practice this part and/or the next part everyday. It's okay to repeat this lesson 2 to 5 times a day.

Part 2 1-Foot Shot
Directions

1. This part is the same as the previous one except that you just shoot the ball. This is a practice-level drill.

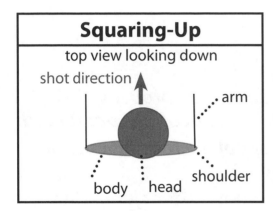

Squaring-Up

top view looking down

shot direction

arm

shoulder

body   head

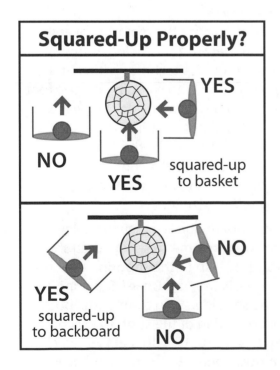

Squared-Up Properly?

NO

YES

YES

squared-up
to basket

NO

YES
squared-up
to backboard

NO

2. Rebound your shot not allowing the ball to hit the floor, then set up and shoot again. You should shoot one shot right after the other, not that you need to go real fast.

3. Make sure to stay 1 foot from the basket. Repeat from right, center, and left.

Key Points

1. Stay 1 foot from the basket.

2. Shoot at a normal speed.

3. Do not let the ball hit the floor.

How To Practice

Practice this every day. This lesson is essential to preserve shooting technique.

Part 3 1-Foot Jump Shot
Directions

1. Repeat the previous part using a jump shot.

2. Just jump and shoot at the same time. You don't want the jump to throw off the shot. Quick releases are better than big jumps.

Key Points

1. Stay one foot from the basket.

2. Shoot off the backboard.

3. Do not let the ball hit the floor at any time.

4. Jump and shoot at the same time.

How To Practice

This lesson is for more advanced players, not novices who need more work on technique.

MOVES LESSONS

29 Jab Fake Moves
30 Pivot Moves
31 Ball Fake Moves

About Moves on the next page gives more information on this topic. Lesson 29, Jab Fake Moves, covers moves involving jab fakes. Lesson 30, Pivot Moves, covers moves with pivots and pivot fakes. Lesson 31, Ball Fake Moves, covers moves that involve ball fakes.

About Moves

The word "move" is this section is considered a scoring move, although this term is often used more broadly to mean any series of movements. The purpose of each move in this section is to score. There are endless possibilities for moves when you consider each type of shot and/or pivot and/or fake involved. A player with sufficient ability can invent a move during a game. This section on moves provides a varied sample that will help even the most advanced player.

The moves in this section are great practice for several reasons.

(a) Players practice short shots, which help with technique, even though most moves can be executed or practiced anywhere on the court.

(b) The many pivots involved improve agility as well as pivoting ability.

(c) Players start to practice many fakes: jab fakes, pivot fakes, and the most difficult ball fakes.

(d) Players love to work on them.

All moves should be done slowly at a relaxed pace so the body can learn the needed balance. Each player must keep his/her head up; looking at the floor is a bad habit. Work 1 foot from the basket, though most moves can be executed anywhere on the floor.

Make every shot—zero misses. Another problem, even with college players, is that they will not properly square-up to the basket, actually the backboard for most moves.

The specific directions for each move are given in each lesson. Here is the general practice routine:

1. Each player needs a basket to properly practice a move. Often several players can alter-nate working at one basket. However, a player can practice a move anywhere on the court without the actual shot at a basket. Just shoot the ball 1-3 feet straight up.

2. Shoot from a distance of 1 foot from the right, center, then left.

3. Shoot 5-10 shots from each position with the strong hand. Do not dribble or let the ball bounce between shots.

4. Start with the left foot as pivot, then repeat the entire lesson with the right foot as pivot.

5. Perform slowly using the backboard on each shot, even from the center position.

6. Optional to repeat the entire lesson with the weak or off hand.

7. Optional to repeat a move using a jump shot. If so, make sure to release on the way up; no big jumps.

8. Another option on each pivot-around move is to pivot around in the other direction. So, after pivoting forward, it is quite worthwhile to repeat the entire lesson pivoting backwards, especially since pivoting backwards is more difficult.

Hook shots, the next group of lessons, should be practiced just like moves. More advanced shots such as fadaways and lean-tos can be practiced just like the moves. However, even most pros need more basic practice.

At least 80 lessons are possible combining the shots with the fakes and other options; 160 if you practice with each hand. Don't try any move without first working on basic pivoting and faking.

29 Jab Fake Moves

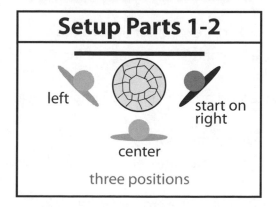

Player's Corner

Parts	1	2
Type	OPT	OPT
Players	1	1
Assist	YES	YES
Ball	○	○
Court	🏀	🏀
Effort	2	2
Time	5-10	5-10

Setup Parts 1-2

left

start on right

center

three positions

Briefs

In Part 1, use a jab fake before shooting.

In Part 2, take a long jab fake before shooting.

Why Do This

These moves involve movements taught in a previous section. In Part 1 you take a jab-step with a ball fake, then gather yourself up for the shot. In Part 2 perform a drive fake, which involves a long jab-step with a ball fake before shooting. Each fake is very difficult to properly perform and is also very effective if done well.

Directions will shorten as we go through the moves assuming you have started from the beginning. Most diagrams with pivoting only show the move with the left foot as pivot foot. Lessons should be repeated with the right foot as pivot.

Part 1 Jab Fake
Directions

1. Start on the right side, one foot from the basket in the half-down position with the ball at waist-height. Left foot pivot foot. **See the diagram Setup Parts 1-2.**

2. Square-up to the point on the backboard where you aim.

3. Jab-step to the right, pushing the ball out with the step. Keep the ball at waist-height. Keep the head up. Do not look down.

4. Bring the feet back to shoulder-width while moving the ball overhead. Shoot using the backboard.

5. Catch the rebound before it hits the ground. No dribbling.

6. Repeat steps 1-5, taking 5 to 10 shots.

7. Move to the center position and repeat. Use the backboard on each shot.

8. Move to the left side and repeat.

9. Now set up on the right side again using the right foot as pivot.

10. Jab-step to the left, pushing the ball left.

11. Bring the feet back together to shoulder-width with the ball overhead. Shoot. Rebound.

12. Repeat steps 9-11, 5-10 times.

13. Repeat steps 9-12 at the center position, then the left side.

•Optional to repeat steps 1-13 with the opposite hand.

•Optional to repeat using a jump shot.

Key Points

1. Square-up properly.

2. No dribbling. Do not let the ball hit the floor.

3. Go slow. No reason to rush.

How To Practice

This is optional.

Part 2 Jump Drive Fake
Directions

1. This is the same as Part 1 except for the drive fake.

2. The drive fake is a long jab-step while pushing the ball low to the fake side.

3. Spring back to starting position but with the ball overhead.

4. Square-up and take a jump shot.

5. Perform on the right, center, and left, then switch pivot foot and repeat.

6. A much more difficult fake is a crossover step fake. To perform this, take a very small jab-step to the right, then a long crossover step to the left pushing the ball low.

7. Spring back to the starting position with the ball overhead, then shoot.

8. Repeat from the right, center, and left. Switch pivot foot and repeat.

Key Points

1. On the drive fake or crossover drive fake the body is close to the ground. The stretch must be as long as possible. This is quite difficult.

2. Keep the head up. Look and act like there is a defender right in front of you.

How To Practice

This is optional.

30 Pivot Moves

Player's Corner

Parts	1	2
Type	OPT	OPT
Players	1	1
Assist	NO	NO
Ball	○	○
Court	🏀	🏀
Effort	2	2
Time	5-10	5-20

Briefs

In Part 1, start with your back to the basket, pivot around, then shoot.

In Part 2, start facing the basket, pivot around 180 degrees with a fake, pivot back 180 degrees, then shoot.

Why Do This

These moves involve a 180 degree or half-turn pivot. Perform these with the head up like there is a defender in front of you.

In Part 1 the initial half-turn just gets you to the starting position. In Part 2 the initial half-turn is part of the move.

Part 1 Pivot Move
Directions

1. Start on the right side with left foot pivot. ***See the diagram Part 1 Steps-Left Foot Pivot.*** Diagram step numbers do not correspond to the numbers in the directions.

2. Here is how to find the optimal starting position. Square-up to the backboard facing the basket like in the previous lesson. ***Step 1 in the diagram Part 1 Steps-Left Foot Pivot.***

Part 1 Steps - Left Foot Pivot

Steps	Right	Center	Left
1 initial position			
2 pivot backward to starting position			
3 pivot forward (a) or backward (b) to shoot			

Part 1 Steps - Right Foot Pivot			
Steps	Right	Center	Left
1 initial position			
2 pivot backward to starting position			
3 pivot forward (a) or backward (b) to shoot			

3. Pivot backwards a half turn. *Step 2 in the diagram.* This is the starting position.

4. Raise the ball overhead, then pivot forward to face the basket. Square-up, then shoot. *Step 3a in the diagram.*

5. It's better to raise the ball as you pivot around than before the pivot. However, it's also better to raise it earlier than late. In a game, you will raise and pivot simultaneously. Because there is a defensive player between you and the basket, keep the ball close to the body and slightly to the side.

6. Rebound without letting the ball hit the ground.

•Repeat steps 1- 6, 5-10 times.

7. Repeat steps 1-6 from the center and left.

8. Switch pivot foot, and set up facing the backboard on the right side. Square-up to shoot a shot off the backboard. *See the diagram Part 1 Steps- Right Foot Pivot.*

9. Pivot backwards to the starting position. *Step 2 in the diagram.*

10. Pivot forward raising the ball overhead first. *Step 3a in the diagram.* Square-up and shoot. Rebound.

11. Repeat steps 8 to 10, 5-10 times then repeat from center and left.

12. It's very worthwhile to repeat the entire lesson pivoting around backwards. *Step 3b in the diagrams.*

Key Points

1. Set up in the final position, then pivot around to the starting position.

2. Keep the head up during this lesson.

3. Keep the ball close to the body and slightly to the side.

How To Practice

This is optional though very worthwhile.

Part 2 - Move 1	
1 initial position	
2 pivot fake backward	ball fake
3 pivot forward to shoot	

Part 2 Pivot Fake
Directions

1. Set up just like the previous part. Right side, left pivot foot. Half-down position. Ball waist-high. Square-up to the backboard. *Step 1 in diagram Part 2 - Move 1.*

2. Pivot backwards 180 degrees so that your back is to the basket. Simultaneously push the ball far to the right as you pivot. This is a pivot backwards fake. *Step 2 in the diagram.*

3. Now pivot forward to the original position pushing the ball from the side to high overhead. *Step 3 in the diagram.* Square-up and shoot.

4. Repeat 5-10 times.

5. Perform steps 1-4 from the center and left.

6. Switch pivot foot and repeat the entire drill. Start with the right foot as pivot foot on the right side, pivot backwards pushing the ball out to the left. Pivot forward while pushing the ball overhead from the side. Square-up and shoot.

7. There are several other ways to perform this lesson. *See the diagram Variations Part 2.* All moves in the diagram start with the left foot as pivot from the right side. Perform from the center and left as well. Then repeat each move with the right foot as pivot.

Move 1 The move previously described.

Move 2 Pivot-backwards fake like in the first part, but then pivot backwards again, instead of forward, to the starting position.

Move 3 Pivot-forward fake, then pivot forward again to the starting position.

Move 4 Pivot-forward fake, then backward to the starting position.

•You can add a jab fake to each move before the initial pivot fake.

Key Points
1. Make sure to perform this and every other move slowly.

How To Practice
This is optional.

Variations Part 2		
Steps	**1st pivot**	**2nd pivot**
Move 1 1-backward 2-forward		
Move 2 1-backward 2-backward		
Move 3 1-forward 2-forward		
Move 4 1-forward 2-backward		

31 Ball Fake Moves

Player's Corner

Parts	1	2
Type	ADV	ADV
Players	1	1
Assist	NO	NO
Ball	○	○
Court	🏀|	🏀|
Effort	2	2
Time	5-10	5-10

Setup Parts 1-2

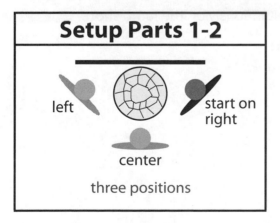

left   start on right

center

three positions

Briefs

In Part 1, pump fake, then shoot.

In Part 2, fake an overhead pass, then shoot.

Why Do This

Ball fakes are incredibly effective if done properly. They not only freeze your coverage, they can freeze and confuse the entire defense. They are also quite difficult to do.

Fakes need to be slow enough so that the defense can react. Go very slow in practice. In a game you will naturally go a bit faster. Too fast makes a fake worthless.

Part 1 Jump Pump Fake
Directions

1. Same setup as the previous lesson. Start on right side facing the basket with the ball at waist height, feet shoulder-width apart, in the half-down position. Left foot pivot. *See the diagram Setup Parts 1-2.*

2. The pump fake is like a fake shot.

3. Here's how to do it. Look at the basket while slowly bringing the ball up to forehead height and simultaneously bending the knees like you are going to jump.

Pump Fake Steps

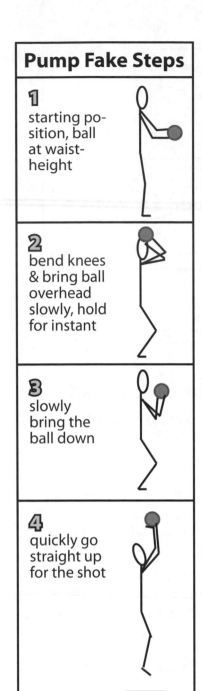

1
starting position, ball at waist-height

2
bend knees & bring ball overhead slowly, hold for instant

3
slowly bring the ball down

4
quickly go straight up for the shot

4. Then bring the ball down to chin height keeping the knees bent. Jump straight up for a jump shot. *See the diagram Pump Fake Steps.*

5. The name, pump, comes from the pumping up and down, and then up again motion of the arms.

6. Repeat 5-10 times from right, center, and left, then switch pivot foot and repeat.

Key Points

1. Keep the head up during this lesson.

2. Go slow on the pump fake. Better too slow than too fast.

How To Practice

This is optional though worthwhile.

Part 2 Jump Pass Fake
Directions

1. This is the same as Part 1 except that the ball starts overhead and a pass fake is used instead of a pump fake. *See the diagram Setup Parts 1-2.*

2. The pass fake is just a flick of the wrist with the ball overhead. The fake involves a short jab-step as well.

3. Simultaneously flick, take a jab-step to the right, and look in a direction away from the basket.

4. Then square-up and take a jump shot.

5. Start with the left foot as pivot foot. Repeat from right, center, and left, then switch pivot foot.

Key Points

1. There is not much movement on this fake. Do it slowly.

2. To convince the defense that you are passing, you must actually look at something or someone like you are going to pass to them.

3. Jump and shoot simultaneously on the jump shot.

How To Practice

Optional though worthwhile.

HOOK SHOTS LESSONS

Hook shots are not for novices or small players. The **About Hooks** page (on the next page) gives information about hooks.

Lesson 32, Regular Hook, teaches the old hook shot. Lesson 33, Step Hook, teaches how to perform the hook starting on the other pivot foot. Lesson 34, Jump Hook, teaches how to do the modern day hook shot. Lesson 35, Underneath Hooks, teaches how to do various hooks starting right under the basket and/or backboard.

About Hooks

Hook shots are not for novices for several reasons. One, to be effective, players need to be able to control the ball with one hand. Young players can't do this because they have small hands. Two, hook shots are used close to the basket when the defense is tight. With novices, tight defenses are seldom encountered.

The power of the hook is that it neutralizes the defense. It allows a player unimpeded 1-2 foot shots with the defense right in his/her face. Two reasons stand out for the effectiveness of the hook. One is that the body of the shooter protects the ball from the defense. The other is that the hook is a quickly executed shot. Players need not even turn around to face the basket to shoot.

A player standing on the opposite pivot foot takes a step hook. A right-hander on the right pivot foot must take a step with the left foot before shooting. A left-hander on the left pivot foot must take a step on the right foot first. Being able to shoot with either hand allows a player to turn either left or right, taking a hook in one direction with one hand or a step hook in the other direction with the other hand.

All directions are given for right-handers (righties). Directions for lefties are given when they are different. Older players should repeat each lesson with the opposite hand.

As with the other shooting lessons, players line up 1 foot from the basket on the right, then center, and then left. Since the hook is most effective as a short shot, I recommend that you practice with each hand. This means twice as much practice.

Two types of hooks are especially effective. On the jump hook, the ball is quickly released from a position higher and closer to the basket than the regular hook. The jump hook is very difficult to block. The other type of hook is taken from directly underneath the basket. This enables players to shoot without needing to take steps outward or turn around, or square-up to the basket. Underneath hooks also catch the defense by surprise because players shoot from an awkward position. The net and the rim are also in the way of taller defenders.

The jump hook is the modern day hook shot. The regular hook is a thing of the past in today's fast-paced game for several good reasons. One, the regular hook takes a lot of time to release, whereas the jump hook is a very quick move. Two, the jump hook can be executed from a jump off of either pivot foot without even taking a step. Three, on the regular hook the shooter needs a lot of space to shoot, whereas the jump hook can readily be shot in traffic.

Like moves, all hook shots should be done slowly at a relaxed pace so the body can learn the needed balance. Make sure to keep your head up; looking at the floor is a bad habit. Work only 1 foot from the basket, though hooks can be executed from slightly greater distances; 5 feet would be a maximum distance.

Make every shot—zero misses. Another problem, even with college players, is that they will not properly square-up to the basket, actually the backboard for most moves. Make sure an assistant watches.

The specific directions for each move are given in each lesson. Hook shots are practiced just like moves, so it is worthwhile to read **About Moves** in the previous section.

32 Regular Hook

Player's Corner

Parts	1
Type	ADV
Players	1
Assist	YES
Ball	◯
Court	🏀
Effort	1-2
Time	5-15

Alignment For Hook

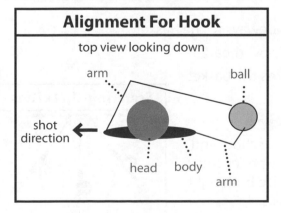

top view looking down

arm   ball

shot direction ←

head   body

arm

Briefs

Take the old fashioned hook shot from right, center, and left.

Why Do This

Learn the regular hook before spending the majority of your time on the jump hook and underneath hooks.

Directions

1. Start on right side, left pivot foot. *See the diagram Two Setups.* Lefties use the right foot as pivot. *See the diagram Lefties.*

2. Start with the ball at waist-height 1 foot away from the basket, squared-up to the backboard for a regular shot. *See setup 1 in the diagram Two Setups.*

3. Turn sideways and push the ball straight out to the right side. Lefties turn sideways the other way and push the ball straight out to the left. Both arms are straight out to the ball side, not in front of the body. *See the diagram Alignment For Hook.* Both shoulders and the ball are in a straight line. The left elbow (right elbow for lefties) is forward and slightly up, often in contact with the defender. The right elbow (left elbow for lefties) is back and slightly down.

4. Square-up on a hook shot by aligning the

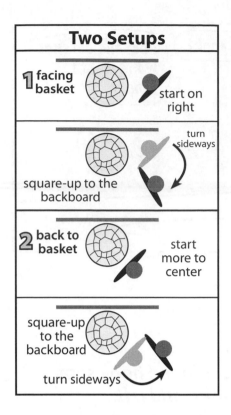

Two Setups

1 facing basket — start on right

square-up to the backboard — turn sideways

2 back to basket — start more to center

square-up to the backboard — turn sideways

Squaring-Up On Hook

Common Mistakes

ball forward

body turned to basket

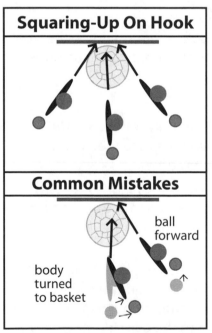

ball and the shoulders in a straight line with the point on the backboard that you're aiming for. *See the diagrams Squaring-Up On Hook and Squaring-Up Lefties.*

6. Raise the ball on the side and release the ball in a direction that takes it directly overhead to the basket. The shot starts from the waist and is released 1-3 feet to the side of the body at about head height. Use the wrist to flick the ball, just as with other shots. Use the shooting arm as little as possible.

7. One common error is to loop the ball in front of the body. In this case the ball does not go overhead. The ball is not protected by the body. A defender can easily block the shot. Another error is to turn the body toward the basket. Often a player makes both mistakes. *See the diagram Common Mistakes.*

8. Perform steps 1-7, 5-10 times from right, center, and left. Use the backboard from each position.

9. Perform steps 1-8 starting with the back to the basket. Righties start slightly more to the center of the court, so that after the turn you do not end up near the baseline. Lefties move slightly to the right of the court, so that after the turn you are not too near the center. *See setup 2 in the diagram Two Setups.*

Key Points

1. Body is lined up sideways to the basket.

2. Ball is shot directly overhead.

3. Do not turn towards the basket on the shot.

How To Practice

This is a must for high school and older players. More experienced players should practice both right and left handed hooks.

Lefties

1 facing basket — start more to center

square-up to the backboard — turn sideways

2 back to basket — start on right

square-up to the backboard — turn sideways

Squaring-Up Lefties

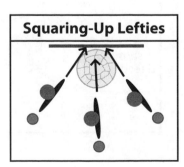

33 Step Hook

Player's Corner

Parts	1	2
Type	ADV	ADV
Players	1	1
Assist	NO	NO
Ball	○	○
Court	🏀	🏀
Effort	1-2	1-2
Time	5-10	5-10

Back To Basket

Step	Righties	Lefties
1		
2		

Facing Basket

Step	Righties	Lefties
1		
2		

Briefs

In Part 1, take a hook shot starting with the other pivot foot (called a step hook).

In Part 2, jab fake before shooting a step hook shot.

Why Do This

To shoot the regular right-handed hook a player uses the left foot as pivot and shoots (or steps) off the left foot. For the regular left-handed hook a player uses the right foot as pivot and shoots (or steps) off the right foot. To shoot a right-handed hook when the right foot is pivot or a left-handed hook when the left foot is pivot, a player steps onto the other foot before shooting. These moves are called step hooks.

The step hook is often more effective than the regular hook because you can use the step to take you farther from the defense. It is worthwhile to practice all hooks with the opposite hand because you then have the option of turning one way to use a step hook or turning the other way to use a regular hook.

In Part 1 the step hook is learned. Once a player learns the move, he/she can take a step of any length in any direction. The fake used in Part 2 makes the step hook more effective.

Part 1 Step Hook
Directions

1. Setup 1-2 feet farther away from the basket than the previous lesson, so that you do not end up under the backboard on the shot. S*ee the diagram Back To Basket.*

2. To shoot a right handed hook when the right foot is the pivot foot, you need to step onto the left foot before shooting. To shoot a left handed hook when the left foot is the pivot foot, you need step onto the right foot before shooting.

3. Start with the right foot as pivot (left for lefties) with the back to the basket.

4. Step onto the left foot (right foot for lefties), pivot on the left foot to square-up to the backboard for the hook, and shoot.

5. If necessary adjust your starting position so that after the pivot you are in a position to easily shoot off the backboard.

6. Repeat 5-10 times from right, center, and left.

7. Repeat facing the basket. *See the diagram Facing Basket.*

Key Points

1. To shoot a step hook, start on the opposite pivot foot used to shoot a regular hook.

2. Step onto the non-pivot foot, square-up sideways to the backboard before shooting. Do not bring the original pivot foot down till after you shoot.

Part 2 Fake Step Hook
Directions

1. A fake makes the step hook a very effective move. The fake is always away from the pivot foot. You can start either facing the basket or with the back to the basket. *See the diagrams Fake Step Hook and Backward Pivot.*

2. For righties start with the right foot as pivot. For lefties just switch the words *left* and *right* in the directions.

3. Start facing the basket first. *Step 1 in the diagram Fake Step Hook.* Jab fake to your left, pushing the ball left *(Step 2)*. Pivot forward (backward for lefties), taking a step towards (away for lefties) the basket with the left foot. Simultaneously push the ball across the body to the right. Square-up to the backboard and shoot *(Step 3)*.

4. When you start with your back to the basket (*Step 1 in the diagram Backward Pivot)* jab fake to your left, pushing the ball left *(Step 2)*. Pivot backward (forward for lefties) for a quarter turn and take a step towards the basket with the left foot. Simultaneously push the ball across the body to the right. Square-up and shoot *(Step 3)*.

5. Perform each shot 5-10 times from right, center, and left.

6. Optional to repeat with the other hand.

Key Points

1. Jab step and ball fake away from the pivot foot.

2. Square-up sideways to the direction that you shoot.

How To Practice

This is a must for older players. Eventually, repeat squaring-up to the basket. Lesson 35, involves more difficult step hooks.

Fake Step Hook	
Step	Forward Pivot
1	
2	
3	

Backward Pivot	
Step	Backward Pivot
1	
2	
3	

34 Jump Hook

Player's Corner		
Parts	1	2
Type	ADV	OPT
Players	1	1
Assist	YES	NO
Ball	◯	◯
Court	🏀	🏀
Effort	1-2	1-2
Time	5 -10	5-20

Briefs

In Part 1, shoot a jump hook.

In Part 2, fake before taking a jump hook, or step jump hook.

Why Do This

The jump hook is more effective than the hook because it is released more quickly from a higher elevation. ***See the diagram Hook Shot Release.*** A player can also square-up in the air, making it easier to shoot in traffic. Practicing with a fake makes the jump hook even more effective. On the jump hook a player jumps off both feet, rather than stepping off one foot, for the shot.

Part 1 Jump Hook
Directions

1. It's better to shoot the jump hook straight in, without use of the backboard. ***See the diagram Squaring-Up.***

2. For right handers, left foot pivot. Square-up to the basket by setting up sideways with the left foot closer to the basket (right foot closer for lefties).

3. On the jump, bring both arms up high overhead. The off arm acts a protection, the ball arm is up high. Do not turn the front of the body or

Hook Shot Release	Squaring-Up

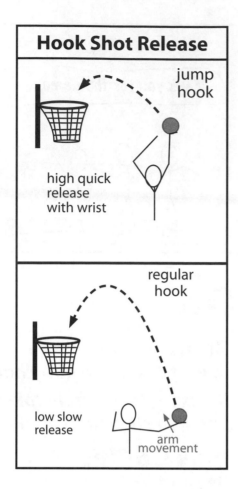

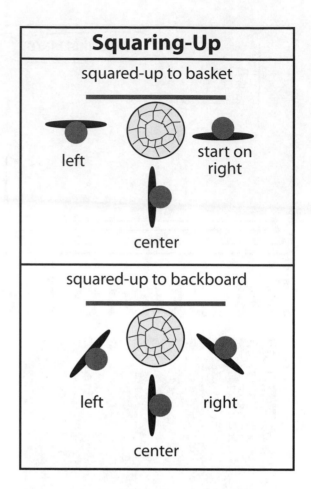

bring the ball forward. *See the first part of the diagram Hook Shot Release.*

4. Keep the ball to the side of the body and the body squared-up properly for the jump hook.

5. The shot is just a flick of the wrist without any arm movement.

•On the regular hook, the shot starts from the waist and is released 1-3 feet to the side of the body at about head height. *See the second part of the diagram.* The jump hook is released high overhead just behind the body.

•You will have a tendency to turn the front of the body forward, moving the body out of proper square. To prevent this, ask another player or assistant to push or hold back the shoulder of your shooting arm when you shoot.

6. Repeat from right, center, and left. Then repeat using the other pivot foot.

Key Points
1. Square-up to the basket.

2. Extend the shooting arm as high as possible.

3. Flick the shot with the wrist.

How To Practice
This is a must for older players. Repeat with the other hand.

Part 2 Fake Jump Hook
Directions

1. The hook, step hook, and jump hook can be practiced with a jab fake. (The fake step hook is Part 2 of the previous lesson.)

2. Repeat each move 5-10 times from right, center, then left. Lefties use the same pivot foot, but pivot in the other direction to square-up. Lefties must also adjust the starting position, so that you are in a good position to shoot after you pivot around for the shot.

3. *Move letters are from diagram Setup/Motion Part 2*, which shows the move from the left side. Do not use the backboard on these moves.

Move A
Face the basket. Left foot pivot. Jab fake to right pushing the ball right. Pivot backward to square-up to the basket and shoot. (Lefties pivot forward to square-up)

Move B
Face basket. Right foot pivot foot. Jab fake to left pushing the ball left. Pivot forward to square-up and shoot. (Lefties pivot backwards to square-up.)

Move C
Back to basket. Left foot pivot. Jab fake to right, pushing the ball right. Pivot forward to square-up and shoot. (Lefties pivot back-

Setup/Motion Part 2				
Move / Steps	A	B	C	D
1	pivot foot			
2	jab fake			
3	pivot			

35 Underneath Hooks

Player's Corner

Parts	1
Type	ADV
Players	1
Assist	NO
Ball	◯
Court	🏀
Effort	2
Time	5-25

Underneath Hooks

1 - Underneath Backboard

2 - Underneath Basket

Briefs
Start underneath the basket and/or backboard before shooting.

Why Do This
It is quite useful to have the ability to shoot a hook from directly under the basket. Picking up a loose ball or a rebound in traffic may not give you much time, or room, to move. These hooks can be shot in awkward and crowded situations. Use the backboard in each case. You can repeat each move shooting directly over the rim without using the backboard. Practice each move at least 5 times in a row from as many directions as possible.

Directions
1. There are 2 starting positions. One, underneath the backboard facing the court, and two, underneath the basket facing the baseline. *See the diagram Underneath Hooks.*

2. These moves can be released high or low. The two shots are quite different. The high release involves jumping high to the backboard releasing the shot as high as possible. The shot is like a jump hook and is released overhead. The low released shot is more like an underhanded pass than the jump hook. The hook is started from the waist and is released right in front of the body, not overhead. High is usually better. A low release allows an easier block. *See the diagram Two Different Shots.*

3. Here are 12 moves to practice. "Taking a half step before shooting" means that you start to take a step in one direction, then shoot before bringing the foot down. "Taking one full step", technically one and a half steps, means that you take one step, then shoot before you bring the other foot down. *See the diagram Moves 1-12.*

4. Lefties follow the directions switching the words *left* and *right*.

Moves 1-3
Stand directly behind the basket under the back-

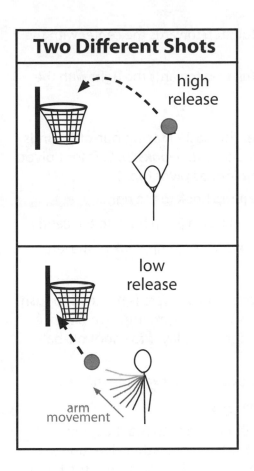

Two Different Shots

high release

low release

arm movement

board facing downcourt *(see Part 1 of the diagram Underneath Hooks).* Left foot pivot foot. Shoot the hook while taking a step forward. Square-up as much as possible. You don't need to be perfectly squared-up, since you are so close to the basket. The more you can square-up, the easier the shot. The direction of the step is relative to the player, not the court. Do not use the backboard.

Move 1 - Take a half step forward with the right foot toward the left, square-up in the air, and shoot a hook.

Move 2- Take a half step forward with the right foot towards the center.

Move 3 - Take a half step forward with the right foot towards the right.

Moves 4-6

From the same starting position shoot a hook off the backboard. This looks like a backward hook.

Move 4 - Take a half step forward with the right foot toward the left. Shoot using the backboard.

Move 5 - Take a half step forward with the right foot toward the center. Shoot using the backboard. This will be more difficult for small players.

Move 6 - Take a half step forward with the right foot toward the left. Shoot using the backboard.

Moves 7-9

Start in the same position with the right foot as pivot foot. (Letties start with left foot as pivot foot.) Take a step hook toward the right, then center, then left. The step puts you in a better position to shoot. Perform these first using the backboard. It is optional to repeat without the backboard.

Move 7 - Take a full step towards the left with the right foot.

Moves 1-12

Move	1	2	3	4	5	6	7	8	9	10	11	12
Initial Position												
Pivot Foot	left	left	left	left	left	left	right	right	right	left	left	left
Steps	1/2	1/2	1/2	1/2	1/2	1/2	1.5	1.5	1.5	1/2	1/2	1/2
Back-board	no	no	no	yes	yes	yes	yes	yes	yes	no	no	no
Final Position												

Move 8 - Take a full step towards the center with the right foot.

Move 9 - Take a full step towards the right with the right foot.

Moves 10-12
Stand directly under the basket facing out-of-bounds *(see the diagram Underneath Hooks 2)*. Left foot pivot. (Lefties use the right foot as pivot foot.)

Move 10 - Take a jump hook to the right.

Move 11 - Pivot and take a jump hook to the center.

Move 12 - Pivot and take a jump hook to the left.

Key Points

1. Perform each move slowly. There is no need to rush. Working slowly allows the body to improve balance and agility. Rushing forces a player to shoot off-balance.

2. This lesson only covers some example moves.

How To Practice

There are many other positions to practice from, including facing the sidelines in either direction and starting under the backboard 1-3 feet from the basket.

Another continuous shooting lesson involves rebounding the shot and then immediately stepping to the other side and going up again.

It is also worthwhile to repeat each lesson with the opposite hand.

PRACTICE SHOOTING LESSONS

36 Driving To The Basket
37 Near To Far
38 Practice Shoot

The key to shooting is developing and maintaining technique. These practice lessons and the ones in the Moves & Hook Shot Lessons (29-35) teach how to practice shooting without destroying technique. All practice shooting lessons are effort level 2 lessons.

The most notable part of the practice shooting section is what appears to be missing: drills that include repetitions from distances greater than 3 feet. Shooting many shots far from the basket usually causes a player to develop a technique *du jour* that cannot be repeated during a game or at any other time. An even better reason for not doing shooting drills involving many repetitions at great distances is that it rarely, if ever, works.

Lesson 36, Driving to the Basket, covers the four basic drives to the basket. Lesson 37, Near to Far, gives a sensible way to determine, then increase, shooting range while maintaining technique. Lesson 38, Practice Shoot, presents sensible, effective ways to practice shooting from any spot.

36 Driving To The Basket

Player's Corner

Parts	1	2	3	4
Type	CORE	CORE	CORE	CORE
Players	1	1	1	1
Assist	NO	NO	NO	NO
Ball	○	○	○	○
Court	🏀	🏀	🏀	🏀
Effort	2	2	2	2
Time	5	5	5	5

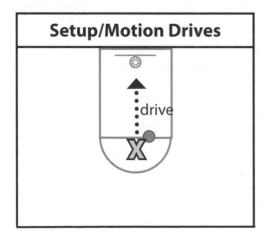

Setup/Motion Drives

Briefs

In Part 1, drive right starting with the left foot as pivot.

In Part 2, fake left, then drive right starting with the right foot as pivot.

In Part 3, drive left starting with the right foot as pivot.

In Part 4, fake right, then drive left starting with the left foot as pivot.

Why Do This

Every player gets their steps together for each of the four drives like a hurdler getting steps together between hurdles. *See the diagram The Four Drives.* Righties (or a player shooting with the right hand) always shoot off the left foot, and lefties (or a player shooting with the left hand) off the right foot. If you also want to shoot with the off-hand then there are eight drives to practice.

Make sure to perform these at a moderate to slow pace; there is no need to go fast. Make sure that your head is up when driving. Remember that the first step of the drive is very long; this is the step used to beat the defense. The last step of the drive is straight up, not forward. After shooting, the driver should be in position to rebound the shot, not land several feet behind the backboard.

The Four Drives

pivot point······ⓧ ◯
pivot foot········◯ ◯

1 Drive Right

2 Crossover Drive Right

1- short jab step

2- long crossover step

3 Drive Left

4 Crossover Drive Left

2- long crossover step

1- short jab step

Part 1 Drive Right
Directions

1. For each drive start at the free-throw line with a ball. *See the diagram Setup/Motion Drives.* Do each drive 5 times with the strong hand before working with the off hand.

2. Start from a half-down position with the ball at waist-height. Left foot pivot foot. *See 1 Drive Right in The Four Drives diagram.*

3. Take a very long first step with the right foot, pushing the ball low and far to the side of the drive. This step gets you by the defense. It's a good idea to practice long jab-steps, Lesson 7, before working on these drives.

4. You must step around the defense, not through them, so move sideways before moving forward. Use a chair or another person as dummy defense to step around.

5. Dribble the ball with the right hand on the first step. Always dribble with the outside arm, because the defense will be inside.

6. Do not drag the pivot foot as you take the long step with the right foot.

7. When using the right hand always shoot the layup off the left foot on either side of the basket and when using the left hand always shoot off the right foot.

8. Take as many steps and dribbles as necessary to complete the move.

9. The last step is up, not forward. You should land in front of the backboard, not behind. After the shot, quickly rebound and go back to the starting position.

10. Repeat this drive 5 times at a comfortable pace. There is no need to go fast. It is better to be too slow than too fast, because slow allows your body to learn balance. Fast does not.

11. Eventually you should repeat this drive (and the others) with these fakes:

(a) Overhead pass fake away from the drive direction.

(b) A more difficult fake involves a waist-high, ball fake away from the drive direction.

12. The eyes are part of the fake, so pay special attention to where you look. You should be looking up toward the basket, not down at the floor or engaged in reverie. Fakes are slow compared to the actual move.

Key Points

1. The first step is long. Do not drag the pivot foot.

2. The last step is up.

3. Keep the head up during the drive. Do not look down when you dribble.

4. Go at a comfortable pace, no need to rush.

How To Practice

Eventually repeat the drive using fakes. An experienced player should repeat this drive with the opposite hand.

Drive 2

pivot point······
pivot foot········

2 Crossover Drive Right

1- short jab step

2- long crossover step

Part 2 Crossover Drive Right
Directions

1. Start from the free-throw line, ball waist-height, right foot pivot foot. *See the diagram Drive 2.*

2. Take a short jab-step to the left with a waist-high ball fake, then take a long crossover step to the right, pushing the ball low to the right.

3. Dribble the ball with the right hand on the first step.

4. Do not drag the pivot foot as you take the long step with the right foot.

5. Shooting right-handed alway go off the left foot on either side of the basket and shooting left-handed always go off the right foot.

6. Repeat using an overhead ball fake with a jab-step to the left.

7. See **Part 1**, steps 10-12.

Key Points

1. The crossover step is long. Do not drag the pivot foot.

2. The last step is up.

3. Keep the head up during the drive. Do not look down when you dribble.

4. Go at a comfortable pace, no need to rush.

How To Practice

Eventually repeat the drive using fakes. An experienced player should repeat this drive with the opposite hand.

Drive 3

pivot point·····
pivot foot·······

3 Drive Left

Part 3 Drive Left
Directions

1. Start at free-throw line, ball waist-height. Right foot pivot foot. *See the diagram Drive 3.*

2. Take a long first step with the left foot, pushing the ball low, far to the side of the drive.

3. Dribble the ball with the left hand on the first step.

4. Do not drag the pivot foot as you take the long step with the left foot.

5. Right-handers shoot off the left foot on either side of the basket and left-handers off the right foot.

6. Repeat using an overhead ball fake or a ball fake to the opposite side.

7. See **Part 1**, steps 10-12.

Key Points

1. The first step is long. Do not drag the pivot foot.

2. The last step is up.

3. Keep the head up during the drive. Do not look down when you dribble.

4. Go at a comfortable pace, no need to rush.

How To Practice

Eventually repeat the drive using fakes. An experienced player should repeat this drive with the opposite hand.

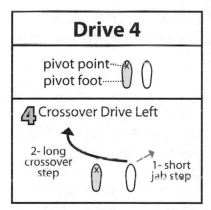

Drive 4

pivot point······
pivot foot·······

4 Crossover Drive Left

2- long crossover step

1- short jab step

Part 4 Crossover Drive Left
Directions

1. Start from the free-throw line, ball waist-height, left foot pivot foot. *See the diagram Drive 4.*

2. Take a short jab-step to the right with a ball fake, then take a long crossover step to the left, pushing the ball low to the left.

3. Dribble the ball with the left hand on the first step.

4. Do not drag the pivot foot as you take the long step with the right foot to the left foot.

5. Shooting right-handed alway go off the left foot on either side of the basket and shooting left-handed always go off the right foot.

6. Another fake that can be used is an overhead pass fake with a jab-step to the right.

7. See **Part 1**, steps 10-12.

Key Points

1. The crossover step is long. Do not drag the pivot foot.

2. The last step is up.

3. Keep the head up during the drive. Do not look down when you dribble.

4. Go at a comfortable pace, no need to rush.

How To Practice

Eventually repeat the drive using fakes. An experienced player should repeat this drive with the opposite hand.

37 Near To Far

Player's Corner

Parts	1
Type	CORE
Players	1
Assist	NO
Ball	◯
Court	🏀
Effort	2
Time	5-15

Setup Near To Far

start in a position close to the basket

Briefs

Start close to the basket, then take one step back after making two shots in a row.

Why Do This

This is the best way to increase shooting range without destroying technique. As a matter of fact, this may be the only way, because this lesson allows you to find your current shooting range and then adjust to longer distances. Make adjustments for longer shots with the legs, rather than the arms. If you have a major technique problem, you are not ready for this lesson.

Directions

1. Start anywhere—left side, right side, or center—as long as it is 1 foot from the basket. *See the diagram Setup Near To Far.*

2. Shoot without using the backboard. Older players must make each shot with the ball hitting the net only, no rim.

3. There are several variations for this drill.

  (a) Make two shots in a row from the same spot, then take one step back away from the basket. Continue shooting and moving back. However, every time you miss, take a step forward toward the basket.

(b) Make one shot, then take a step back. Miss one shot, then take a step forward.

4. Continue this drill for 5-15 minutes.

5. A player usually starts missing shots at his/her maximum range. Don't be surprised if this is only 1-4 feet from the basket. Continue to use proper technique.

6. An assistant should check your shooting technique as you move away from the basket.

Key Points

1. Start close to the basket.

2. Move towards the basket on each miss.

3. Have an assistant check your technique as you move away from the basket.

How To Practice

Only practice this if your technique is together. Most players are not ready for this lesson. Remember that shooting improvement only comes with technique improvement.

38 Practice Shoot

Player's Corner			
Parts	1	2	3
Type	CORE	CORE	OPT
Players	1	1	1
Assist	NO	NO	NO
Ball	◯	◯	◯
Court	🏀|	🏀|	🏀|
Effort	2	2	2
Time	5-15	5-15	5-15

Briefs

In Part 1, dribble back and forth full-court taking only one shot at each time.

In Part 2, run or dribble through a half-court circuit before shooting.

In Part 3, dribble a circuit then move left or right before shooting.

Why Do This

The overriding concern in any practice shooting drill from more than 4 feet is to maintain a consistent shooting technique. Making 10 or 100 shots in a row in practice while rested with a feeder retrieving balls does not insure that technique has either improved or been maintained. Shooters in-the-zone in practice often develop a technique *du jour*, just for the day, that cannot be duplicated come game time.

Several precautions included in the lessons that follow prevent technique *du jour*:

(a) No rapid-fire shooting from one spot. Run for 5-15 seconds before shooting again from the same spot.

(b) No shooting from outside your range. Your range is the maximum distance you

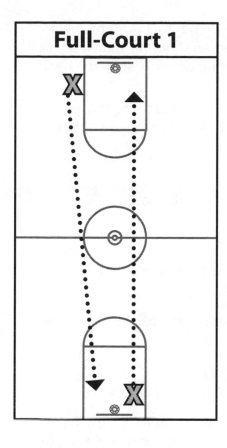

Full-Court 1

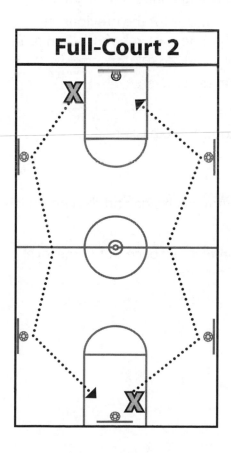

Full-Court 2

can shoot while maintaining a consistent technique. Shooting from outside the range destroys technique. The best example of this involves youngsters throwing, not shooting, 3-point shots at the basket. However, even college-level players, who have not developed shooting technique, may only have an actual range of 4-6 feet. Use the Near To Far lesson to determine range.

(c) No perfect, easy passes from feeders. Expecting near perfect soft passes is not realistic, especially if the lesson is run at the game level. Instruct feeders, if and when they are used, to intentionally throw off-the-mark and hard passes. Often it's better for a player to retrieve his/her own shots.

Initially perform these drills at the practice level before running them full speed at game level. I remember running a 5-foot shooting drill at the game level first with an experienced college men's team: they missed 90% of the shots. Working between levels can result in a drill that is too fast for learning agility and too slow for real game-level practice.

In these lessons, more time is spent dribbling than shooting, so make sure your head is up. Regularly switch the dribbling hand. On long runs its okay to use behind-the-back and between-the-legs-type dribbles as long as the head is up. All three lessons are good CM drills if you run for at least 15 minutes.

You can practice any type of shot in these lessons, including jump shots and jump hooks. However, make sure to move straight downcourt, alternating shooting from the right side, then center of the court, then left side. Do not waste time dribbling around and making dribbling moves. Go directly to the shooting position. In Part 3, players move either right or left before shooting.

Part 1 Full-Court Shoot
Directions

1. Run down one end of the court, shoot, get the rebound, run down the other end and shoot. It is optional to follow it up if you miss. Pace yourself. You do not need to go fast. *See the diagram Full-Court 1.* With many baskets available run a circuit taking one shot at each basket. *See the diagram Full-Court 2.*

2. If you want to speed things up, run this at the game level for only a few minutes. Sprint as fast as you can go before shooting. However, this drill is more beneficial if run as a practice level drill.

3. Regularly switch the dribbling hand. Do not tricky dribble before the shot. Just dribble straight to the chosen shooting spot. Keep the body and ball low, even though there is no defense. Keep the head up at all times, look around.

4. Shoot from any distance, any place on the court: free-throw line, corners, top of the key, 1 foot from the basket. Stay in your range.

5. Run from 5-20 minutes.

Key Points

1. Keep the head up while dribbling. Look at the basket.

2. Stay in your range on the shot.

3. Pace yourself.

4. Vary the shot, making sure to shoot from each side and the center.

How To Practice

It is best to do this drill running at a comfortable pace. For game level practice you must sprint as fast as you can go.

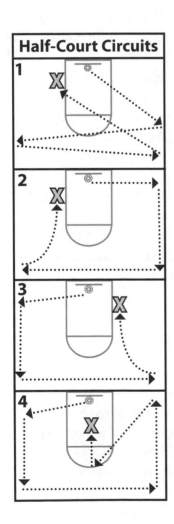

Half-Court Circuits

Part 2 Half-Court Shoot
Directions

1. If a full-court is not available or if you just want to just run half-court, then run and/or mark a half-court circuit. Run at a moderate pace. *See the diagram Half-Court Circuits to get ideas for circuits.*

2. The directions for this lesson are the same as for the previous lesson. Since there is only one basket, shoot one shot, rebound, then run the circuit before shooting again at the same basket.

3. Make sure to shoot from the right, center, and left.

Key Points

1. Keep the head up while dribbling. Look at the basket.

2. Stay in your range on the shot.

3. Pace yourself.

4. Vary the shot making sure to shoot from each side and the center.

How To Practice

It is best to do this drill running at a comfortable pace. For game level practice you must sprint as fast as you can go.

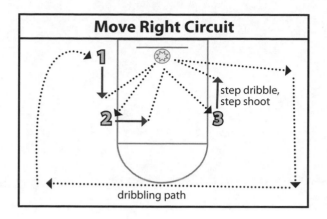

Move Right Circuit

step dribble, step shoot

dribbling path

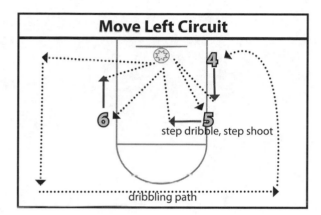

Move Left Circuit

step dribble, step shoot

dribbling path

Part 3 Move Left/Right Shoot

Directions

1. This is a more advanced lesson for older or pro players. *See the diagrams Move Right Circuit and Move Left Circuit.* It's optional to use a feeder in this lesson.

2. In the previous practice shooting lessons, you usually dribbled straight toward the basket before shooting. In this lesson, you run a circuit, taking three shots while moving right and then three moving left. Get your own rebound after each shot.

3. Run the circuit 5 times moving right, then 5 times moving left.

4. Go at a slow, relaxed pace.

5. The movements when moving right just before the shot *(positions 1-3 the diagram)* are step dribble with the left foot, then step with the right foot, bring the ball up and shoot. You can get this together without much instruction as long as you go slowly.

6. The footwork when moving left just before the shot *(positions 4-6 the diagram)* are step dribble right, then step with the left foot, bring the ball up and shoot.

Key Points

1. Do the footwork slowly.

2. Initially shoot from only 3-5 feet.

3. Keep your head up when dribbling.

How To Practice

This part is for older players.

PRESSURE SHOOTING LESSONS

Real game situations are easy after these pressure shooting lessons, because the shooter will not be negatively affected by pressure. No longer will the shooter miss a layup or short shot in a game. These lessons are also great for defensive coverage on the shooter.

Pressure shooting is the last level (level 3) of shooting practice. The key is to excite a player and simultaneously require that he/she not react to the pressure. Let me explain. To feel game-level pressure, an assistant attempts to excite a player by yelling "faster, faster, faster" or by any other verbal means. Younger players initially react to even a "Yo" while shooting, whereas college players may not react to any verbal harassment. So with older players, pressure comes from the defense and the assistant just telling them to move more quickly. To combat pressure, the shooter learns to slow down at the last moment and shoot at normal speed making the shot.

Defenders must play with 100% effort following the directions in the lesson. Lax defense makes these lessons worthless!

In Lesson 39, Quick Shot, the ball starts on the floor right next to the shooter. In Lesson 40, Run Shoot, the shooter sprints for the ball. In Lesson 41, Catch Up, the shooter dribbles in for a layup. In Lesson 42, Defense In Face, the shooter starts with the ball 1 foot from the basket. In Lesson 43, Fouled Shooting, a player must make a short shot even when fouled. An assistant is needed for each lesson.

39 Quick Shot

Player's Corner

Parts	1	2	3
Type	CORE	CORE	OPT
Players	1	2	2
Assist	YES	YES	YES
Ball	◯	◯	◯
Court	🏀	🏀	🏀
Effort	3	3	3
Time	5	5	5

Briefs

In Part 1, go for a ball on the floor, quickly pick it up and shoot.

In Part 2, a defender harasses the shooter.

In Part 3, two players go for the ball.

Why Do This

These lessons simulate shooting under game-type pressure. After grabbing a ball off the floor, the shooter positions the feet and body to shoot. Perform this part quickly, although the shot need not be taken too quickly. An assistant tries to excite the shooter by yelling, "Hurry up," or anything that has the appropriate effect. This is an important part of the lesson. Defense in Part 2 adds even more pressure. This part is also a great defensive lesson. Going for the ball before shooting against an opponent in Part 3 adds even more pressure. Parts 2 and 3 are not for novices.

Part 1 Quick Shot Close
Directions

1. Set up right next to the basket. Put the ball down so it does not roll and then stand up. *See the diagram Setup Part 1.*

2. When the assistant says "Go," pick up the ball as

Setup Part 1

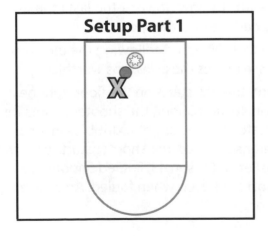

quickly as possible, then shoot. Use the backboard.

3. Make sure to properly square-up and not walk.

4. The assistant yells "Faster, faster, faster" while a player does the lesson.

5. The shooter should quickly pick up the ball and setup quickly for the shot. Slow down on the actual shot.

6. Repeat 5-20 times.

Key Points

1. Move quickly to set up, then shoot at a normal pace.

2. Make sure not to shuffle your feet.

3. Square-up to the direction of the shot.

4. The assistant must always yell, "faster, faster".

5. Make 100% of the shots.

How To Practice

If you want to do this more than once or twice, face another direction before going for the ball. Line up facing either sideline or facing downcourt.

Defense Part 2

one hand straight up for ball

one hand in line of vision

Part 2 Shot With Defense
Directions

1. This is the same as Part 1 with the addition of a defensive player.

2. The defensive player harasses the shooter after he/she picks up the ball. Harass means that the defense bothers the shooter by playing tough defense without fouling.

3. One arm of the defender should be extended straight up to block the shot. The other should block the shooter's line of vision to the basket. This hand should be above the eyes, at least 6 inches away. *See the diagram Defense Part 2.*

4. Do not bring either arm down to snuff the shot. Do not block the shot. If necessary, move the arms at the last moment to not block the shot. It's okay to yell at the shooter as well. This is great defensive practice if correctly done.

5. The shooter gets the rebound after the shot and places the ball on the ground. The defender now becomes the next shooter.

6. Switch roles after each shot. Repeat 5-10 times.

Key Points

1. The defender must play at 100% and cause the shooter problems.

2. The defender does not block the shot and does not foul the shooter.

3. The assistant makes sure the defense plays properly.

4. The shooter makes 100% of the shots.

How To Practice

Repeat this only once or twice.

Part 3 Go Shoot
Directions

1. Place the ball on the floor near the basket.

2. Two players set up in the ready position, elbow-to-elbow, body-to-body, about 1-3 feet from the ball. *See the diagram Two Setups for Part 3.* Use either setup.

3. Players go for the ball when the assistant yells "Go."

4. Players should attempt to step in front of one another, then go for the ball.

5. The player who gets his/her hands on the ball first is on offense and should just shoot. No moves or fakes. Set up quickly to shoot, then slow down to shoot. Make the shot.

6. The other player harasses the shooter, but does not block the shot or foul the shooter. Move the hands at the last second to avoid the block.

7. Repeat 3-10 times.

Key Points

1. The defense must play at 100% and make an effort to block the shot.

2. The defense ultimately does not block the shot, even if he/she has to move the arms slightly at the last moment.

3. Players should attempt to step in front of one another before going for the ball.

4. The shooter makes 100% of the shots.

How To Practice

This is optional.

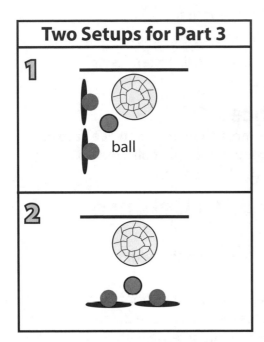

Two Setups for Part 3

1

ball

2

40 Run Shoot

Player's Corner

Parts	1	2	3
Type	CORE	CORE	OPT
Players	1	2	2
Assist	YES	YES	YES
Ball	○	○	○
Court	🏀|	🏀|	🏀|
Effort	3	3	3
Time	5	5	5

Briefs

In Part 1, sprint to the basket for the ball, quickly pick it up, then shoot slowly.

In Part 2, a defensive player harasses the shooter.

In Part 3, the shooter cuts for a pass underneath and then is harassed by a defender on the shot.

Why Do This

When a player sprints to the ball before shooting, he/she often shoots just as quickly as they run. This results in many missed easy shots. These drills slow down the shooter on the shot, after a sprint to the ball.

Part 1 Run Stop Shoot
Directions

1. Start between the free-throw line and the top of the key facing the basket. Place the ball under the basket. *See the diagram Setup Part 1.*

2. The assistant yells "Go" to start. The player sprints for the ball, stops, picks it up, then takes the shot in a relaxed, unhurried way.

3. The assistant makes the player feel the pres-

Setup Part 1

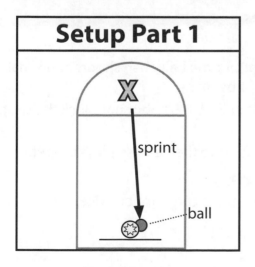

sprint

ball

sure. Yell "Go, go, go, faster, faster, faster." Without this urging the lesson is worthless. After all this yelling the player needs to slow down and make the shot.

4. Rebound, then place the ball on the floor near the basket. Go back to the starting position.

5. Repeat 3-10 times.

Key Points

1. Run fast, set up quickly, then slow down on the actual shot.

2. Make sure to make the shot.

How To Practice

This only needs to be practiced a few times.

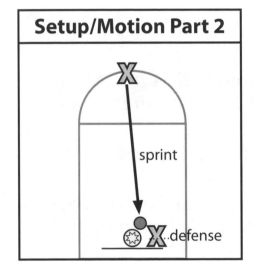

Setup/Motion Part 2

sprint

.defense

Part 2 Run Stop With De
Directions

1. This is the same as Part 1 except that a defender is positioned under the boards. *See the diagram Setup/Motion Part 2.*

2. The defender attempts to block the shot as described in the previous lesson, 39-2.

3. From the starting position sprint to the ball, pick it up, and shoot with a defender right in your face.

4. Either player rebounds the shot, then places the ball on the floor for the next shooter.

5. The original shooter sticks around to play defense.

6. The original defender runs to the starting position between the free throw line and the top of the key.

7. At a signal, or when ready, he/she sprints for the ball repeating the lesson.

8. Repeat 3-10 times.

Key Points

1. The shooter sprints for the ball, then shoots at normal speed. The shot must be made.

2. The defense must play at 100%, but not block the shot nor foul.

3. The assistant makes sure the defense plays properly.

How To Practice

This only needs to be practiced once or twice.

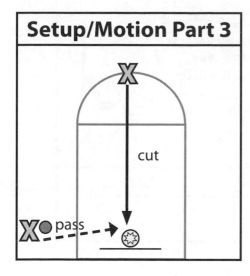

Setup/Motion Part 3

cut

X○ pass ⟶ ✿

Part 3 Run Catch Shoot
Directions

1. This is similar to the previous part except that the defender passes the ball before playing defense. *See the diagram Setup/Motion Part 3.*

2. The cutter/shooter is near the top of the key.

3. The passer/defender is about 5 yards from the basket towards the corner.

4. At a signal from the passer, the cutter sprints to the basket to catch the ball. Make eye contact with the passer before the cut. Catch the ball, stop, square-up, shoot, and go for the rebound. Then go to the passing position with the ball.

5. Fake a pass to the cutter as a signal to cut. Pass the ball so that it meets the cutter at the basket. Follow the pass to the basket. Sprint to the shooter, then play tought defense and harass the shooter by yelling as well. To avoid a block, slightly move the arms at the last moment. Go for the rebound. Give the ball to the shooter. Go to the position of the shooter at the top of the key.

6. Repeat 5-15 times.

Key Points

1. The passer sprints to the ball immediately after passing.

2. The defense harasses the shooter as much as possible. No fouls. No flailing arms or body. Stay in control.

3. The assistant makes sure the defense plays properly.

How To Practice

This lesson is optional.

41 Catch Up

Player's Corner

Parts	1
Type	CORE
Players	2
Assist	YES
Ball	○
Court	🏀
Effort	3
Time	5

Briefs
A defender sprints to catch up to a player who is driving to the basket.

Why Do This
This is a great lesson for both the offense and defense. The offense hears the footsteps, but learns not to react. The defense learns hustle, because he/she must catch up to the dribbler. The defender also learns not to play defense from behind or reach in from the side. This lesson focuses on the offense. An assistant makes sure the defense does not try to run directly in front of the driver.

Directions
1. Two players line up at midcourt. *See the diagram Setup Catch Up.*

2. The offense starts near midcourt. Move closer to the basket with younger players. The defense starts directly behind.

3. The offense has 5 seconds to start a drive to the basket. The driver can use many fakes before driving, but once he/she takes a step he/she must go.

4. The defense pursues immediately.

5. The offense sprints to the basket and then shoots the layup slowly. Go up on the layup. Do not float forward under the backboard. An assistant can stand under the basket or use a chair or

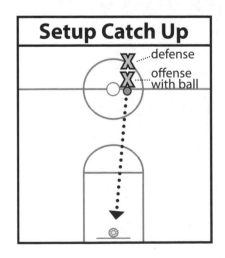

Setup Catch Up

defense
offense with ball

other obstacle to slow down the driver. The driver slows down, then goes straight up for the layup.

6. The defense must run 3 feet past the offense before stepping in front to prevent the layup. If the defense is not able to run past the offense, then they can only harass from a distance.

7. Do not try to block the shot by throwing your body in front of the driver. This is an error as well as a foul. There should be no contact.

8. The defense gets no closer than 3 feet from the driver unless he/she catches up, which rarely occurs. If the defense does catch up, he/she stops 3 feet in front of the offense and turns to play defense. The offense must change direction or, if close enough to the basket, stop and take a short shot.

9. Both players go for the rebound, whether or not the shot is missed.

10. Repeat switching positions.

11. Continue for 3-5 minutes.

12. To make this more demanding for the defense and more fun, allow the shooter to set up and go without waiting for the defense. ***See the diagram Sprint Back.***

In the diagram *A* is the initial shooter who just sprinted to the basket; *B* is the initial defender. As soon as *B* gets the ball under the boards, he/she sprints back to midcourt without waiting for *A*.

Setup and go, sprint in for a layup, when ready. Do not wait for a defender who is slow to setup. This forces the new defender to sprint back to midcourt with the new shooter.

Sprint Back

starting positions

new offense with ball **B**   ▼**A** new defense

Key Points

1. Younger players think that if they run fast, they must shoot fast as well. Slow down on the shot.

2. Only practice this drill if you are expert at doing layups. You are not an expert if you either miss the layup or you float under the backboard after the shot.

3. The defender must catch up and pass the dribbler before playing defense. No reaching in from the side.

How To Practice

Practice this 2-5 times or till the offense slows down and makes 100% of the layups.

42 Defense In Face

Player's Corner

Player's Corner	
Parts	1
Type	CORE
Players	2
Assist	YES
Ball	◯
Court	🗑
Effort	3
Time	5

Setup

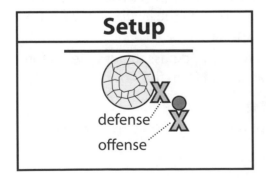

defense

offense

Briefs
The offense shoots a 1-foot shot with the defense in their face.

Why Do This
The offense shoots with close defensive harassment. Initially, the defense neither touches the ball nor the offense. The defense must make an extra effort to maneuver out of the way of the shot, especially when the offense is a much shorter player.

This is very beneficial for both offense and defense for the following reasons. One, the offense learns to shoot with contact or in traffic. Two, the defense learns not to hack the shooter.

Directions
1. The shooter sets up 2 feet from the basket with the defense in his/her face. *See the diagram Setup.*

2. The offense takes a normal 1-foot shot using the backboard.

3. The defense stands 3-4 inches away, directly between the shooter and the basket, with arms outstretched. One hand is in the face of the offense, no closer than 6 inches, impairing his/her vision to the basket. *See the diagram Defensive Setup.* This hand can move. The other hand is outstretched

Defensive Setup

one hand straight up for ball

one hand in line of vision

straight up to block the ball. This hand is stationary; do not slash forward at the ball. Yelling and talking about relatives enhances the harassment.

4. If the shooter is right-handed, the defense should extend the left arm straight up. With a left-handed shooter, the defense should outstretch the right arm.

5. The defense may jump, but no flailing arms.

6. The defense does not block the shot. Move your hands slightly at the last moment if necessary, so that the shot is not deflected.

7. Offense and defense switch roles after each shot. Continue for 3-5 minutes.

8. It's optional for players to go for the rebound on the shot. Go for the rebound whether or not the shot is made.

Key Points

1. The defense sets up close and makes an attempt to block the shot and harass the shooter.

2. Only at the last moment does the defense slightly move the arms to avoid the block.

3. The offense must make every shot.

How To Practice

This only needs to be practiced a few times.

43 Fouled Shooting

Player's Corner

Parts	1
Type	CORE
Players	1
Assist	YES
Ball	○
Court	🏀
Effort	3
Time	5

Setup Parts 1-2

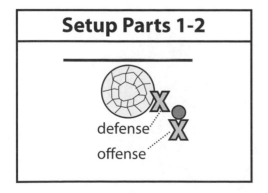

defense

offense

Briefs
The defense deliberately fouls the shooter.

Why Do This
In a game a player is often fouled on a short shot. Whether or not the foul is called by the referee, the player must make the short shot. This lesson teaches the shooter to make the short shot even when fouled. It's better to use an assistant, than another player, to do the fouling. However, the fouling is so deliberate that the fouler may not develop bad habits.

Directions
1. Use the same directions as the previous lesson except that the defender deliberately fouls the shooter.

2. The shooter starts 1 foot from the basket with a defender in his/her face.

3. Initially the foul is a soft push on the shooting arm and/or shoulder.

4. As the offense adjusts, the foul should increase in intensity. The foul involves contact anywhere on the body. Eventually the foul should be substantial, though not life-threatening.

Key Points
1. The shooter must make the shot.

2. The fouler increases the intensity of the foul as the shooter improves.

How To Practice

Practice this 3-5 times increasing the intensity of the foul.

Free-Throw Shooting Lessons

44 Free-Throw Technique
45 Free-Throw Practice

See **About Free Throws** on the next page for more information on this topic. Lesson 44, Free-Throw Technique, presents a special technique to calm and focus players on the free-throw line. Lesson 45, Free-Throw Practice, applies this technique to more game-like, free-throw practice.

About Free Throws

Improving free throws has been a difficult, if not impossible, task for most coaches. The problem stems from a lack of development of both shooting and free-throw technique. As I have said before, you can't improve shooting and maintain consistency without working on technique. Since a free throw is a long shot, practicing improperly quite often yields negative results—players get worse!

Two poster children for the wrong way to practice may be two great NBA players. Though I have no firsthand knowledge of their practice regime, I've heard stories that these players would practice 100 free throws a day, often making most of them. The problem lies in the fact that they did not use the same technique every day. So, by shooting 100 in a row a player develops a "technique *du jour*." Unfortunately on game day this technique is "not available," so a player is back to step one. If a player first develops a consistent technique, then free-throw shooting can improve.

I once had a team of mostly 10th grade girls who were terrible shooters. Because players kept missing the rim on a free-throw transition drill, meaning we couldn't run the drill, I had to move the shooter closer to the basket. For most of the season I kept players shooting from 1-3 feet maximum. Mid-season we lost a game by two points, missing 17 out of 19 free throws. The reason for this loss bothered me, but I knew players needed technique first. So, I continued to keep practicing close. In the last game of the season against an undefeated opponent we hit the rim 100% of the time on our free throws, making about 50%; we also nearly doubled their points. Working on basics did pay off in the long run.

At every level, junior high to professional, players regularly miss free throws in game-deciding situations. One reason is that players do not shoot at their normal speed. Being more cautious, they slow down the movements of the arms, legs, and wrists to prevent mistakes. This becomes the mistake–a player must shoot at a normal speed. Another reason players miss free throws at the end of the game is that they are tired and their muscles, especially the leg muscles, are stiff. As a result, they arm the ball–shoot with their arms– to the basket, instead of shooting with the wrists and legs. This lesson shows how to relax and focus on the free-throw line and prepare for the mechanics of the shot.

44 Free-Throw Technique

Player's Corner

Parts	1
Type	CORE
Players	1
Assist	NO
Ball	◯
Court	X
Effort	2
Time	5-15

Setup Part 1

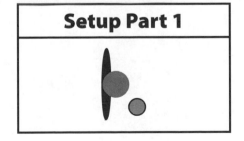

Brief

The four-step, free-throw shooting technique is introduced.

Why Do This

Free throws are always shot under great pressure in a game. Often the score is close. The game is momentarily stopped, so every person in the gym focuses on the shooter. This lesson helps the player to relax and concentrate on the mechanics of the shot.

Directions

1. Put the ball on the ground. The feet are shoulder-width apart.

2. Shake the wrists for 5 slow seconds to loosen up. In a game you can start loosening up before the ref hands you the ball.

•The cue word for this step is "wrists". *See the diagram Free-Throw Cues.*

3. Pick up the ball, handle it with your fingertips. Overdo it. It's okay, but not necessary to dribble with the fingertips a few times. In the game you have very little chance to touch the ball. Handling it helps your touch and wrist movement.

•The cue word for this step is "ball".

4. Bend the knees a few times to the half-down position. This helps you loosen up and also re-

Free-Throw Cues
1 Wrists
2 Ball
3 Knees
4 Breath

minds you to bend the legs while shooting. Many missed free throws are due to a player not bending the knees resulting in a shot armed to the basket.

•The cue word for this step is "knees".

5. Take a deep breath or two. This helps you to calm down. Hold your breath to steady body movement while you take the shot. Shoot the ball, 1 or 2 feet, straight overhead at normal speed. Do not shoot slowly or cautiously. Just shoot.

•The cue word for this step is "breath".

6. Repeat this procedure 20 times using the cue words–Wrists, Ball, Knees, Breath. Do not rush.

Key Points

1. Memorize the cue words.

2. Take your time, do not rush.

3. Shoot the ball at normal speed. Do not slow down on the shot.

How To Practice

Practice using cue words everyday for 2 weeks or until they are part of your regular thinking. Use them when you practice free throws or shoot free throws in a game.

45 Free-Throw Practice

Briefs

In Part 1, sprint downcourt before shooting two short free throws using the free-throw technique.

In Part 2, sprint downcourt before shooting two free throws from the line.

In Part 3, shoot in a one-on-one situation with a penalty for missing.

Why Do This

Most free-throw practice that involves repetition, 10 to 100 shots in a row, does not help a player for several reasons:

(a) Players need to work on shooting technique, rather than shooting. To develop technique a player must work on technique lessons, shooting a maximum of 1 foot from the basket.

(b) The free throw may not be in a player's shooting range. A player's range is the maximum distance from which a player can shoot while maintaining a consistent technique. And I'm not just talking about 10-year-olds. Many 20-year-olds have a shooting technique that breaks down between 4 and 8 feet from the basket. Use the Near To Far lesson (37) to determine

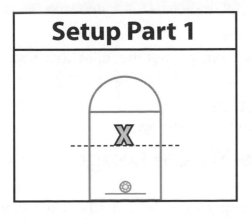

Setup Part 1

Motion Parts 1 & 2

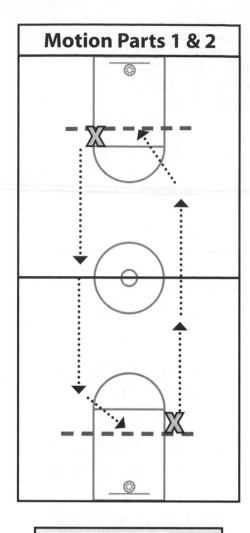

Free-Throw Cues

1 **Wrists**

2 **Ball**

3 **Knees**

4 **Breath**

Setup Part 2

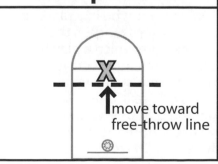

move toward free-throw line

range. Using poor or inconsistent technique from the free-throw line only teaches bad habits.

(c) In a game a player is more tired and under greater pressure than when shooting in practice. Players often tighten up in games. Usually only two shots are taken.

These lessons remedy free-throw practice pitfalls. Part 1 only involves a short shot so you can focus on the special free-throw shooting technique introduced in the previous lesson. You also only shoot two in a row before sprinting to the other basket. Part 2, repeats Part 1, backing up to the free-throw line or as far as the shooter's range permits. In Part 3 special added pressure is put on a player because there is a penalty for missing. This simulates game pressure.

Part 1 Free-Throw Short
Directions

1. Start 5 feet from the basket on an imaginary line parallel to the free-throw line. *See the diagram Setup Part 1.*

2. Use the free-throw technique cues- wrists, ball, knees, breath - explained in Lesson 44. *See the diagram Free-Throw Cues.*

3. After two shots sprint, dribbling the ball to the other end of the court, before shooting again. *See the diagram Motion Part 1 & 2.* If you only have a half-court, then run back and forth between the endline, midcourt and the sidelines. You need to sprint for 10-20 seconds before shooting again.

4. Repeat as many times as possible within a 5-15 minute time period.

Key Points

1. Do not rush through the cues.

2. Shoot at normal speed.

3. If you are not out of breath after the sprint, then sprint for a longer period.

How To Practice

Do this for a few minutes every day.

Part 2 Free-Throw Longer
Directions

1. Same as Part 1 except players set up farther back, eventually shooting from the free-throw line. *See the diagram Setup Part 2.*

2. An assistant needs to closely watch for incorrect and strained shooting technique. Some players may need to shoot from 3 feet, some from 8 feet from the basket. Some may even be able to shoot from the free-throw line. Don't assume that all high-school and college players initially can shoot from the free-throw line with proper technique.

•Without an assistant, use the Near To Far Lesson, 37, to determine your maximum shooting range.

3. A player does not need to line up exactly at the center of the free-throw line. It's okay to shoot 1 or 2 yards to one side or the other. Players must always square-up to the shooting direction.

4. Don't shoot from the full distance until ready. Doing so only prevents you from developing a more proper and consistent technique.

5. Practicing in a crowded or busy gym is helpful. Overcoming the distraction provided by other nearby players forces the shooter to concentrate on business, not the surroundings.

Key Points

1. Determine your maximum shooting range before repeating Part 2.

2. Shooting from further than your range will make you worse!

3. Take your time using the cues, then shoot at a normal speed.

How To Practice

Practice this on a regular basis increasing your range only as you improve. You may need to shoot short of the free-throw line all season.

Part 3 Free-Throw Game
Directions
Setup

1. Near the end of a practice session when you are tired, shoot a one-and-one, free-throw situation. If you make the first, then you take the second shot.

2. An assistant makes sure the shooter is within his/her range; some players may need to shoot 3 feet from the basket. The assistant also makes sure the penalty described below is enforced.

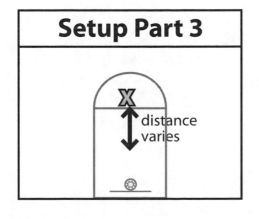

Setup Part 3

distance varies

3. The shooter must make both shots to avoid a penalty. If they make the first, then miss the second, the penalty is still in force.

4. Here are some ideas for penalties. Penalties can vary, however make sure the shooter knows the penalty before shooting.

(a) Repeat the drill only once after running 2-20 laps.

(b) Run 1-5 minutes of full-court layups or 10 full-court layups for each missed shot. A player may enjoy the running, but he/she most certainly does not like being penalized.

(c) Just show the free-throw results to the shooter after practice. Players hate to be reminded about missed shots. After a few weeks they will regularly be making two in a row without any additional penalty.

Key Points

1. Only do this once per day.

2. Make sure the shooter shoots from his/her range.

How To Practice

Practice this every day that you practice free throw shooting.

PASSING LESSONS

Passing is by far the most difficult ball skill to learn for many reasons. One, most short passes are flicks of the wrist with little arm movement. Two, a player needs to twist the body into unusual positions to pass by a defender. Three, passing also involves all the TLC skills.

To prevent the development of a favorite pivot foot, make sure to switch the pivot foot every minute or two. A player can even alternate the pivot foot in a lesson if possible. Having a favorite foot makes catching, grabbing a loose ball, and rebounding more difficult.

Lesson 46, Passing Technique, covers the touch and wrist movement needed to pass. Lesson 47, Overhead Pass, covers the overhead pass along with passing fakes. Lesson 48, Fake Pass, covers fakes used from the overhead pass position. Lesson 49, Side Pass, covers the difficult side pass. Lesson 50, Bounce Pass, covers the side bounce pass. Lesson 51, Back Pass, covers the very difficult back side pass. Lesson 52, Baseball Pass, covers the long baseball pass used to break a press. The chest pass is not covered because it is a telegraphed arm pass that cannot be used when a passer or catcher is closely covered.

46 Passing Technique

Player's Corner

Parts	1	2	3
Type	CORE	CORE	CORE
Players	1	1	2
Assist	NO	NO	NO
Ball	○	X	◉
Court	X	X	X
Effort	1	1	2
Time	5	5	5

Setup Part 1

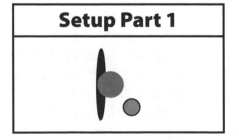

Briefs
In Part 1, hold the ball with the fingerends.

In Part 2, loosen the wrists and do wrist work.

In Part 3, two players tap the ball back and forth using the fingerends.

Why Do This
Passing is another skill that is rarely taught properly though it is an integral part of an effective offense. Passing starts with touch and wrist movement, just like shooting and dribbling. Touch affords control whereas proper wrist movement allows flicking the pass without arm movement. Defenders have less time to react to a wrist pass than an arm pass.

The fingertips should be controlling the ball when you shoot, dribble, pass, and catch. In Part 1, holding the ball with the fingerends sensitizes the control area. You can improve your ability to shoot, pass, catch, and dribble without even practicing these skills. Work on holding the ball at any time during practice or at home. You will readily note an improvement in control on shots, passes, and dribbles.

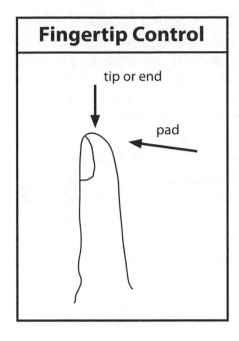

Fingertip Control

tip or end

pad

Part 1 Touch
Directions

1. This is a repeat of Lesson 1. Start by placing the ball on the floor. Spread the fingers apart as far as possible. Shape each hand into a claw and growl. The growl must be fierce.

2. Pick up the ball with your claws, so that only the fingerends touch the ball. *See the diagram Fingertip Control.*

3. The palm and fingers should not touch the ball.

4. Hold the ball tightly for 1 minute.

Key Points

1. Fingers spread apart as far as possible.

2. Fingers clawed, only slightly bent at joints.

3. Hands clawed, not flat.

4. Only fingerends contact the ball.

How To Practice

Practice this as much as possible both on the court and at home.

Part 2 Flick
Directions

1. This is a combination of several wrist work lessons, Lessons 12-13. With arms at the sides, shake the wrists and arms to loosen up. Older men will be tighter than younger players and women. Continue 1-2 minutes or until you are loose.

2. Place the arms at the sides, elbows straight, palms facing back. Flick the hands forward and then let the hands come back naturally. Keep the arms stationary and the wrists loose. *See the diagram Flick Up Steps.*

3. Now, move your arms straight up overhead, elbows straight, palms facing forward.

4. Slightly claw the hands, spread the fingers apart. Flick the hands back and let them come forward naturally. Continue to do this while you follow the ensuing directions. *See the diagram Flick Back Steps.*

5. Slowly start to move the arms from the straight up position towards the right side till they are horizontal. Keep the elbows as straight as possible. The

Setup Part 2

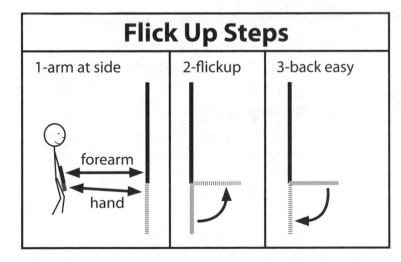

Flick Up Steps

1-arm at side	2-flickup	3-back easy

forearm

hand

Flick Back Steps

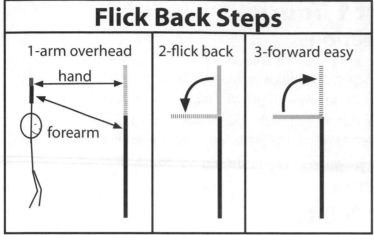

1-arm overhead	2-flick back	3-forward easy
hand ← → forearm		

Moving Through Positions

Up	Half-Down	Full-Down

Arm Extension On Pass

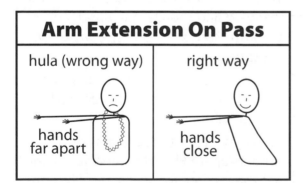

hula (wrong way)	right way
hands far apart	hands close

palms face forward. As the arms move down, bend the legs as well. Bend through the half-down position to the full-down position. At this point the arms are horizontal. *See the diagram Moving Through Positions.*

6. This will look like a hula dance if not done properly. *See the diagram Arm Extension On Pass.* The upper body should be twisted toward the extension direction. The hands should be close to each other.

7. Continue flicking the hands as you move back to the original position standing straight up with arms overhead. Then, move the arms to the left side as you bend the legs to the full-down position.

8. Repeat steps 5-7 at least 3 times.

Key Points

1. "Stay loose man".

2. Do not move the forearms when flicking the hands.

3. When flicking on the side, keep the hands together like you are going to pass.

4. Make sure that the palms always face forward, that the flicking is back, not forward.

5. Does it look like a pass could be thrown this way? The hands must be close enough to hold the ball.

6. The fingers need to be spread apart, not closed, in a claw-like position.

7. This is very difficult to do properly. The more spastic you feel, the more effort you are putting into this lesson. Remember that you are working on agility. Give yourself the opportunity to improve.

How To Practice

Continue to work on loosening up every free moment at home and on the court.

2-4 feet

Part 3 Fingertip Tap

Directions

1. Two players start 2-4 feet apart. One with a ball.

2. Both players start with arms outstretched overhead. Hands are clawed, fingers separated as much as possible.

3. The passer flicks the ball using only wrists, hand movement, and fingerends. Flick the ball overhead to the hands of the catcher.

4. The catcher catches the ball with wrists bent back and flicks a pass back. The ball only touches the fingerends. This looks like a volleyball set pass.

5. Continue flicking fingertip passes back and forth for 1-5 minutes. The ball is tapped back and forth without hesitation.

Key Points

1. Contact the ball with the fingerends.

2. There is no arm movement, only wrist movement.

3. Arms are outstretched, not bent.

How To Practice

Do this at least once.

47 Overhead Pass

Player's Corner

Parts	1
Type	CORE
Players	2
Assist	NO
Ball	◯
Court	X
Effort	2
Time	5-10

Setup

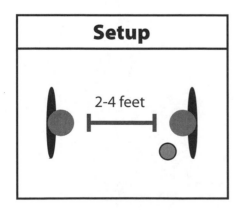

2-4 feet

Briefs
Two players flick overhead passes.

Why Do This
The overhead pass is the mainstay of the half-court offense for several reasons. One, fakes from the overhead position can be seen by the entire defense and thus affect the entire defense, not just the defender on the ball. And players need to be faking every second they hold the ball. On the other hand, a ball fake when the ball is at waist-height can't be seen by other players. This is one reason the so-called "triple threat" position is problematic.

Two, executed properly, a quick flick from the overhead position does not give the defense time to react. In the triple threat position with the ball at waist-height, the ball must be moved to either pass or get into position to pass.

Three, the overhead pass is the easiest, most effective pass from the periphery of a half-court offense. On the other hand, the chest pass, which I do not teach, has one major disadvantage without any advantages. The disadvantage involves the use of the arms, which means that all chest passes are telegraphed.

Another advantage of the overhead-pass position is that the player is in position to shoot with the ball overhead. The ball does not need to be brought up overhead from the waist. A good move from the overhead pass position is to simply pass fake, then shoot. Drives to the basket from a pass fake are also very effective. The most obvious advantage of the overhead pass over a chest pass is that the entire offense and defense can easily see the ball.

Directions

1. Two players start 2-4 feet from each other.

2. One starts with the ball overhead, elbows straight, hands clawed. Only the fingertips touch the ball.

3. Bend the wrists back as far as possible. Then, flick the ball using the wrists without the arms.

4. The other player flicks the ball back. Continue to flick passes for 2-10 minutes.

5. As the flicking improves move back several feet every 30 seconds.

6. Move back to the starting positions for one minute to end the drill.

7. Switch the pivot foot on a regular basis so a favorite foot does not develop.

Key Points

1. No arm movement. It's okay if you look spastic attempting to pass without arm movement.

2. Flick mostly at the close position. Flicking longer passes does not help as much as short flicks because players tend to use more arm motion.

How To Practice

Repeat this 5-10 times.

48 Fake Pass

Player's Corner

Parts	1
Type	CORE
Players	2
Assist	YES
Ball	◯
Court	X
Effort	2
Time	5-15

Setup

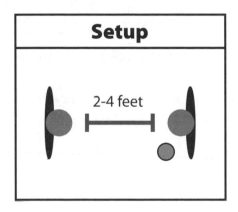

2-4 feet

Briefs

Each player fakes before flicking an overhead pass.

Why Do This

Each second you have the ball you need to be faking and misleading the defense. Faking from the overhead pass position is very effective. A fake can freeze your individual coverage or even the entire defense. And the fake need not involve more than a look in a particular direction.

Directions

1. Players setup 2-4 feet apart. *See the diagram Setup.*

2. Fakes must be slow enough so that the defense can react. Fast faking is self defeating.

3. The ball is always in the overhead passing position for these fakes.

4. On each fake you need to be looking somewhere, not in reverie. Act like you are going to pass in the looking direction.

5. Pass back and forth for 1-3 minutes using each fake. In a game you use combinations of these pass fakes.

6. Switch your pivot foot after each pass to avoid the habit of passing off the same foot each time.

Fake 1 Look Away

1. Set up to throw a normal overhead pass facing the catcher. Slightly turn or twist your body, from the hips up, arms and head away from the direction of the catcher. Look in the direction you are facing, not at the catcher. Don't dream or be in reverie, really look straight ahead.

2. Change the fake direction on each pass. *The diagram Fake Setups* shows four possible faking positions or directions – *A, B, C, D* – that you can use and the starting position.

3. Fake for 2 seconds before passing.

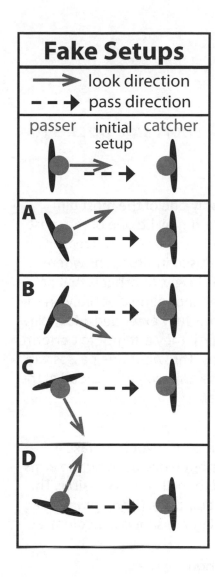

Fake Setups

→ look direction
- - ➔ pass direction

| passer | initial setup | catcher |

4. Continue passing and faking back and forth.

5. Use steps 1-4 for each fake.

Fake 2 Head Fake

Set up to throw a normal overhead pass. Only turn your head to one side, not the body, ball or arms. Look in this one direction only. Throw a pass from various head-looking positions. Again, you need to really look at something or someone. The defense can tell if you are simply looking into space.

Fake 3 Wrist Head Fake

Set up to throw a normal overhead pass. Look in one direction and slightly flick the wrists in that same direction. Do not use the body. Fake slowly from left to center to right before passing. Look like you are actually going to throw a pass on each fake.

Fake 4 Body Fake

Slightly turn the entire body by pivoting in one direction or another. Look in that direction. Only the body moves, no extra arm or wrist movement. Fake left, center, then right before passing. Fake 4 is similar to Fake 1, but involves multiple movements.

Fake 5 Jab Fake

Another pass fake involves a short jab-step with a ball fake. The ball fake involves moving the arms and the wrists in one direction. The jab-step usually goes to one side, away from the pivot foot; the ball fake can be straight ahead or to the side. Try it both ways.

Key Points

1. Fakes are slow.

2. To make a fake convincing you must really look at something.

3. Switch pivot foot after each pass.

4. Fake in a slightly different direction on each pass.

5. Do not overdo the motion. Little motion is needed for most fakes.

How To Practice

Practice this 2-5 times.

49 Side Pass

Player's Corner

Parts	1
Type	CORE
Players	2
Assist	NO
Ball	◯
Court	X
Effort	2
Time	5-15

Setup

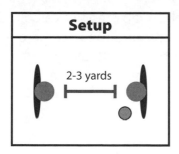

2-3 yards

Side Pass Positions

the more the stretch, the better

left foot pivot

stretch right   stretch left

right foot pivot

stretch left   stretch right

Briefs
Two players flick short side passes to each other.

Why Do This
The side pass is not only one of the most difficult passes to execute, it may be one of the most difficult basketball skills to master. One reason is that side passes are used in situations where the passer is covered closely. Another is that an effective side pass depends almost entirely on the wrist flick with the arms fully extended. Most players should look spastic if they attempt to perform these lessons correctly. Throwing side passes with bent arms or using the arms to pass instead of the wrists is not beneficial.

Directions
1. Start with the left foot as pivot foot. Take a long jab-step to the right while pushing the arms and the ball as much to the right as possible. The elbows should be straight. *See the diagram Side Pass Positions.* The diagram shows a medium jab-step.

2. Flick a pass. Not a bounce pass.

3. The farther to the right you can move, the better because you are moving past the defender. Go slow, don't worry about throwing a hard pass. Continue for 1-3 minutes.

4. With the same foot as pivot, the left foot, stretch left as far as possible before extending the arms and passing. Only spend a minute on this.

5. Repeat steps 1-4 with the right foot as pivot.

Key Points
1. Keep the elbows straight.

2. Bend as far as you can.

3. It's okay to feel spastic, especially if you are properly performing the lesson.

How To Practice
Do this every day for 1-3 minutes.

50 Bounce Pass

Player's Corner

Parts	1
Type	CORE
Players	2
Assist	NO
Ball	◯
Court	X
Effort	2
Time	5-15

Setup

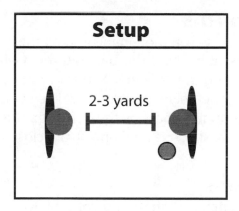

2-3 yards

The Bounce Pass

pass bounces
2/3rds of the way

Briefs
Two players flick bounce passes to each other.

Why Do This
The side bounce pass is a very effective pass both inside and out. The pass is slower than the regular side pass because of the bounce. This gives the catcher more opportunity to run to the ball. It is also an easier pass to throw because the flick direction is down rather than straight out to the side. Most inside short passes are bounce passes.

Directions
1. The directions for this lesson are similar to the previous lesson. Start with the left foot as pivot foot. Take a jab-step to the right while pushing the arms and the ball as much to the right as possible. The elbows should be straight.

2. Flick a bounce pass. The bounce should be 2/3 of the way, not halfway, to the catcher. ***See the diagram The Bounce Pass.*** For clarity in the diagram, the passing arms are not in the side-pass position.

3. Go slow, don't worry about throwing a hard pass. Continue for 1-3 minutes.

4. With the same foot as pivot, the left foot, stretch left as far as possible before extending the arms and passing. This is awkward. Only spend a minute on this.

5. Repeat steps 1-4 with the right foot as pivot.

Key Points
1. Keep the elbows straight.

2. Bounce the ball 2/3 of the way to the catcher.

3. It's okay to feel spastic; do the lesson properly.

How To Practice
Do this each day for 1-3 minutes throughout the season. Each player needs to improve his/her agility in order to throw an effective side pass.

51 Back Pass

Player's Corner

Parts	1
Type	CORE
Players	2
Assist	NO
Ball	◯
Court	X
Effort	2
Time	5-15

Setup

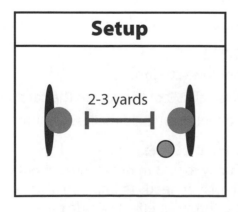

2-3 yards

Brief
Two players flick short, back passes to each other.

Why Do This
The back pass is even more difficult than the previous passes because this pass is thrown with your back facing the defender. You start by facing your partner, then pivot 180 degrees. Then twist your body around to pass by the defender. This is a very effective short pass when you are closely covered.

Directions
1. Face the catcher. Right foot pivot; ball overhead. Take a short jab fake left and pass fake, then pivot forward 180 degrees. This is like a long, crossover jab-step. ***See the diagram Back Pass Steps.***

2. Extend the arms as far as possible to the left.

3. The back is now facing the direction of the pass. This is why it is called a back pass.

4. Slightly twist the head, body, and arms to the passing direction and flick a bounce pass. Use the bounce pass first, because it is easier. Continue for 3-5 minutes.

5. Repeat starting with the left foot as pivot. Fake right, then pivot forward 180 degrees. Extend

Back Pass Steps

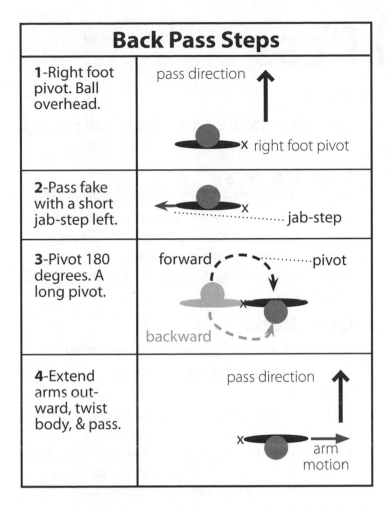

1-Right foot pivot. Ball overhead.	pass direction ↑ **x** right foot pivot
2-Pass fake with a short jab-step left.	←............... **x** .... jab-step
3-Pivot 180 degrees. A long pivot.	forward ⤢⋯⋯⋯pivot **x** backward
4-Extend arms outward, twist body, & pass.	pass direction ↑ **x** ➔ arm motion

Passing Near Pivot Foot

4-Extend arms outward, twist body, & fake a pass.	pass fake in this direction ↑ **x** ➔ fake
5-Stretch to the right and pass.	↑ pass direction **x** ← stretch & pass

the arms and body to the right. Use a bounce pass.

6. Repeat steps 1-5 using a back pass without a bounce. This is more difficult.

7. It is worthwhile to repeat steps 1-6 pivoting backward 180 degrees, *step 3 in the diagram Back Pass Steps*, before passing.

8. It's optional to repeat this lesson, steps 1-7, stretching in the other direction towards the pivot foot on the back pass.

9. To do this move start in the position shown in *step 4 in the diagram Back Pass Steps*. In step 4, the stretch to the left side to pass is now a fake to the left side. The fake can involve just a look with the ball in passing position. *See step 4 in the diagram Passing Near Pivot Foot.*

10. After the fake, quickly stretch the arms to the right towards the pivot foot to pass on the right side of the body. Make sure to keep the pivot foot in place. *See step 5 in the diagram Passing Near Pivot Foot.*

Key Points

1. Keep the arms extended. Flick the pass with the wrists.

2. It's okay to feel spastic.

3. Imagine there is a defender covering you on the pass.

How To Practice

This drill concentrates on the agility needed to properly throw the pass. The more you practice the better you will do. However, this will never be easy. Practice at least 1-5 minutes everyday.

52 Baseball Pass

Player's Corner

Parts	1
Type	CORE
Players	2
Assist	YES
Ball	◯
Court	X
Effort	2
Time	5

Setup

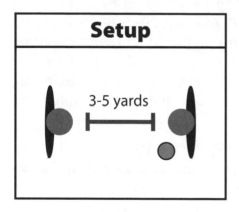

3-5 yards

Briefs

Two players fire short baseball passes back and forth.

Why Do This

The one-handed, baseball pass is more important than you think. It is the best way, and the only way for novices, to throw a long pass. Long two-handed passes require more strength. The long baseball pass is also necessary for beating a full-court press.

Directions

1. Start 3-5 yards apart. ***See the diagram Setup.***

2. Throw one-arm, baseball passes back and forth for 3 minutes.

3. For 1 minute, fire passes as hard as possible. This is especially important for younger players and women. Stronger players may need to move further apart to prevent injury. Firing hard, short passes improves the technique for throwing longer passes.

4. For 1 minute alternate pivot foot on each pass.

5. Take 2 steps away from each other and continue passing for 1 minute.

6. Every 10-20 passes take another 1-2 steps away until players are as far apart as possible. Use the technique for throwing hard, short passes at these greater distances. Don't worry about the ball hitting the ground. The catcher can catch it on a bounce.

7. If passes are weak go back and practice hard passes from a distance of 3-5 yards.

Key Points

1. Use the technique for hard, short passes for the longer passes.

How To Practice

This only needs to be practiced several times or until a player can throw a long accurate pass.

Catch Cut Lessons

Another basic skill that even most college players lack mastery of is catching. Catching and cutting always go together, which is why this section is called Catch Cut. Half-court offenses, especially with younger players, routinely fail because of a lack of catching and cutting ability. Effective catching and cutting makes it difficult for an opponent to run a successful press.

Lesson 53, Basic Catching, covers two basic catching techniques. Lesson 54, Catching On The Move, teaches players to run through the ball, to not slow down until after the catch. Lesson 55, Catching Bad Passes, teaches a player to go after bad passes. Lesson 56, Flash To Ball, introduces a third way to catch that is mainly used in the lane. Lesson 57, Loose Ball Drill, involves going for a loose ball against an opponent.

53 Basic Catching

Player's Corner

Parts	1	2
Type	CORE	CORE
Players	1	1
Assist	NO	NO
Ball	X	◯
Court	X	X
Effort	1	1
Time	5 -25	5-15

Setup Part 1

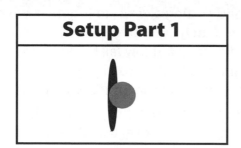

Briefs

In Part 1, practice four different types of footwork to catch the ball.

In Part 2, catch a self-tossed ball using the footwork in Part 1.

Why Do This

Catching, even at the basic level, is a skill most college players have not mastered. Basic catching involves a slight jump, then a catch-one-two, where the one and two are steps. The first step is on the pivot foot, so players with a pivoting deficiency will have great difficulty learning how to properly catch. That's one reason it is so important that you work on pivoting.

Part 1 Catch-One-Two
Directions

•There are four catch-one-two's: **A**, **B**, **C**, and **D**.
See the diagram Starting Positions & Steps Parts 1 & 2.

> **(A)** Face forward, jump, extend arms for the catch, land left, right.
>
> **(B)** Face forward, jump, extend arms, land right, left.
>
> **(C)** Face sideway, jump and turn 90 degrees to the right, extend arms, land inside, outside or leading foot, back foot.
>
> **(D)** Face sideways the other way, jump and turn 90 degrees to the left, extend arms, land inside, outside or leading foot, back foot.

Directions For A

1. Jump forward landing first on the left foot, then the right. A small jump will do.

2. Say, "Catch-one-two." Jump and extend the arms on the jump like you are catching the ball. Hands should be in a position to catch the ball. Land on the left foot on "one," then right on "two." *See the diagram Catch-One-Two.*

3. Catch-one-two across the floor at your own

Starting Positions & Steps Parts 1 & 2		
Starting Body/Feet Direction	Jump, Then Land 1, 2	Ending Body/Feet Direction
A jump direction →	left(1) then right(2)	1 / 2
B →	right(1) then left(2)	2 / 1
C →	right(1) then left(2)	2 / 1
D →	left(1) then right(2)	1 / 2

Catch-One-Two

1-start position	2-jump, extend arms to catch	3-land one two

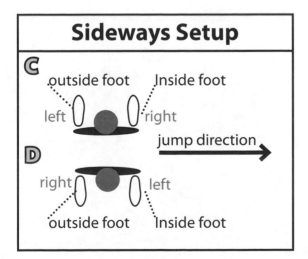

Sideways Setup

C outside foot   Inside foot
left   right

jump direction →

D right   left
outside foot   Inside foot

pace. Make sure to say, "Catch-one-two."

4. Pivot around 360 degrees after each catch to make sure you have a pivot foot, then continue. Go across the court and back or practice for 2-10 minutes.

Directions For B

5. Now, repeat landing on the right foot first.

6. Go across the floor and back.

Directions For C

7. Line up sideways to the jump direction. *See the diagram Sideways Setup.* Jump forward, turning 90 degrees in the air, landing on the inside or forward foot first. Make sure to say "Catch-one-two."

8. Continue the move going across the court and back.

Directions For D

9. Set up facing sideways the other way, and then repeat the lesson landing on the other foot first.

Key Points

1. This is not an easy lesson even for advanced players.

2. You need to be expert at pivoting before attempting this lesson.

3. If you are having trouble with the footwork don't worry about extending the arms. Nail the footwork first, then extend the arms on the jump.

4. Do this slowly so you can improve your agility. Fast indicates you are not doing this right.

5. Make sure the arms and fingers are extended on the catch.

6. Make sure to practice each lesson using both the right and left foot as pivot.

How To Practice

A player that has problems catching the ball while running needs to work on this to the exclusion of everything else except pivoting! Work on these drills and pivoting for an hour or two each day.

It's optional, though worthwhile, to repeat **C** and **D** landing first on the outside or back foot.

Setup Part 2

Part 2 Catch With Ball
Directions
1. Repeat Part 1 with a ball. Start with the first jump position **A**, then do **B** through **D**.

2. Toss or drop the ball 1-2 feet in the jump direction; do not throw the ball any farther.

3. Then jump, extend and catch the ball while both feet are still in the air, then land one, two. The object is to catch the ball before either foot touchs the floor.

4. Pivot around 360 degrees, then continue.

5. Repeat this move across the floor and back. Take your time. You need to learn the agility to catch.

Key Points
1. Make sure to extend your arms on the catch.

2. Do not work on Part 2 till you can readily do Part 1.

How To Practice
You will be amazed at the improvement in your offensive play after 1-2 weeks.

54 Catch On The Move

Briefs

In Part 1, go after and grab a loose ball.

In Part 2, catch while running straight toward the ball.

Why Do This

The second step in learning how to catch involves catching a ball while running. It sounds easy, but most players slow down before the actual catch, not coming to or meeting the ball.

This topic is a diagnostic test for catching without walking. The faster you go, the more difficult the drill. Start off easy or slow. Make sure to slow down only after the catch, not before nor while catching.

This skill is crucial for team offense, and most offenses at all levels have problems because players have not been trained to properly catch. In this section players catch a ball while running in two situations: picking up a loose ball and coming directly to the ball.

Part 1 Fetch It
Directions

1. Set up about 10 yards from the passer (the assistant). *See the diagram Setup Part 1.*

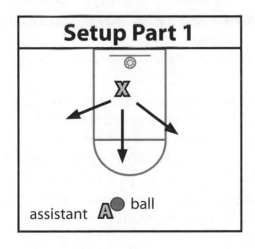

Setup Part 1

assistant **A**● ball

2. The passer throws a grounder 2-5 yards to the left or right of you. Initially just throw easy grounders. Increase the speed and difficulty of the pass as the catcher improves.

3. Go after the ball, grab it, thinking catch or grab-one-two, and then slow down. Don't slow down until after you grab the ball.

4. Raise the ball overhead, pivot around and pass the ball to the assistant. Then go back to the original position.

5. Repeat 10-20 times.

Key Points

1. This is not where a player learns to catch. A player learns how to catch in the previous lesson.

2. The catcher must extend his/her arms on the catch.

3. The catcher runs for the ball, then slows down only after the catch.

How To Practice

Practice this till you can catch the ball properly going at a moderate speed.

Part 2 Come To Ball
Directions

1. This is a continuation of the Part 1. *See the diagram Setup Part 2.*

2. Run towards the passer for the ball. Don't run directly towards the passer. Take a path just to the side, so that you can run past.

3. Do not stop running until after you catch the ball. Initially run or jog at medium speed. Speed up as you perform better.

4. Do not slow down for faked passes. Slowing down on a faked pass means that you are slowing down before the catch. The objective is to catch the ball without slowing down.

5. The passer throws the ball at any point in the run. It's okay to fake a pass. If the catcher slows down on the fake, then keep on faking. You can even let the catcher run by and then pass while he/she is running away. It's also okay not to throw a pass if the catcher keeps slowing down.

6. Slow down only after the catch, not before. Perform the catch-one-two move, then pivot around and pass to the assistant.

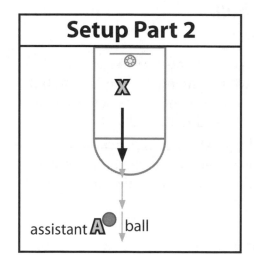

Setup Part 2

assistant **A** | ball

7. Go back to the starting position. Continue for 3-5 minutes.

Key Points

1. The objective is to run through the ball and not slow down before the catch.

2. If you have trouble with the footwork, then go back to the previous lesson.

3. When running fast it's initially okay to take 3 or 4 steps to slow down after catching.

How To Practice

Practice as many days as needed till you can correctly perform this part running full speed.

55 Catching Bad Passes

Player's Corner	
Parts	1
Type	CORE
Players	1
Assist	YES
Ball	◯
Court	X
Effort	2-3
Time	5

Brief
Catch a pass thrown off the mark.

Why Do This
Players often receive poorly thrown passes in a game. This lesson teaches players to catch bad passes as well as emphasizes the need to go after them. Catching Bad Passes is a particularly important lesson.

Directions
1. This is a continuation of the previous lesson. ***See the diagram Setup.*** The assistant throws a real bad pass to one side or the other. The pass can also bounce right in front of the player. Increase the pass speed as the catcher improves.

2. The catcher plays like a baseball shortstop attempting to prevent the ball from going by. Catch it, then pass the ball back to the assistant.

3. Repeat for 1-5 minutes.

Key Points
1. Stop the ball. Do not let the ball go by.

How To Practice
This usually only needs to be practiced once.

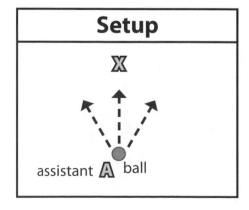

Setup

assistant **A** ball

56 Flash To Ball

Player's Corner

Parts	1	2
Type	CORE	CORE
Players	1	1
Assist	NO	YES
Ball	◯	◯
Court	🗑	🗑
Effort	1	1-2
Time	5-10	5-10

Briefs
In Part 1, practice a long jump or flash to the ball.

In Part 2, flash into the lane for a pass, counting 3 seconds.

Why Do This
Flashing is a different type of catch than the catch one-two, because on a flash a player lands simultaneously on both feet. Either foot can be the pivot foot after catching the ball via the flash method. Flashes are primarily used when jumping into an open area near the basket or when a catcher is close enough to the passer to just jump for a ball. If you think this is confusing after learning catch-one-two, then perform all these lessons as catch-one-two lessons.

Part 1 teaches the last step of the flash, which is a long jump in the appropriate direction. Part 2 combines a flash into the lane with a 3 second counting lesson and finally a shot.

Part 1 Long Jump To Ball
Directions
1. This is similar to Lesson 53. Setup on a sideline facing the endline. You are sideways to the direction of the jump which is across the court. *See the diagram Setup Part 1.*

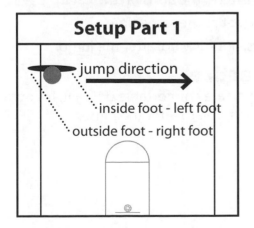

Setup Part 1

jump direction

inside foot - left foot
outside foot - right foot

Moving Back & Forth

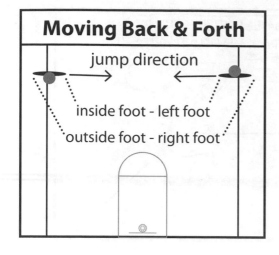

jump direction

inside foot - left foot

outside foot - right foot

The Jump

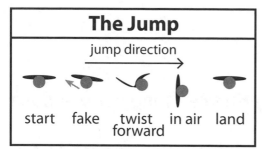

jump direction

start | fake | twist forward | in air | land

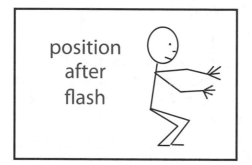

position after flash

2. For this lesson the outside foot is away from the direction of motion. The inside foot is near the direction of motion. *See the diagram Moving Back & Forth.*

3. Fake away from the direction of motion with the body before jumping. *See the diagram The Jump.* The fake involves taking a very short step with the outside foot and slowly turning the body away from the direction of movement.

4. Just before the jump, quickly turn to face the jumping direction and jump. When in the air turn back to the original sideways position before landing.

5. On the jump say, "Jump, catch (extend the arms), land." Both feet should land at the same time.

6. Land facing the starting direction. It is optional to repeat this lesson landing facing forward.

7. Pivot completely around before continuing. If you land on both feet simultaneously you can pivot on either foot. However, if you land on one foot first, then this is your pivot foot.

8. You do not need to break Olympic records on the jump. You can perform the required movements with a small jump. And if the detailed instructions make this more difficult, then just jump forward extending the arms and land sideways.

9. Continue jumping across the gym and back at your own pace. On the way back your body faces the other sideways direction. Continue for 2-10 minutes till you feel comfortable doing this.

10. Repeat steps 1-8 starting sideways the other way. Just turn around to face the opposite direction.

Key Points

1. Make sure to extend the arms on the catch.

2. Land on both feet at the same time.

3. Face sideways, not forward, after the jump.

How To Practice

Practice this till you are comfortable doing it. It's optional to repeat facing forward after the jump.

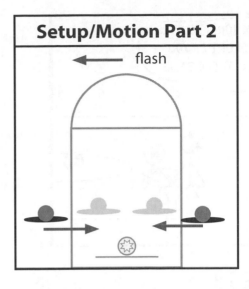

Setup/Motion Part 2

flash

Position After Flash

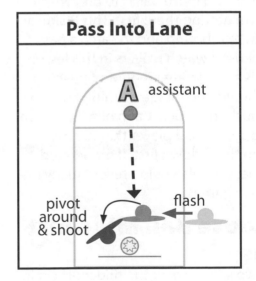

Pass Into Lane

A assistant

pivot around & shoot

flash

Part 2 Flash & Count
Directions

1. Line up on one side of the lane, as close as possible to the low post. Do not stand on the line. *See the diagram Setup/Motion Part 2*

2. Start counting when you step into the lane. Count out loud, "one thousand one, one thousand two, one thousand out." As you say "out," step out of the lane.

3. When ready just step into the lane and start counting.

4. Repeat this 10 times. It should take about 1 minute.

5. Repeat the drill except this time flash, rather than step into the lane. Fake away, then jump into the lane ready to catch the ball. Arms are extended for the pass. *See the diagram Position After Flash.* Hold this position while you count.

6. Count to three again to yourself. Jump out on "out."

7. Repeat 10 times.

8. Repeat steps 1-7 from the other side of the lane.

9. Repeat steps 1-8 with an assistant near the free throw line or key area throwing a pass on the flash. *See the diagram Pass Into Lane.*

10. Pivot around slowly and shoot off the backboard. Rebound, then pass the ball back to the passer. Repeat steps 9 and 10, 5 times.

11. You can practice this lesson on your own without the pass. Just place a ball in the center of the lane, then flash into the lane to the ball as though you are going to receive the pass. Pick up the ball, pivot around, and shoot.

Key Points

1. Do everything slowly in this lesson. Speed of performance will not help.

2. Fakes are slow, compared to the actual move.

3. After the pass, slowly pivot around, get your bearings, and shoot off the backboard.

How To Practice

Practice this lesson 1-3 times. Practice the flash, catch, and pivot-around move in step 10, till you feel comfortable.

57 Loose Ball Drill

Player's Corner		
Parts	1	2
Type	CORE	CORE
Players	2	2
Assist	YES	YES
Ball	◯	◯
Court	X	🏀
Effort	3	3
Time	5	5

Setup Part 1

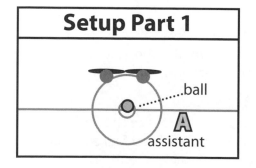

Briefs

In Part 1, two players go for a loose ball at midcourt.

In Part 2, two players go for a ball under the basket; the winner shoots.

Why Do This

Going for a loose ball is another catch-cut skill. The key to retrieving a loose ball is to prevent the other player from getting there first. This is similar to actions taken to rebound and to catch a pass. An assistant needs to watch players in this lesson because there is a moderate amount of pushing. The assistant should encourage a timid player to overdo it and push too much. Calm him/her down later. Do the opposite for a player that is very aggressive; calm them down first. If moderated properly these lessons also help prevent many unnecessary fouls in games.

Part 1 Loose Ball Midcourt
Directions

1. A group of two sets up near the midcourt circle. An assistant watches. If no midcourt is available set up anywhere. *See the diagram Setup Part 1.*

2. Set up side-to-side, elbow-to-elbow, leaning on each other at midcourt on the jump restraining circle.

3. When the assistant yells "Go," step in front of the other player before going for the ball. Move your foot and arm in front of the other player first, and then your body. This is called *getting position*.

4. The assistant should allow inexperienced players to foul at first to get the feel for contact. When they are more experienced, demand more legal contact.

5. Players get position first, then go for the ball.

6. Repeat 3-10 times.

7. The assistant can vary the distance between the ball and the players from 1 foot to 5 yards. It's also okay to repeat tossing the ball slowly in any direction, even toward the players, instead of just placing it on the floor.

Key Points

1. Go for position first, then go for the ball.

2. The player who gets to the ball first, rips the ball away and pivots away from the opponent.

3. Younger players usually need to push more; older players less.

How To Practice

This part only needs to be practiced once or twice till it is properly performed.

Part 2 Loose Ball At Basket
Directions

1. Two players set up elbow-to-elbow, leaning against each other about 2 yards from the basket. *See the diagram Setup Part 2.*

2. An assistant places a ball near the basket and says "Go." The assistant alternately can just drop the ball, so players go after a moving ball.

3. Players get position, step in front of the opponent, then go for the ball.

4. The player who gets to the ball first shoots. The other plays harassing defense. Play 100% defense, but do not foul or block the shot. See Lesson 42 for defensive information.

5. Only take one shot, even if it is missed. Rebound, place the ball on the floor in the original position. Then set up again.

6. Repeat 3-7 times.

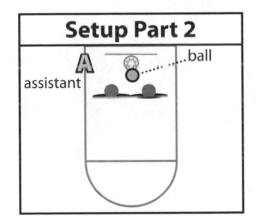

Setup Part 2

assistant · · ball

Key Points

1. Go for position, then for the ball.

2. Go straight up to shoot.

3. The defender must play harassing defense, no fouls, no blocking the shot.

4. The assistant must make sure that play is rough enough, but not too rough.

How To Practice

This only needs to be practiced once.

TLC Skills Lessons

58 Cut Fake Technique
59 Timing
60 Communication
61 Pass Off The Dribble

The TLC skills are the key to team offense. They are the most difficult skills to learn for several reasons. One, only instants of time are involved. A pass, cut or look that is one tenth of a second late can spoil a play. Two, TLC skills involve more than one player. Two or more players must coordinate movements. Three, TLC skills depend on passing, catching, cutting, and faking ability. Properly performing TLC lessons is difficult even without defense.

Lesson 58, Cut Fake Technique, presents four basic fakes used before any cut. Lesson 59, Timing, involves passing, cutting, and catching routines. Lesson 60, Communication, improves communication between catcher and passer. Lesson 61, Pass Off Dribble, involves making a pass while dribbling. Note that many lessons throughout the book involve TLC skills. However, Lessons 62-65, the next section, are especially worthwhile TLC lessons if they are practiced slowly focusing on the skills, rather than running or the actual play. If practiced properly, these lessons will not look anything like a cool quickly run play.

58 Cut Fake Technique

Player's Corner

Parts	1	2	3	4
Type	CORE	CORE	CORE	CORE
Players	1	1	1	1
Assist	YES	YES	YES	YES
Ball	○	○	○	○
Court	X	X	X	X
Effort	2	2	2	2
Time	3	3	3	6

Briefs

In Part 1, relax then sprint to the ball.

In Part 2, walk away from the passer before sprinting to the ball.

In Part 3, step behind the defense, then sprint to the ball.

In Part 4, the catcher reacts to a fake from the passer before sprinting to the ball.

Why Do This

Faking without the ball is a crucial offensive skill that is often overlooked by coaches. Faking before cuts frees up closely-covered players, allowing the offense to better function. Every second on offense, off-ball players should be misdirecting the defense in some way. It is hard to think of an offensive situation where a player would not fake. Overtly faking a cut is used to keep the defense close. This move allows other players to operate more freely.

Remember that the key to all faking is that it be slow enough for the defense to react. Fast fakes are counterproductive. Most of the time players will use the fakes learned in this lesson in combination. For example, the step-away fakes works well with the sleep fake.

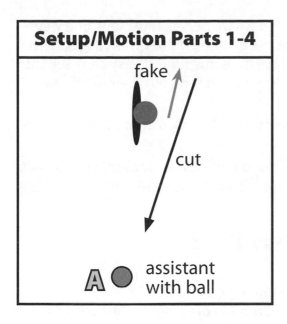

Setup/Motion Parts 1-4

fake

cut

A assistant with ball

Part 1 The Sleep Fake
Directions

1. An assistant holds the ball at one end of the gym. The faker sets up 10 yards away. *See the diagram Setup/Motion Parts 1-4.*

2. The first fake is one that is accomplished only too readily. It is the sleep fake. Relax. Appear to be uninvolved. Slowly turn away from the action and the ball. Actually, pay close attention to everything. You are waiting for the right moment to cut.

3. Before cutting count to three slowly: one-thousand one, one-thousand two, one-thousand three. Alternatively an assistant can signal the cut. The signal must be non-verbal, silent, so that the cutter closely watches.

4. Turn and sprint to the ball with arms extended. An assistant passes the ball to the cutter.

5. Repeat 5 times.

Part 2 Step-Away Fake
Directions

1. Take several lazy steps in the opposite direction that you plan to cut. *See the diagram Setup/Motion Parts 1-4.*

2. Slowly count to three while you are walking before sprinting forward with arms extended.

3. An assistant can throw a pass to the cutter.

4. Repeat 5-10 times.

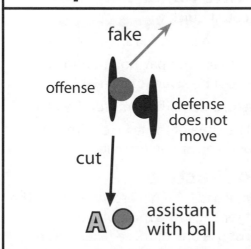

Step-Behind Fake

fake

offense

defense does not move

cut

A assistant with ball

Part 3 Step-Behind Fake
Directions

1. Use a chair or other object in lieu of a defender. If a live defender is used he/she should be in the half-down position and line up sideways 1 foot closer to the ball than the offense. *See the diagram Step-Behind Fake.*

2. Defenders do not move an inch in this drill! Stay in position! A defender only counts to three, then turns his/her head to look at the offense. This look is the signal for the offense to cut.

3. The best way to perform this fake involves sleepily stepping behind the defense away from the ball. You want the defense to be in the position where he/she must look one way to see you and the other way to see the ball. You do not want the defense to be able see both you and the ball at the same time. If they can't see the ball, they can't help-out. If they can't see you, then you can more easily make a successful cut.

4. The offense starts beside the defense. Sleepily step behind and count to three.

5. On three or when the defense turns to look, sprint forward. An assistant passes to the cutter.

6. Repeat 5-10 times.

Part 4 Pass-Response Fake
Directions

1. The pass-response fakes involves two fakes, one fake from the passer and a response fake from the cutter. *Step 1 in the diagram Steps Pass-Response Fake* shows the setup*.*

2. The cutter looks at the passer while jogging away. Ask for the ball using your arms. This looks like a football player asking for an overhead pass. *Step 2 in the diagram.*

3. When the passer fakes a pass, within 1-3 seconds, act like you are going to catch it, then pivot around and sprint forward. *Step 3 in the diagram.* The fake arrow next to the cutter is towards the passer to show communication. The actual fake for the cutter involves two parts: one, looking back towards the passer; two, asking for a pass over the head in a direction away from the passer.

4. Ask for the ball again using arms and hands while sprinting forward.
Step 4 in the diagram.

5. The passer throws you a pass.

6. Repeat 5-10 times.

Key Points Parts 1-4

1. Do not count quickly.

2. Fake slowly, then cut full speed to the ball.

3. Act like you are not paying attention on most fakes, but be aware of everything.

4. On the cut, extend the arms for the ball.

5. You will use one of these fakes virtually every second you are on offense.

How To Practice

Only repeat Parts 1-3 if necessary. Part 4 is the only must repeat. From this point onward, players must use one of these fakes before each cut in each and every lesson in the book.

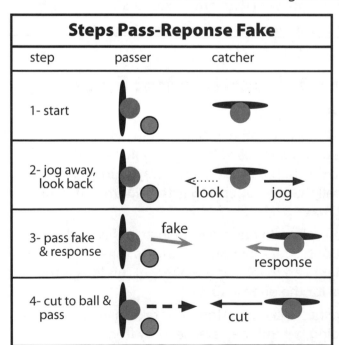

Steps Pass-Reponse Fake		
step	passer	catcher
1- start		
2- jog away, look back		look jog
3- pass fake & response	fake	response
4- cut to ball & pass		cut

TLC SKILLS: LESSONS 58-61

59 Timing

Player's Corner

Parts	1	2	3
Type	CORE	CORE	CORE
Players	2	2	2
Assist	YES	YES	YES
Ball	◯	◯	◯
Court	X	X	🏀
Effort	2	2	2
Time	5-10	5-10	5-10

Setup Parts 1-2

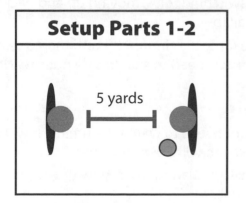

5 yards

Briefs

In Part 1, two players execute the pass-response fake maneuver before the cutter sprints to the ball.

In Part 2, the cutter jumps to the ball.

In Part 3, the cutter runs down-and-out before cutting to the basket.

Why Do This

The most difficult of the most difficult skills to teach is timing. One reason is that good and bad timing involves instants of time. Another is that every other offensive skill is involved. Usually timing evolves over a period of time, so don't expect great improvement overnight. Try to separate poor timing from other catching, passing, and TLC problems. Work on each problem separately. An assistant can make sure that the timing improves by watching and pointing out the exact problem.

Though many lessons in the book involve timing and TLC skills, the three lessons in this topic are particularly useful. The assistant is essential because players will not notice that the timing is off. Attempting to figure out *why* timing is off, is quite difficult even when a video of a play is available. Usually it involves the catcher either starting too soon or not cutting through the ball.

Steps Part 1

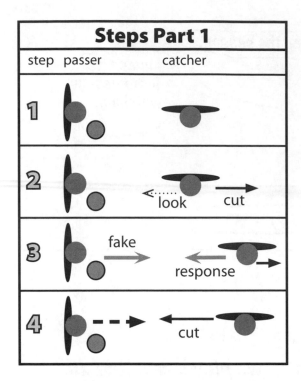

step	passer	catcher
1		
2		look — cut
3	fake	response
4		cut

How To Catch A Pass

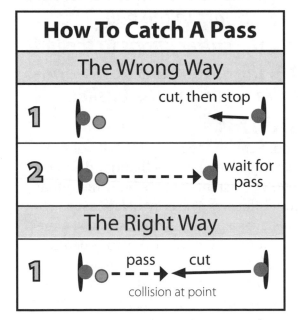

The Wrong Way

1. cut, then stop

2. wait for pass

The Right Way

1. pass — cut
collision at point

In these lessons, players also get great practice pivoting, ball faking, faking before the cut, communicating, and looking. In Part 3 a player shoots a shot.

Part 1 Cut To Ball
Directions

1. Players setup 5 yards apart. *See the diagrams Setup Parts 1-2 and Steps Part 1.* The passer starts with the ball overhead.

2. The catcher jogs away and looks back at the passer asking for the ball by waving the arms overhead. *See Step 2 the diagram Steps Part 1.*

3. The passer fakes a pass that the catcher acts like he/she will catch. This is a pass-response fake. Passer and catcher need to look at each other. *Step 3 in the diagram.*

4. The catcher then sprints forward for the ball. *Step 4 in the diagram.*

5. The passer passes using an overhead pass as soon as the cutter starts forward. Step 4 in the diagram.

6. The catcher stops running only after he/she catches the ball. Think– jump, catch, one, two. Stop on the one, two. It's okay if you end up next to the passer. *See the diagram How To Catch A Pass.*

7. Pivot around with the ball overhead, ready to repeat the lesson now as the passer. No need to go back to the original positions.

8. On the pass fake, the new catcher should fake away enough, maybe 5-10 yards, to keep the catcher and passer separated by at least 5 yards instead of being on top of each other.

9. Continue switching roles, moving up and back in the space available.

10. Continue for 5-15 minutes. It's optional to switch the pass from overhead to side to side bounce. No chest passes.

Key Points

1. The assistant needs to watch the timing. It will be terrible at first and will slowly improve.

2. Catchers will regularly stop or slow down before catching the ball.

3. Passers will often pass late.

4. Timing is difficult to nail down because only instants of time are involved.

5. Catchers need to extend the arms for each pass.

How To Practice

You can't practice this enough. Start slow. Increase running speed only as timing improves. It's okay to go back to more basic lessons.

Part 2 Flash To Ball
Directions

1. This is similar to Part 1 except that the catcher sets up by standing sideways and takes a long jump forward for the ball instead of running. *See the diagram Steps Part 2.*

2. The catcher sets up standing sideways by turning right. The catcher then takes one or two small steps, at most, away from the ball. On the pass-response fake, the catcher acts like he/she is going to catch the ball overhead by raising an arm. This is like a football player going out for a pass with the back arm raised. After the fake, pivot around and jump to the ball with arms outstretched, fingers extended.

3. The passer must hit the cutter before he/she lands, preferably in the middle of the jump. The timing is difficult.

4. Catch, then pivot around with ball overhead ready to repeat.

5. Again the catcher moves away on the fake just enough to keep the distance around 5 yards. Remember that after the fake, the cutter is going to just jump forward. No running forward in this part.

6. The passer must fake when the catcher is about 5 yards apart. The fake is the signal for the catcher to jump forward.

7. After a few minutes, the flasher starts sideways the other way.

Key Points

1. The passer must fake when the catcher is about 5 yards away.

2. The catcher acts like he/she is catching the ball overhead, then jumps forward to catch the pass.

3. Arms must be extended on the jump forward and catch.

4. Timing will be even more difficult in this lesson.

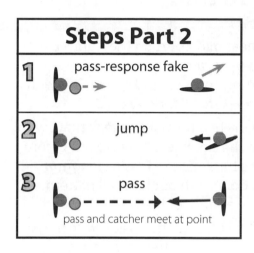

Steps Part 2

1 pass-response fake

2 jump

3 pass

pass and catcher meet at point

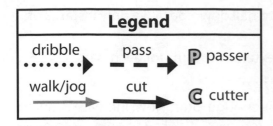

Legend

dribble ······▶	pass --▶	Ⓟ passer
walk/jog ──▶	cut ──▶	Ⓒ cutter

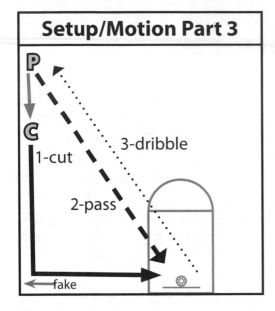

Setup/Motion Part 3

3-dribble
1-cut
2-pass
fake

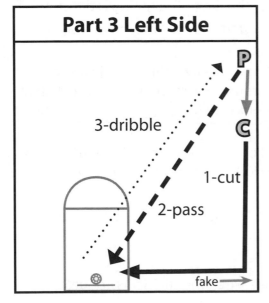

Part 3 Left Side

3-dribble
1-cut
2-pass
fake

How To Practice

Practice as much as possible, but not more than 15 minutes per session. Like the previous part, other skills like catching, passing, and pivoting are important for your success. If necessary, go back and work on these skills.

Part 3 Run To Ball
Directions

1. The passer starts near mid-court on the right side-line. The cutter starts 5-10 yards closer to the basket on the sideline. The starting spots should be marked with cones. *See the diagram Setup/Motion Part 3.*

2. Before the cutter cuts he/she makes eye contact with the passer. Cut down the sideline, then fake out before cutting straight to the basket. *Step 1 in the diagram.* This is like running a down and out football pattern. Then cut to the basket asking for the ball.

3. The passer leads the cutter to the basket with a pass. *Step 2 in the diagram.* It's okay if the pass bounces. Move closer to the basket with younger players.

4. The cutter catches the ball and then stops. This prevents crazy off balance shots. Take a one-foot shot or dribble to the basket for a layup or one foot shot. You must make 100% of shots. No misses.

5. Rebound the shot and dribble to the passing position with the head up. *Step 3 in the diagram.*

6. The passer moves to the cutting position.

7. Repeat steps 2-6 for 5-10 minutes.

8. Switch to the other side of the court and repeat steps 2-7. *See the diagram Part 3 Left Side.*

Key Points

1. The cutter looks at the passer before cutting.

2. The passer leads the cutter to the basket.

3. The cutter and pass meet near the basket.

4. The cutter stops after the catch, then shoots a short shot or layup.

How To Practice

Repeat till players can properly time the pass with a cutter going full speed.

60 Communication

Player's Corner

Parts	1	2
Type	CORE	CORE
Players	2	2
Assist	YES	YES
Ball	⭕	⭕
Court	X	X
Effort	2	2
Time	3-5	3-5

Setup Parts 1-2

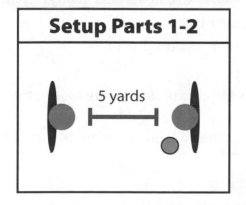

5 yards

Briefs

In Part 1, the catcher tells the passer where to throw the pass.

In Part 2, the passer directs the catcher.

Why Do This

Although TLC skills are inseparable, this lesson zeros In on communication. When players see the need for communication, they get in the habit of looking for each other, and communication skills Improve.

Part 1 Catcher Directs
Directions

1. If you do not have much room to run this lesson, then run it with players only moving up and back. No sideways motion.

2. The catcher fakes either toward or away from the passer. You decide. Then cut in the opposite direction, asking for the ball by extending the arm. Always give the passer a target like a baseball catcher.

3. After the pass, the new passer faces the catcher. The new catcher directs. Do not change or go back to the original positions. Start from the positions after the pass.

4. Continue for 2-5 minutes.

5. Now use other types of fakes and/or signals like: point with your finger, hand, elbow, or nose; nod your head in any direction; move your eyes and/or head in any direction; turn your body or just your head in any direction; gesture with any part of your body.

6. The catcher can fake and cut a few times before asking for the ball. When you want the passer to actually throw the pass either nod your head or use any other above signal or use a secret signal. It's okay to discuss the signal before play. Do not use verbal communication.

7. After the pass, the new passer faces the catcher. The new catcher directs. Do not change or go back to the original positions. Start from the positions after the pass.

8. Continue for 2-5 minutes.

Key Points

1. Use non-verbal communication.

2. The passer must lead the catcher.

3. The catcher catches the pass on the run, then slows down.

4. An assistant, if available, needs to watch the timing.

How To Practice
This only needs to be done once or twice.

Part 2 Passer Directs
Directions

1. Use the same directions as Part 1 except in this part the passer directs the catcher. Use the arms, eyes, head, or any part of the body to signal where you want to throw the pass. The catcher must follow each direction signal given by the passer and be ready to catch a pass at any instant.

2. It's okay if players are obvious at first.

3. Eventually make some secret signals.

Key Points

1. The passer directs the catcher. Make sure to lead the catcher.

2. The catcher catches the ball running at normal speed, then slows down.

How To Practice
This only needs to be practiced once or twice.

61 Pass Off The Dribble

Player's Corner

Parts	1	2
Type	OPT	OPT
Players	2	2
Assist	NO	NO
Ball	○	○
Court	🏀	🏀
Effort	2	2
Time	5 - 10	5-10

Setup Parts 1-2

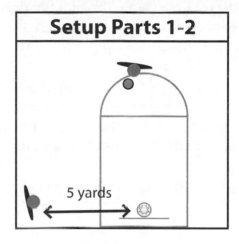

Motion Part 1

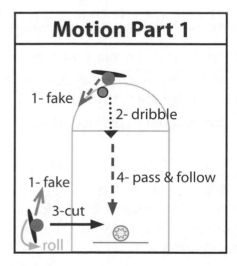

Briefs

In Part 1, a running dribbler passes to a cutter at the basket.

In Part 2, the dribbler receives a return pass.

Why Do This

These two lessons involve throwing a pass while moving. Making a good pass when stationary without a defender is quite difficult. Doing the same while moving is even more difficult. Do not throw a chest pass, because it cannot be used when covered. Only more experienced players should attempt this lesson.

Part 1 Pass On The Run
Directions

1. The dribbler sets up near the top of the key. The cutter starts near the corner or 5 yards from the basket near the endline. *See the diagram Setup Parts 1-2.*

2. Begin with a pass-response fake toward the ball. The cutter moves to the ball with arms extended asking for the pass. The passer fakes an overhead pass. *This is step 1 in the diagram Motion Part 1.*

3. The dribbler then starts to dribble to the basket. *Step 2 in the diagram.*

4. The cutter cuts or rolls to the basket. A roll is a (backward) pivot away from the ball, then a cut. *Step 3 in the diagram.*

5. After one or two dribbles, the passer stretches to one side to throw a side pass, not a chest pass, to the cutter at the basket. Then continue to the basket for the rebound. *Step 4 in the diagram.*

6. The cutter shoots a 1-foot shot.

7. Switch positions, then repeat.

8. Continue for 5-15 minutes.

9. To make the pass more difficult, the dribbler

Part 2 Step 1

pass-response fake

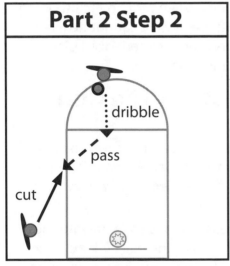

Part 2 Step 2

dribble

pass

cut

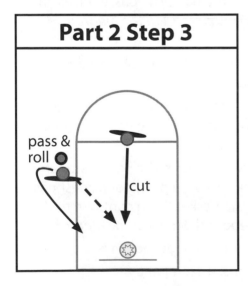

Part 2 Step 3

pass & roll

cut

can initially move toward the left or right side instead of to the basket.

Key Points

1. Do not use a chest pass!

2. The side pass is very difficult to throw while moving.

3. The cutter rolls away from the ball before the cut.

4. The pass and cutter meet at the basket.

How To Practice

This is only for experienced players. Perform this till the timing is correct using a side pass, not a chest pass.

Part 2 Pass Back
Directions

1. This is similar to Part 1 with an added step. The dribbler pass-response fakes toward the basket. The cutter responds by moving toward the basket and asking for the ball. *See the diagram Part 2 Step 1.*

2. The cutter cuts to the mid-post area. The dribbler dribbles toward the basket and throws a side bounce pass to the cutter at the mid-post area on the right side. *See the diagram Part 2 Step 2.*

3. After the pass, the dribbler cuts to the basket. The mid-post player immediately throws a no-look side bounce pass back, then rolls away from the pass to the basket. The roll is a backward pivot away from the ball. *See the diagram Part 2 Step 3.*

4. The cutter shoots a 1-foot shot rather than a layup. Both players rebound.

Key Points

1. Use a side bounce pass. Assume a defender is covering the dribbler.

2. The ball and the cutter meet at the mid-post area.

3. The return pass to the dribbler is a no-look pass. No need to look away, just don't overtly look at the cutter.

4. Jog through this lesson in order to perfect the timing. Do not go full steam.

How To Practice

There are a myriad of difficult skills in Part 2 that even the most advanced players will have trouble performing together. This is only worthwhile if done correctly with proper fakes and proper timing.

PLAY TRANSITION LESSONS

In this section, the 3-person plays from **The Basketball Coach's Bible** are transformed into 2-person plays, so players can practice all the TLC skills. However, this is not the place to start learning offense. Start with the most basic lessons and then work up to these. With a transition, these are worthwhile CM lessons. See **About Plays** on the next page for more information.

Lessons 62-64, cover Plays 1-3 respectively. The transition for each play, which is similar to a fast break, is exactly the same Lesson 65, In & Out Pattern, covers a repeating pattern where players cut inside and then out for the ball. There is no transition for this lesson.

About Plays

Each defense presents particular problems and opportunities for an offense. It is difficult to predict what these will be. Practicing predetermined specific plays ignores this fact and thus defeats the purpose of the offense, which is to react to the defense. Sensible preparation involves understanding offensive objectives and how to achieve them. The objective, in general, of any offense is to pass the ball inside and score from the inside. There are three different areas to pass the ball from–the center, the side, and the corner. Each one of the three numbered plays covers one of these possibilities. The fourth lesson, In & Out Pattern, involves repeatedly cutting in and out, to and from the basket.

In games, plays are seldom run. If players have learned the offensive tools—the individual skills—they recognize an opportunity and then go for it. Do not spend a lot of time mindlessly running these plays or any other expecting that repetition will bring success. With plays, too much repetition can be problematic. However, when these plays are practiced, spend a lot of time on the TLC skills involved. This entails running these plays very slowly and concentrating on timing and faking.

Cardinal Rules For Plays 1-3

• The passer always uses a pass-response fake to the other player before passing. The cutter must react to the pass fake. This is the response part of the pass-response fake. So, if player *A* pass-response fakes to player *B*, then two things occur simultaneously. One, player *A* fakes the pass toward player *B*. Two, player *B* responds like he/she is going to catch the ball. The pass fake and response are usually in a different direction than the actual pass and cut.

• The cutter always fakes away before cutting. In the 2-person plays, this will usually be part of the pass-response fake.

• The ball and the cutter meet at a spot. The cutter does not wait in position for the pass.

• The passer uses overhead and side passes for outside passes; use side or back bounce passes inside.

• Inside passes must be no-look passes because the cutter and passer are so close. The passer does not turn the head to look at the cutter.

• After an inside pass, the passer always turns (rolls) away from the pass direction before cutting. Turning away prevents the defender on the cutter from both watching the ball and the cut.

• After a catch on the periphery, the cutter pivots around to face the basket.

• For these lessons only, after a catch in the low or mid-post areas, the cutter does not turn around to face the basket. In a game a player can pivot around and make a move to score.

• Execute these lessons at a moderate to slow pace. Speeding things up to make the play work better, defeats the purpose of the lesson which is to improve TLC skills.

• In a game each offensive player, with or without the ball, should be faking just about every second. Eventually players should run these plays the same way and be faking continuously.

The starting setup for each play is similar. *A* starts outside. *B* starts in the right side low post. Repeat each play starting from the other side of the court. *A* & *B* regularly switch starting positions as well.

Walk through each play the first time without the fakes. Use more fakes as players become more experienced. The more fakes the better, even though the more fakes the slower the play must be run. Do not run any play for more than 15 minutes after the first day.

62 Play 1

Player's Corner

Parts	1	2
Type	OPT	OPT
Players	2	2
Assist	YES	YES
Ball	◯	◯
Court	🏀	🏀
Effort	2	2
Time	5-15	5-15

Briefs

In Part 1, two players run Play 1.

In Part 2, players run Play 1 with a transition.

Why Do This

In Play 1 the inside, or entry, pass is made from the center of the court. Part 2 involves a transition.

Part 1 Play 1
Directions

Walk through each play the first time without fakes. Add more fakes as players become more experienced. **See the diagram Setup Play 1.** The setup for each play is the same.

Directions Without Fakes

Pass 1 *A* passes to *B*, who is cutting up the lane to the mid-post area. **See the diagram Play 1 Pass 1.** Numbers in diagram show sequence of movements.

Pass 2 *B* passes back to *A*, who is cutting down the lane. *B* then rolls away from the pass to the basket. **See the diagram Play 1 Pass 2.**

The Shot *A* shoots a layup or 1-foot shot. Both players follow for the rebound.

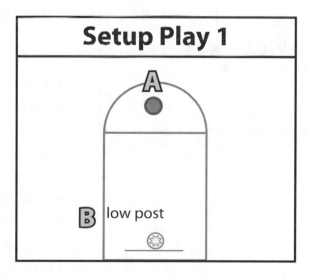

Setup Play 1

A

B low post

Diagram Legend

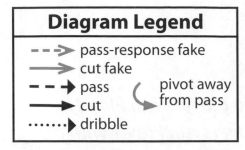

- - -> pass-response fake
———> cut fake
- - -> pass
———> cut
·······> dribble
↰ pivot away from pass

Play 1 Pass 1

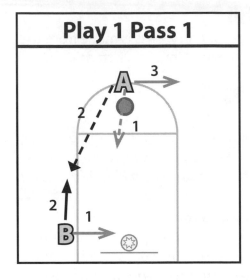

Play 1 Pass 2

after pass

Directions With Fakes
Pass 1

A uses an overhead pass-response fake towards the basket. *B* reacts by acting like he/she is catching a pass near the basket. *1 in the diagram Play 1 Pass 1.*

A passes to *B* cutting to the mid-post area, *2 in the diagram Play 1 Pass 1,* then fakes away, *3 in the diagram.*

B does not pivot around to face the basket. *B's* back is to the basket.

Pass 2

B pass-response fakes towards the side to *A*. *A* responds. *1 in the diagram Play 1 Pass 2.*

A cuts down the lane. *B* hits *A* with a side or back, bounce pass near the basket. Don't overtly look at *A*. *2 in the diagram Play 1 Pass 2.*

After the pass *B* rolls away from the pass to the basket. *3 in the diagram Play 1 Pass 2.*

The Shot

A shoots a layup or 1-foot shot. Both players go for the rebound. Do not let the ball hit the ground. Missing the shot is not an option. Each and every shot must be made.

- Players switch positions every 2 minutes.

- Repeat running the play from the other side of the court with *B* setting up on the left side low post.

- Each play needs to look realistic, like there is a defense.

- Add more fakes each time the lesson is performed.

- An assistant needs to point out bad timing on cuts, so players can improve.

Key Points

1. The ball should meet the cutter at a spot.

2. The catcher should not wait for the ball.

3. The ball should be caught with outstretched arms.

4. No chest passes from the front. Side passes only.

5. On inside passes do not overtly look at the catcher.

6. The inside passer rolls away from the pass direction.

7. The slower you do this drill, the better.

8. Add another fake each time you work on this.

9. Each shot must be made. 100% of the shots go in.

10. The drill should look realistic like there is defense.

11. Work on this for 15 minutes maximum after the first time.

Setup Part 2

Pass to sidelines, no dribbling, no walking.

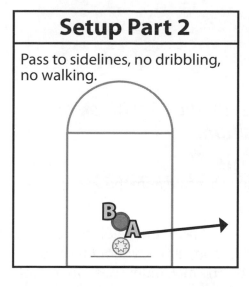

Transition Motion

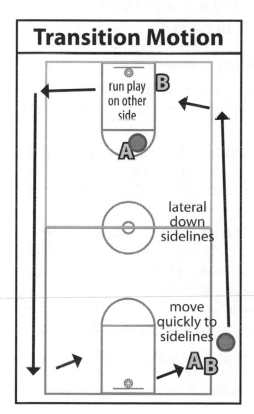

How To Practice

Don't expect good timing to occur overnight. This is something to work on all season.

Part 2 Play Transition
Directions

1. Part 2 starts at the end of Play 1 with players under the basket with the ball. *See the diagram Setup Part 2.*

2. One player rebounds, the other runs to the sideline.

3. The rebounder passes to the sideline then follows the pass.

4. Lateral back and forth down the sidelines to the other basket.

5. No dribbling at any time during the lesson. No walking either. After catching a pass you can only take one step before passing. You must look and pass to each other to advance the ball to the next basket. *See the diagram Transition Motion.*

6. At the next basket, keep the same positions, but run the play from the other side.

7. The assistant must make sure there is no walking at any time during the transition.

8. The transition for plays 2 and 3 are identical.

Key Points

1. Proper timing develops if you do not try to do everything quickly.

2. If you just want to run, then do this as a CM drill skipping most play fakes. Do the play as a TLC drill at another time.

3. No walking. You can only take one step after you catch the ball.

How To Practice

Work on this over the season.

63 Play 2

Player's Corner

Parts	1
Type	OPT
Players	2
Assist	NO
Ball	◯
Court	🏀
Effort	2
Time	5-15

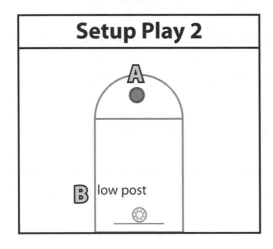

Setup Play 2

Briefs
Two players run Play 2 with an optional transition.

Why Do This
Play 2 works the ball inside from the side.

Directions
This play is similar to Play 1, but involves 3 passes. Walk through this many times without fakes before adding fakes. The maximum speed for players is a jog. *See the diagram Setup Play 2.*

Directions Without Fakes
Pass 1 *A* passes to *B*, who is cutting to the side. *See the diagram Play 2 Pass 1.*

Pass 2 *B* passes to *A*, who is cutting across the lane to the high post. *See the diagram Play 2 Pass 2.*

Pass 3 *A* passes back to *B*, who is cutting via the endline back to the basket. *A* then rolls away from the pass to the basket. *See the diagram Play 2 Pass 3.*

Shot *B* shoots a layup or 1-foot shot. Both players go for the rebound. The shot must be made. It is optional to run this with a transition. The transition is the same one made for Play 1.

Directions With Fakes
Each player fakes away from the direction of the cut or the play each second on the court. For the sake of clarity, some fakes had to be left out of the diagrams and directions.

Pass 1
A pass-response fakes to *B* in the lane, *1 in the diagram Play 2 Pass 1,* then passes to *B*, who is cutting toward the sideline. *2 in the diagram Play 2 Pass 1.*

Pass 2
B pass-response fakes to *A* in a direction away from the basket. *1 in the diagram Play 2 Pass 2.*

B hits *A* with a pass on the side of the lane at the

Play 2 Pass 1

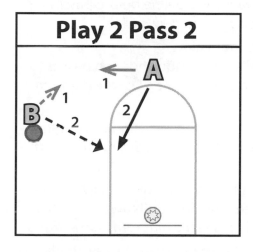

Play 2 Pass 2

Play 2 Pass 3

Diagram Legend

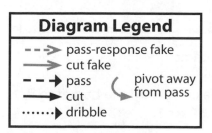

- - - > pass-response fake
- —> cut fake
- - - + pass
- —+ cut   pivot away from pass
- ····+ dribble

mid-high post area. *2 in the diagram Play 2 Pass 2.* After catching the pass *A* faces away from the basket and does not turn around.

Pass 3

A pass-response fakes to *B* in a direction away from the basket. *1 in the diagram Play 2 Pass 3.*

B cuts to the basket via the baseline. *A* hits *B* with a no-look side bounce pass near the lane. *2 in the diagram Play 2 Pass 3.*

A then rolls away from the pass, into the lane, towards the basket. *3 in the diagram Play 2 Pass 3.*

Shot

B shoots a layup or 1-foot shot. Make the shot. Both players follow for the rebound.

The transition is optional. Make sure to run the play from each side if no transition is made. Also switch positions.

Key Points

1. The ball should meet the cutter at a spot.
2. The catcher should not wait for the ball.
3. The ball should be caught with outstretched arms.
4. No chest passes.
5. On inside passes do not overtly look at the catcher.
6. Roll away from the pass direction.
7. The slower you do this drill, the better.
8. Add another fake each time you work on this.
9. Each shot must be made. 100% of the shots go in.
10. The drill should look realistic like there is defense.

How To Practice

Don't expect good timing to occur overnight. This is something to work on all season. Practice as much as possible, but not more than 15 minutes per session. Like the previous part, other skills like catching, passing, and pivoting are important for your success. If necessary, go back and work on these skills.

64 Play 3

Briefs
Two players run Play 3 with an optional transition.

Why Do This
Play 3 works the ball inside from the corner.

Directions
The one exception to the no-dribble rule involves *A* dribbling toward the sideline before passing to *B*. **See the diagram Setup Play 3.**

Directions Without Fakes

Pass 1 *A* dribbles to the side and then passes to *B*, who is cutting to the corner. **See the diagram Play 3 Pass 1.**

Pass 2 *B* passes to *A*, who is cutting toward the basket near the mid-post area. **See the diagram Play 3 Pass 2.**

Pass 3 *A* passes to *B*, who is cutting toward the basket via the endline, then rolls away from the pass to the basket. **See the diagram Play 3 Pass 3.**

Shot *B* shoots a layup or 1-foot shot. Both players follow for the rebound. The transition is optional.

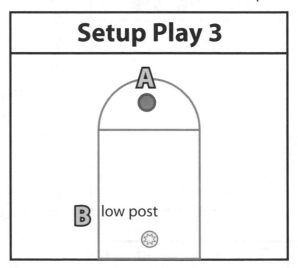

Setup Play 3

Directions With Fakes
Pass 1
A pass-response fakes toward the basket to *B*. *1 in the diagram Play 3 Pass 1..*

Play 3 Pass 1

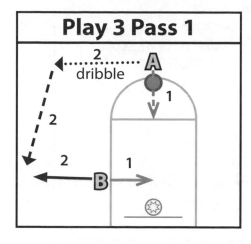

Play 3 Pass 2

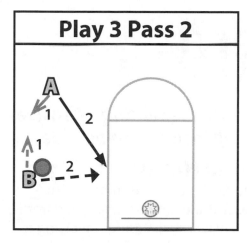

Play 3 Pass 3

Diagram Legend

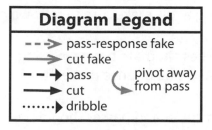

- - - > pass-response fake
------> cut fake
- - -> pass
------> cut
·······> dribble

pivot away
from pass

A dribbles toward the side and passes to *B* cutting to the corner. **2 in the diagram Play 3 Pass 1.** After the catch *B* pivots around to face the basket. .

Pass 2

B pass-response fakes to *A* toward the sideline. **1 in the diagram Play 3 Pass 2.** *A* cuts to mid-post area.

B hits *A* with a pass in the mid-post area near the lane. **2 in the diagram Play 3 Pass 2.** *A* continues to face away from the basket and does not turn to face the basket.

Pass 3

A pass-response fakes toward the sideline to *B*. **1 in the diagram Play 3 Pass 3.**

B rolls to the basket via the endline. *A* hits *B* with a no-look side bounce pass near the lane. **2 in the diagram Play 3 Pass 3.**

A rolls away from the pass direction into the lane to the basket. **3 in the diagram Play 3 Pass 3.**

Shot

B shoots a layup or 1-foot shot. Both players follow for the rebound. Make 100% of the shots.

The transition is optional. Make sure to run the play from each side if no transition is made. Rotate positions as well.

Key Points

1. The ball should meet the cutter at a spot.
2. The catcher should not wait for the ball.
3. The ball should be caught with outstretched arms.
4. No chest passes.
5. On inside passes do not overtly look at the catcher.
6. Roll away from the pass direction.
7. The slower you do this drill, the better.
8. Add another fake each time you work on this.
9. Each shot must be made. 100% of the shots go in.
10. The drill should look realistic like there is defense.

How To Practice

Don't expect good timing to occur overnight. This is something to work on all season. Practice as much as possible, but not more than 15 minutes per session. Like the previous part, other skills like catching, passing, and pivoting are important for your success. If necessary, go back and work on these skills.

65 In & Out Pattern

Player's Corner

Parts	1
Type	OPT
Players	2
Assist	NO
Ball	○
Court	🏀
Effort	2
Time	5-15

Briefs
Two players run a repeating offensive pattern cutting inside then outside.

Fundamental Notes
In this lesson the All-Around Pattern from **The Basketball Coach's Bible** has been modified from a team drill to a 2 player drill. Besides involving a host of TLC skills, this could be used as a CM lesson.

Directions
1. *A* starts at the top of the key with a ball. *B* is in the low post. ***See the diagram Setup/Pass 1.***

2. Run this lesson slowly.

3. Initially do not bother with fakes, just concentrate on passing and cutting.

4. Passes and cuts need to be realistic like there is a defense.

5. On short passes there is no need to look directly at the cutter.

6. On cuts involving a roll, make sure to roll away from the ball.

7. Every 5-10 minutes alternate between using overhead passes and side bounce passes. No chest passes.

8. Eventually each cutter and passer should be faking just about every second of the lesson. There is no down time.

Setup/Pass 1

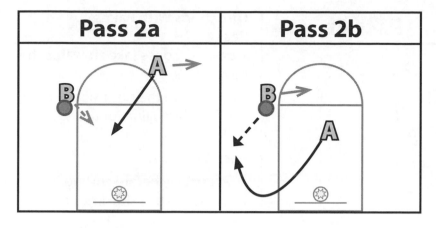

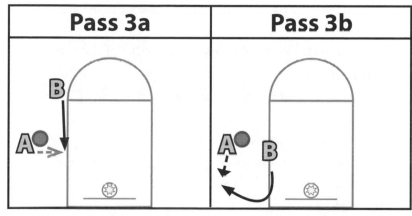

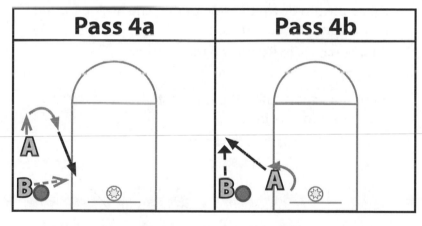

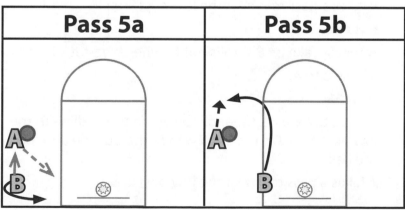

9. The directions only give you the idea for the cuts. You do not need to explicitly follow each one.

Directions Without Fakes

Pass 1 *B* cuts out to the right side near the free throw line for a pass from *A*. **See the diagram Setup/Pass 1.**

Pass 2a & 2b *A* cuts in towards the ball side low post, then out towards the sideline for a pass from *B*. **See the diagrams Pass 2a & Pass 2b.**

Pass 3a & 3b *B* cuts in near the right side of lane, then out towards the corner for a pass from *A*. **See the diagrams Pass 3a & Pass 3b.**

Pass 4a & 4b *A* rolls towards the low post, then rolls out to where the cut started for a pass from *B*. **See the diagrams Pass 4a & Pass 4b.**

Pass 5a & 5b *B* rolls to the low post, then cuts up the side of the lane to the free throw line, then out towards the sideline for a pass from *A*. **See the diagrams Pass 5a & Pass 5b.**

Pass 6a & 6b *A* cuts in towards the ball side low post, then up the side of the lane to just right of the top of the key for a pass from *B*. **See the diagrams Pass 6a & Pass 6b.**

Continuation Repeat steps moving towards the left corner and then back to the right. *A* and *B* continue to cut in and out.

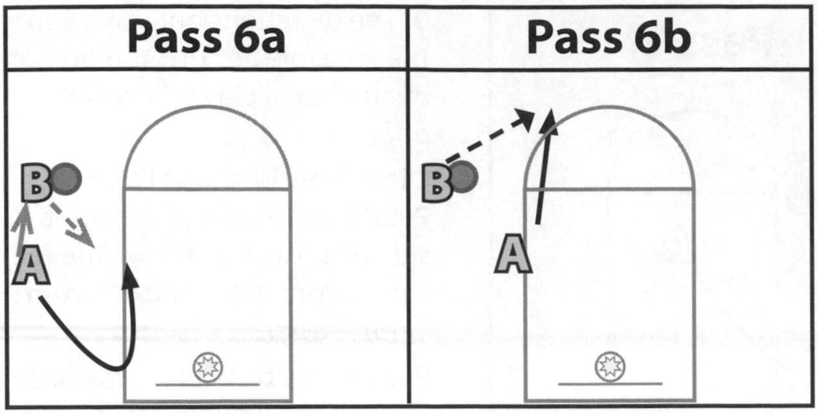

Pass 6a	Pass 6b

Directions With Fakes

Pass 1

A pass-response fakes towards the basket to B.

B cuts out to the right side near the free throw line for a pass from A.

Pass 2a

A fakes away before cutting in towards the ball side low post. On the cut, A asks for the ball waving the outside arm (left arm).

B fakes a pass when A is near the center of the lane.

Pass 2b

A continues the cut to the low post, then out towards the sideline for the ball.

B hits A with a pass when only a few yards away.

B fakes away the other side of the court before a cut inward.

Pass 3a

B cuts inward down the side of the lane asking for the ball waving the outside arm.

A fakes a pass to B near the mid-post area.

Pass 3b

B continues the cut to the low post, then out towards the corner for the ball.

A hits B with a pass in the corner.

Pass 4a

A fakes away then rolls to the basket asking for the ball with the arm farthest away from the ball.

B fakes a pass to A near the low post area.

Pass 4b

After the fake by B, A rolls out to where the cut started

B passes to A.

Pass 5a

B fakes towards A, then rolls away via the endline to the low post area. On the cut B waives the outside arm for the ball.

A fakes a pass to B near the low post area.

Pass 5b

B continues the cut up the lane to the free throw line, then out towards the sideline for the ball.

A hits B with a pass when only a few yards away.

Pass 6a

A fakes away before cutting in towards the ball side low post, then up the lane. While cutting, A waives the outside arm for the ball.

B fakes a pass to A at the mid-post area.

Pass 6b

A continues the cut to the original starting position near the top of the key.

B hits A with a pass when only a few yards away.

Continuation

Repeat steps moving towards the left corner and then back to the right. A and B continue to cut in and out.

Key Points

1. Do this lesson slowly.

2. The cutter meets the ball with arms outstretched.

3. Before the pass fake, the cutter asks for the ball by waiving the outside arm and looking at the passer

4. On short passes there is no need for the passer to look directly at the catcher.

5. Eventually passers should be faking every second they have the ball.

6. Use overhead, then side and/or side bounce passes. No chest passes.

How To Practice

There are a myriad of difficult skills that even the most advanced players will have trouble performing together. This is only worthwhile if done correctly with proper fakes and proper timing.

REBOUNDING LESSONS

Being tall, strong, and able to jump well are attributes helpful to a rebounder. However, the keys to rebounding are watching shot arcs, predicting where the ball will go, heading to the ball, and getting position on the opponent. Believe it or not, offensive and defensive rebounding are similar. Defenders have the advantage of inside position to start, but also have the disadvantage of having to watch the offense and the ball. Offensive players are more free to move around, and can go for the rebound from the baseline. Smart offensive rebounders box out and/or get position on the defense.

Boxing out for the defense always involves two steps. First, the defense must collide with the offense, stopping their momentum. Second, the defense must keep the offense on his/her back.

Each lesson covers a different aspect of rebounding. Lesson 66, Rebound Grab, covers grabbing the rebound like you own the ball. Lesson 67, Watch Arcs, involves watching shot arcs and predicting where the ball will go. Lesson 68, Ready Position, works on the rebound-ready position. Lesson 69, Positioning, works on getting good position against an opponent. Lesson 70, Block and Box Out, works on blocking and holding-on-the-back skills. Lesson 71, Box Out, involves actually boxing out a player going for a rebound.

66 Rebound Grab

Player's Corner	
Parts	1
Type	CORE
Players	2
Assist	NO
Ball	◯
Court	X
Effort	2
Time	5

Grab Rebound

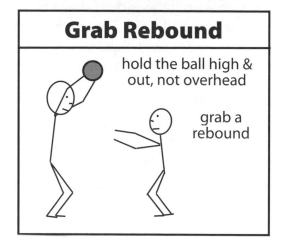

hold the ball high & out, not overhead

grab a rebound

180 Degree Pivot

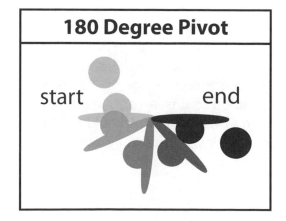

start   end

Briefs
One player grabs, then rips the ball away from the other.

Why Do This
To effectively rebound, a rebounder must forcefully rip the ball out of the air, simultaneously pivoting away from each opponent.

Directions
1. One player holds the ball high, but not directly overhead. It's okay to make your partner slightly jump, but do not hold the ball too high. **See the diagram Grab Rebound.**

2. The other player grabs the ball using the fingertips for control. Grab the ball hard. Slam your hands (fingertips) on the ball.

3. Now forcefully rip it away, and simultaneously pivot away a half-turn. You want to make sure no one takes the ball from you. **See the diagram 180 degree pivot.**

4. The rebounder now holds the ball overhead for the other player. Alternate grabbing for 1-5 minutes.

Key Points
1. Forcibly rip the ball away.

2. Simultaneously pivoting and ripping needs time to develop.

How To Practice
One player can perform this drill solo by just tossing the ball 1-2 feet in the air and then grabbing it. Work on this till you can do a forcible rip which includes a pivot away.

67 Watch Arcs

Player's Corner

Parts	1
Type	CORE
Players	1
Assist	YES
Ball	○
Court	🏀
Effort	2
Time	3-5

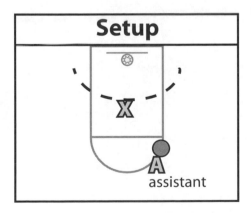

Setup

assistant

Briefs
Closely watch shot arcs attempting to predict where a ball will rebound.

Why Do This
Great rebounders will tell you that a key to rebounding is watching the shot arc, then predicting where the ball will go. All rebounders watch a little. Great rebounders watch very closely and also become familiar with how each shooter usually misses.

If its not obvious, the laws of physics apply to rebounds as well. The harder the shot, the longer the rebound. Softer shots yield short rebounds. The angle that the ball hits the rim or backboard equals the angle the ball bounces off the rim or backboard, etc. Predicting where the ball will go requires closely watching the shot.

Directions
1. Set up on a spot on a semicircle 6 feet from the basket. The assistant sets up near the free-throw line. *See the diagram Setup.*

2. The assistant shoots the ball from the free-throw line or elsewhere, trying to miss the shot one way then another. One way would be short, another long, another to the left or right; shoot long backboard shots off to the right and left as well. Move around so the ball rebounds in different directions.

3. Closely watch the arc of the shot and the rim.

4. Yell the instant you think you know where the ball will ricochet. Use words like short, left, center, right, and/or far as soon as you can. It is okay to yell more than one direction.

5. Don't worry about being correct. If you take the time to look, predicting will become easier.

6. The assistant shoots 10-15 shots. It is okay for a player to change his/her position on the semicircle.

Key Points

1. You want to get into the habit of closely watching shots.

2. Closely watching will make you a better predictor.

How To Practice

Practice this at least 2-3 times.

68 Ready Position

Player's Corner

Parts	1
Type	CORE
Players	1
Assist	YES
Ball	X
Court	X
Effort	2
Time	3

Setup Part 1

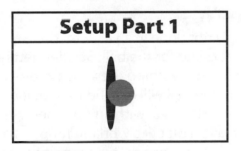

Rebound-Ready Position

Briefs
Snap to the rebound-ready position.

Why Do This
Another rebound basic is being ready to grab the ball with the body, arms, and hands in the best position. It is difficult to determine exactly when a rebound will bounce your way. Even after the rebound, a player often needs to scramble on the floor for the ball. You must be ready to catch or grab the ball at any moment. The rebound-ready position is the best starting position for going after a rebound.

Directions
1. Start in the half-down position ready to run.

2. To get into the ready position, the forearms need to be bent toward the upper arm all the way, hands slightly above shoulder height. The wrists are bent back; the fingers are spread and clawed. *See the diagram Rebound-Ready Position.*

3. Stand in a normal position. When ready snap to the ready position.

4. Repeat 5-15 times.

5. Repeat the previous lesson, Watching Arcs, snapping into ready position before each shot.

6. The assistant takes 5-10 shots.

7. Go for each rebound from the ready position.

Key Points
1. Make sure your forearms are vertical, hands clawed, and fingers spread apart.

2. The knees are bent, so you are ready to move to the rebound.

3. After snapping into position, watch the shot arc before going for the rebound.

4. Change your court position on the semicircle on a regular basis.

How To Practice
Practice this 2-3 times.

69 Positioning

Player's Corner

Parts	1
Type	CORE
Players	2
Assist	YES
Ball	◯
Court	🏀
Effort	3
Time	5

Setups

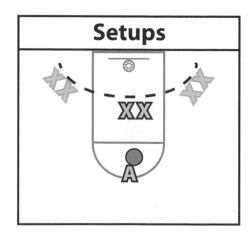

Briefs

Two players maneuver for a better rebounding position.

Why Do This

Rebounding is not done in a vacuum, there are lots of players going for the ball. Besides getting ready to rebound, watching the shot arc, predicting where the ball will go, and then going, rebounders need to deal with an opponent. In this lesson two players practice working for position before going for a rebound. There is no need to discriminate between offense and defense because these skills apply to both.

Directions

1. Two players start in the ready position shoulder-to-shoulder on an arc 3 yards from the basket. Change positions on the arc after each shot.

2. Watch the shooter and the ball, not your opponent. Stay in contact with your opponent using your arms and body. From this contact you can determine his/her whereabouts and movements.

3. This is like boxing out. Keep your eye on the ball. Predict where it will go, then go for it. Step in front of your opponent as soon as you go for the ball

4. Even if the shot is made, play the ball like a miss.

5. The assistant tries to miss each shot a different way. Here are some ideas for shots:

  (a) a hard shot off the backboard;

  (b) a soft shot that misses everything;

  (c) a short shot that just contacts the front rim;

  (d) a shot that hits the left side of the rim;

  (e) a shot the hits the backboard then the left side of the rim;

  (f) a hard shot that bangs the rim, etc.

Shoot from different positions on the floor as well.

6. After the rebound, pass the ball to the shooter and set up in a different position on the arc.

7. Repeat 7-15 times.

Key Points

1. Start in the ready position.

2. Watch the ball.

3. Step in front of your opponent, then go for the ball.

How To Practice

Do this 2-5 times.

70 Block & Box Out

Player's Corner		
Parts	1	2
Type	CORE	CORE
Players	2	2
Assist	NO	NO
Ball	X	X
Court	X	X
Effort	1-3	1-3
Time	5	5

Setup Part 1

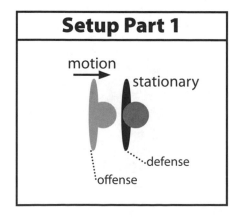

Briefs

In Part 1, one player keeps another on his/her back.

In Part 2, offense and defense start facing each other.

Why Do This

A player running unimpeded to the basket for a rebound is nearly impossible to stop. Stopping the charge to the basket is one key to boxing out. This is the block. The next part of boxing out involves pivoting around and keeping the player on your back. Players usually only have to box out for 1-3 seconds in a game. However, these drills are more difficult, requiring defenders to hold the opponent longer. Initially don't worry about fouling because players need to get used to the contact.

In games, boxing out is often easier for several reasons:

(a) The court is more crowded, so players can't freely roam around.

(b) Once the shot is up, the rebounder only has a few seconds to act.

(c) In a game, rebounders usually go right for the ball without faking around.

The defense must know how to overplay (Lesson 83) for Part 2.

Motion Part 1

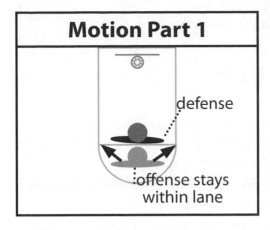

defense

offense stays within lane

Box-Out Position

Not Allowed

Part 1 Hold On Back
Directions

1. The offense starts at the free-throw line if a court is available. *See the diagram Motion Part 1.* The objective is to get into the lane. You may only move a maximum of 2-3 steps to the left or right of the defense. You are bounded by the lane.

2. The defense sets up in defensive position with their back to the offense.

3. The offense walks straight into the back of the defense. Only make a nominal attempt to go by. Keep pushing at the back of the defense and keep trying to get around, but not too hard. Slowly count to five while you are doing this.

4. Defense, keep the offense on your back. Spread out your body by pushing your elbows out to the side, keeping your feet far apart, and sticking your behind out. Your knees should be positioned almost directly above your feet. Move to the left or right in order to keep the offense on your back. *See the diagram Box-Out Position.*

5. Don't worry about offensive or defensive fouls at this stage. The offense is not allowed to push through the defense. The defense is not allowed to extend the arms like a elementary school street-crossing guard. *See the diagram Not Allowed.* A defender is also not allowed to push back, only block the offense.

6. It's important that the offense cooperates with the defense. Don't push too hard or too little. Work just hard enough to give the defense practice.

7. Switch roles after 5 seconds and repeat.

8. The more you do this lesson, the more effort the offense makes.

9. Continue for 5-10 minutes.

Key Points

1. This part can be done anywhere. Better if you have a court.

2. The offense bangs into the defense. Only move a few steps one way or the other after the initial contact.

3. The defense holds the offense on the back.

4. The defense cleans up their act, no fouls, as they improve.

How To Practice
Do this 2-10 times.

Part 2 Block Box
Directions

1. This lesson is the same as the previous lesson except the offense sets up facing the defense and a block is added prior to the boxing out. *See the diagram Setup Part 2.*

2. The offense does the same thing they did in the previous lesson. Walk directly into the defender.

3. The defense blocks the offense like a football player with the forearms close to the body and close to the chest. You are not initiating contact! Wait and let the offense run into you.

4. After the block, turn around and keep the offense on your back for 5 seconds like you did in the previous part.

5. The offense must work just hard enough to give the defense practice, but not so hard that he/she gets by.

6. It's much better to push too much than too little. The correct effort level is needed by both players.

7. Switch positions and repeat.

8. The offensive intensity increases as the defense improves.

9. Repeat for 5-10 minutes.

Key Points

1. The offense must make the right amount of effort to get by. Too little makes the drill worthless. Too much does not give the defense practice.

2. Initially it's okay to foul till players better understand the drill.

How To Practice
Do this 2-10 times.

Setup Part 2

motion →

offense

defense

71 Box Out

Player's Corner

Parts	1	2
Type	CORE	CORE
Players	2	2
Assist	YES	YES
Ball	○	○
Court	🏀|	🏀|
Effort	2-3	2-3
Time	5-15	5-15

Briefs
In Part 1, the defense boxes out a moving player.

In Part 2, the defense overplays, then boxes out the offense on the shot.

Why Do This
Once a defender can box out a nearly stationary player, it's time to box out a moving one.

Part 1 Front & Box Out
Directions
1. The defense sets up right in front of the offense fronting them. (See Lesson 77 for more information on fronting.) Use the free throw line as a starting place if one is available. However, this part can be done anywhere on the court. ***See the diagram Setup/Motion Part 1.***

2. When the assistant yells "Go," the offense makes a moderate effort to get by the defense, but not such a big effort that they get by. The defense fronts and blocks the path of the offense.

3. A few seconds later when the assistant yells "Shot," the offense goes straight to the basket or where a basket would be. The offense should run into the defense.

4. The defense blocks the offense using the fore-

Setup/Motion Part 1

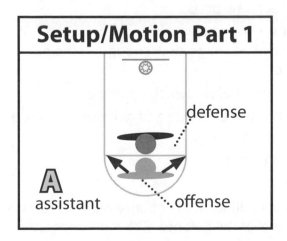

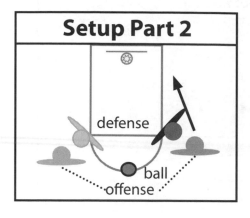

Setup Part 2

defense

ball
offense

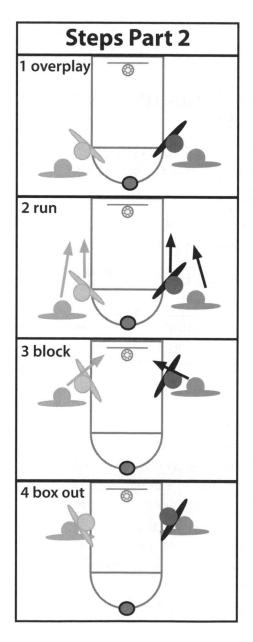

Steps Part 2

1 overplay

2 run

3 block

4 box out

arms for protection, then turns around on the shot, keeping the offense on the back for 5 seconds.

5. Switch roles and repeat.

6. Work on this for 5-15 minutes.

7. The offense makes more effort as the defense improves.

Key Points

1. The assistant signals the start and a few seconds later signals the offense to go directly to the basket for the rebound.

2. The defense fronts, blocks when the offense charges to the basket, turns around and keeps the offense on his/her back.

How To Practice
Continue working on this till players have some success.

Part 2 Overplay & Box Out
Directions

1. Put a ball at the top of the key. The offense first starts on the right side just outside the free throw line. The defense sets up overplaying the offense. (See Lesson 83 for more information on overplaying.) The overplay position is based on the location of the ball. ***See the diagram Setup Part 2 and the diagram Steps Part 2.*** The steps in this diagram correspond to the direction numbers.

2. When the assistant yells "Go," the offense jogs down the side of the lane toward the basket. The defense continues to overplay. Watch the ball. Stay in contact with the offense.

3. When the assistant yells "Shot," the offense goes straight to the basket.

4. The defense blocks, then turns around and holds the offense on the back for 5 seconds.

5. The offense must cooperate with the defense. Just don't run by. The offense needs to go slow enough so the defense can get practice.

6. Repeat several times before switching roles.

7. Repeat the drill with the offense and defense setting up on the other side of the lane.

8. Continue for 5-15 minutes.

Key Points

1. Because this is very difficult, the offense must cooperate and work at the level of the defense. Girls will cooperate.

Guys just want to run by the defense. Work on the cooperation.

2. Work on overplaying before doing this lesson.

How To Practice

You need to work on this on a regular basis till you can properly box out going full speed. When players are more expert, the assistant should actually shoot the ball.

REBOUND BOX OUT: LESSONS 66-71

SCREENING LESSONS

72 Setting A Screen
73 Using A Screen

Screening is an integral part of the game when the defense is tough. Pros screen the most, college next, and so on. With younger players, screening may not even be needed.

Screening is usually the best way to shake a tough, tenacious defender. A screen can free up a player to shoot, cut, dribble, or pass. Screening away from the ball is both more common and more effective than a screen on the ball. That's because an off-ball defensive player is not as ready for a screen as an on-ball player. However, against lesser defenses screening is not as helpful. Why screen if a simple fake will work? In my experience, most teams under high-school level do not need to spend a lot of time on screening. On the other hand, in pro and top-level college ball, screening plays a major role. Just about every cut involves a screen.

Screens can be used many ways:

(a) A dribbler can simply run a defender into a screen.

(b) A close screen can be set up after a player receives a pass. The screener should not run into the defender.

(c) A cutter can use a screen to shake a close defender in order to cut out, or cut inside, for a pass.

(d) A cutter can cut behind a screen to receive a pass.

Lesson 72, Setting A Screen, shows how to properly set a screen. Lesson 73, Using A Screen, shows how to use a screen and how to perform a screen and roll. The screen and roll starts after the screen is set. In a game a player can set a screen near, or next to, the player with the ball. This may be the most worthwhile screening lesson for all ages.

72 Setting Screen

Player's Corner

Parts	1
Type	ADV
Players	2
Assist	NO
Ball	X
Court	🗑
Effort	2
Time	5-10

Setup/Motion Screen

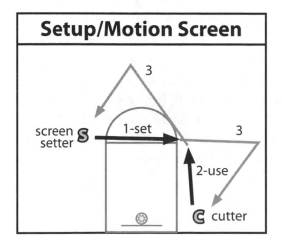

Briefs

A player learns how to set a screen.

Why Do This

It only takes about 15 minutes for a player to learn how to set a screen. However, setting a good screen at the proper moment in a game is not so easy. The proper time and direction to set the screen depend on the user's ability and the defense. With younger players, screens are rarely needed.

Directions For Players

1. Each player sets a screen in 3 diferent locations. For each location the screen setter, *S*, starts just outside the free throw line on the right side. The cutter, *C*, (screen user) sets up on the left side low post area. *See the diagram Setup/Motion Screen.*

2. The screener fakes away in any direction then jogs to the screening location. *See 1 in the diagram Setup/Motion Screen.* For the first location, the screener cuts across the lane to set up just outside the free throw line on the left side. *See 1 in the diagram Setting Locations.*

3. The feet of the screener are slightly more than shoulder-width apart; legs bent. Cross the forearms on the chest for protection. Move the elbows out slightly to take up more space. *See the diagram Elbows Of A Screen.*

Elbows Of A Screen

too much   too little   just right

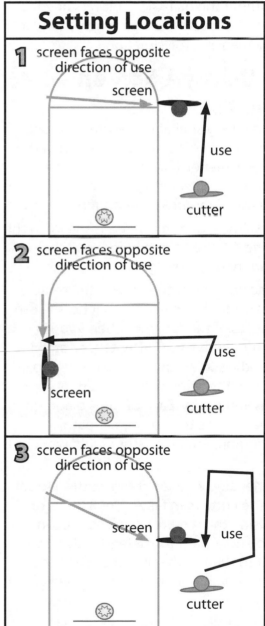

Setting Locations

1 screen faces opposite direction of use

screen
use
cutter

2 screen faces opposite direction of use

use
screen
cutter

3 screen faces opposite direction of use

screen
use
cutter

4. After setting up, remain frozen in this position. It is a violation or foul to move or lean into the defense.

5. The cutter fakes away in any direction, then jogs past the screen rubbing shoulders. *See step 2 in the diagram Setup/Motion Screen.* For location 1 the cutter jogs straight out.

6. Switch setup positions and repeat steps 1-5. *See step 3 in the diagram Setup/Motion Screen.*

7. Repeat directions 1-6 once more, so each player screens twice from the first position.

8. Repeat directions 1-7 from the other two locations.

Location 2

From the starting position the screener fakes then only runs a few steps to the mid-post area before setting the screen. Face across the lane. *See 2 in the diagram Setting Locations.*

The cutter fakes then takes a few steps out before cutting across the lane to use the screen.

Location 3

From the starting position the screener cuts across the lane to the left side and sets up facing away from the basket near the high post. *See 3 in the diagram Setting Locations.*

The cutter cuts out, running towards the left sideline to the top-of-the-key extended. Take a few steps to the right, then cut straight in to use the screen.

Key Points

1. The screen may not move or lean into the defense after it is set. It's the user's or cutter's job to rub off the defense.

2. The screener needs to put the forearms across the chest for protection. The elbows can not be used as part of the screen.

3. The screener usually faces the direction that the user cuts.

How To Practice

This lesson only needs to be practiced once or twice.

73 Using A Screen

Player's Corner

Parts	1	2
Type	ADV	ADV
Players	2	2
Assist	NO	NO
Ball	X	◯
Court	🏀	🏀
Effort	2	2
Time	5-10	5-15

Setup/Motion

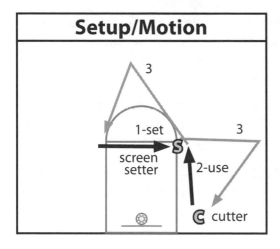

Briefs

In Part 1, each player learns how to use a screen.

In Part 2, players learn how to screen and roll.

Why Do This

Screens are used to free up players with the ball and even without the ball. Older players need to know how to effectively use a screen and how to handle the screen and roll situation.

Part 1 Using A Screen

Directions For Players

1. This lesson is very similar to the previous one except that we concentrate on the motion of the cutter, not the screener. If it's easier, the screener can just start in the screening position rather than run to it. *See the diagram Setup/Motion.*

2. Run each of the 4 different screens shown in the diagram *Using A Screen* twice before switching positions and then repeating.

3. For each screen, the cutter adjusts the route taken before using the screen, so that he/she can cut into the eyes of the screener. Then about 1 yard before the screen, the cutter takes a step inward, toward the screen, in order to better rub off the defender on the screen. Rub shoulders with the screen as you cut by. Each of the 4 diagrams in *Using A Screen* shows the best direct path, although other more indirect paths would work just as well.

4. The screener always fakes before cutting to set the screen. The cutter can fake several times on the way to using the screen. However, keep in mind that you may want the defender closer to you (the cutter) than farther when close to the screen, so that he/she can be better rubbed off on the screen.

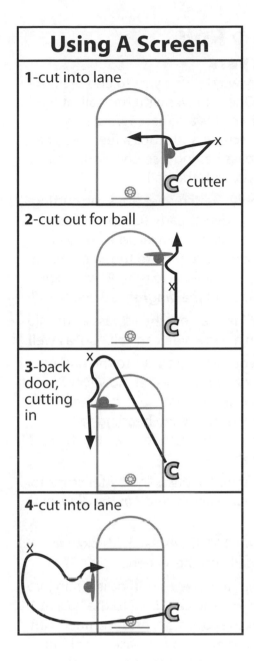

Using A Screen

1-cut into lane

2-cut out for ball

3-back door, cutting in

4-cut into lane

Screen 1

Starting from the right side high post, the screener cuts across the lane and sets up at mid-post on the left side. Face the sideline. Make sure your feet are not on the line. See *1 in the diagram Using A Screen.*

The cutter fakes, then cuts to a position to best use the screen as indicated by an *X* in each diagram. The cuts do not need to be fast. Jogging is fine.

About one yard before the screen take a step inward toward the screen. This makes it more difficult for a defender to slip through. Rub shoulders with the screen as you pass.

The screen may not move or even lean. Just set up to protect yourself, by placing the arms across the chest, from the collision with the defender.

Screen 2

The screener cuts to the left side to set up on the free-throw line facing the basket. *See 2 in the diagram Using A Screen.*

The cutter fakes, then runs right up the lane. Take an inward step about a yard before the screen. This screen can be used to free a player up for a pass, although there is no pass in this lesson.

Screen 3

The screener moves to set up on the right side of the free-throw line facing downcourt. This is called a back-door screen, used to rub off the defender of a player cutting to the basket. *See 3 in the diagram Using A Screen.*

The cutter cuts out past the top-of-the-key extended on the right side. For the back-door cut to be successful, the defender must be maneuvered into a position to be rubbed off when the cutter cuts inward.

Screen 4

The screener moves to set up at the mid-post, right side facing the sideline. This screen is used by a player cutting into the lane. *See 4 in the diagram Using A Screen.*

The cutter must run to the far sideline, then up court a few yards, before cutting across court into the lane.

Key Points

1. Cut to the screen from the best position to use it.

2. When about one yard from the screen, take a step inward in order to rub the defense off on the screen.

Screen & Roll

1 offense with ball

screen

1-3 feet

2 roll away from the ball to the basket

3 look for ball over left shoulder

Part 2 Screen & Roll
Directions For Players

Here are a few of the many ways for players to end up in the screen and roll situation. One, a player with the ball laterals to a close player and then sets a screen. Two, a player with the ball dribbles by a screen and stops a few feet away. Three, a cutter receives a pass behind a screen. Four, a player sets a screen near the player with the ball.

1. In the screen and roll, only the screener does the cutting. The lesson starts with the screen already set up 1-3 feet in front of a player with the ball. The player with the ball remains stationary and attempts to pass to the screener cutting to the basket. Hopefully a defensive miscue will allow the screener to be open. *See 1 in the diagram Screen & Roll.*

2. The player with the ball fakes an overhead pass as the signal for the screen to cut. In a game you can yell, "Go" as well.

3. The screener rolls or pivots around to cut to the basket. The screen can roll either way to the basket, however it's usually better to roll away from the ball, so the defense has more difficulty with the coverage. When heading to the basket keep the leading arm outstretched as a target. *See 2 in the diagram Screen & Roll.*

4. The passer hits the cutter with a pass. The cutter stops to take a 1-foot shot rather than a layup. *See 3 in the diagram Screen & Roll.*

5. Players switch roles. Repeat 10 times each. It's okay to move the position of the ball and the screen.

•The player with the ball has another option other than just passing to a rolling screen. He/she can drive to the basket using the screen to rub off the coverage. After contact with this defender, the screen rolls away to the basket looking for a pass. The driver can continue to drive to the basket or make a pass, usually a bounce pass, to the former screen rolling to the basket. Even though we did a drill like this in high school, I think it involves too many skills and is not as worthwhile as other basic drills.

Key Points

1. The roll is away from the defense and the ball.

2. The roller catches the pass, stops, and shoots a 1-foot shot.

How To Practice

Only older players need to work on Parts 1 and 2. Practice each lesson 2-5 times.

DEFENSE BASICS LESSONS

Defense is a dance that involves two types of steps: jump-steps and defensive runs. Slides, walks, and long steps don't work well because a defender's feet and body must be in position at every instant to sprint in any direction. These movements cause the feet to get out of position. And the offense only needs an instant to gain an advantage. Reaching with the arms instead of moving the feet, besides resulting in unnecessary fouls, allows the offense to do whatever he/she wants.

Defensive footwork is the key to defense, because proper footwork allows a defender to stay with the offense. A misstep or a lack of readiness allows the offense to gain the advantage.

Lesson 74, Defensive Position, covers the best body position for defense. Lesson 75, Jump-Steps, shows how to make small adjustments to correspond to the movement of the offense. Lesson 76, Defensive Runs, shows how to run from the defensive position. Lessons 77-79 present intense drills to work on proper defensive footwork.

74 Defensive Position

Setup

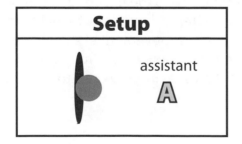

assistant

A

Briefs

Tap in place while maintaining the proper defensive position.

Why Do This

This lesson covers the defensive body position from which a player can readily sprint in any direction. This position is very similar to the dribbling position, so practicing one benefits the other.

Directions

1. Start in the half-down body position. This is a position where your knees are bent and you are ready to run. The feet are slightly more than shoulder-width apart. The back should be straight, not bent. Weight should be on the balls of the feet. An assistant needs to watch and correct your stance. *See the diagram Defensive Positions.*

2. Defense is a race and a dance. For the race you need to be ready to start running in any direction. For the dance you need to know the steps.

3. Go to the full-down position. Go down as far as possible.

4. On the assistant's cue move between the full-down to the half-down to the up position for 1-2 minutes. Make sure to keep the back straight and knees bent in the half-down position. *See the diagram Half-Down Position.*

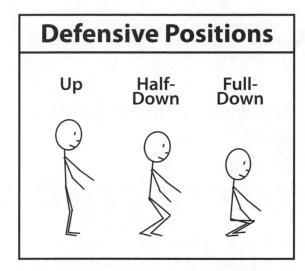

Defensive Positions

Up	Half-Down	Full-Down

Half-Down Position

Right	Wrong

straight-back-bent
down-behind-up
bent-legs-straight

Forcing Positions

starting position	step or pivot →	to forcing position
step 1	2	3 force left
step 1	2	3 force right

5. In the half-down position start tapping on the balls of the feet. This is like a football drill. Stay in the half-down position with knees bent and back straight. Continue tapping for 20-60 seconds.

6. Turn the body 45 degrees to the right side by taking a step forward with the left foot or pivoting an eighth of a turn, while maintaining defensive position. This is the force left position. *See the diagram Forcing Positions*.

7. Turn the body back to the starting position. Now turn partially to the left. This is the force right position.

8. Jump from force right to force left 10 times on a cue from the assistant. Stay in defensive position. The forcing position will be explained in Lesson 80. Jumping from one position to another requires a jump-step.

9. Set up in the force left position and start tapping. Continue tapping for one minute, changing the forcing direction on cue every 2-10 seconds.

Key Points

1. Bend the knees, not the back.

2. Keep the back straight.

3. Weight is on the balls of the feet.

4. Maintain defensive position when jumping

5. The assistant must correct problems.

How To Practice

Practice this 2-10 times.

75 Jump-Steps

Player's Corner

Parts	1
Type	CORE
Players	1
Assist	YES
Ball	X
Court	X
Effort	2
Time	5-10

Briefs

Jump-step while maintaining defensive position.

Why Do This

A jump-step is a short quick jump in one direction while staying in defensive position ready to run. You use jump-steps all the time without knowing it. The advantage of a jump-step over sliding is that you are always in a position to run or change direction. With a slide you are at a disadvantage when the feet are either too far apart or too close together because you must reposition your feet before running. ***See the diagram Jump-Steps vs. Sliding.***

This lesson introduces the jump-step, which all players normally use in tight defensive situations. However, defenders need to regularly use jump-steps. If you have great difficulty with the jump-steps in this lesson, skip to Lesson 77 before returning.

Directions

1. Start in the force-left defensive position with feet shoulder widtch apart and keep the feet separated by this distance during the lesson. ***See the diagrams Setup and Possible Jump Directions.***

2. Moving left and right and forcing left and right are different directions. Directions like "left, left, right" means to move left or right in whatever position you are in. "Force left" or "force right" means to change forcing position. See Lesson 80 for more information on forcing.

Jump-Steps vs. Sliding

feet stay shoulder-width apart
Jump-Steps: always in best position to run

feet too far   feet too close
Sliding: rarely in best position to run

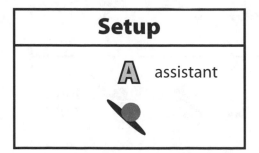

Setup

A assistant

DEFENSE BASICS: LESSONS 74-79

Possible Jump Directions

Forcing Left

assistant **A**

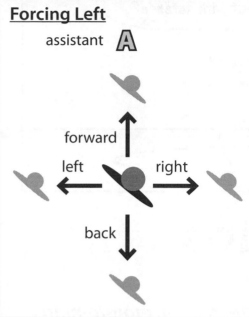

forward

left right

back

Forcing Right

assistant **A**

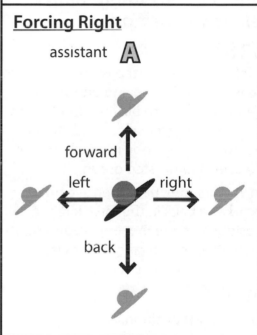

forward

left right

back

3. An assistant points, no talking, in the direction that you jump. You don't need to jump high or far.

4. Sample directions for the assistant: left, left, left, right, left, left, right, right, right, left, left, left, right, right, left, left, right, right, right, and so on for a minute or two.

5. Repeat steps 2 & 3 from the force right position for a minute or two.

6. Return to the force left position. Now jump forward and back instead of left and right for 1-2 minutes.

7. Repeat from the force right position.

8. Once you can do the basic jumps, repeat, adding tapping between directions. Tap during the entire lesson while jumping left, right, back and forward in either the force left or force right position. Continue for 1-5 minutes. This is the best part of the lesson if a player can do it.

9. Sample directions: <u>force left</u>, right, right, right, forward, forward, left, back, back, back, left, right, left, left, <u>force right</u>, left, left, right, forward, left, back, right, and so on. As players become more proficient, switch forcing directions on a more regular basis.

Key Points

1. Keep the back straight and knees bent.

2. Keep weight on the balls of the feet.

3. Steps 8 & 9 are the most important part of the lesson.

4. Beside giving directions, the assistant must correct problems.

How To Practice

Repeat this lesson 2-5 times. If a player has difficulty skip to Lesson 77, Front, before returning.

76 Defensive Runs

Player's Corner	
Parts	1
Type	CORE
Players	1
Assist	YES
Ball	X
Court	X
Effort	1-3
Time	5-20

Setup

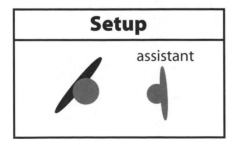

assistant

Brief
Run two steps while maintaining proper defensive position.

Why Do This
The second defensive dance step is the defensive run. Use defensive runs for moving one step or more on defense. One key to playing good defensive is to stay in defensive position ready to run. Another key is to correctly choose which type of dance step to use– a jump-step or run.

In this lesson you first practice defensive runs moving forward and back in the force left and force right positions before moving left and right. Moving in each direction, forcing either way is very important. Don't skip any steps.

Directions
1. Start in the force left position.

2. Run two steps in the direction that the assistant points, then set up in the force left position again. It's okay to go slow at first. Initially it's okay to run 4 steps. *See the diagram Possible Run Directions.*

3. Never run backwards. Always turn the body in the direction that you need to run before running. After running turn the body back to the original position. *The T's in the diagram Possible Run Directions* indicate that a player needs to turn before running and then back again after the run.

Possible Run Directions

Forcing Left

leader $\llcorner$

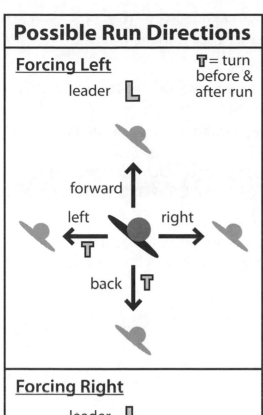

$\top$ = turn before & after run

forward

left   right

back

Forcing Right

leader $\llcorner$

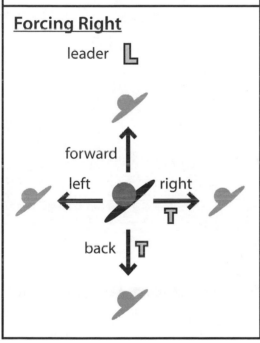

forward

left   right

back

4. As indicated in the diagram, four moves involve turns before and after the run: running left or back in the force left position; running right or back in the force right position. Use jump-steps for these turns. It takes 10-20 minutes to get your steps together.

5. The assistant just points for forward, backward, left or right movement. Verbally give the "force left" and "force right" instructions. Work on each set for 2-5 minutes. Gradually increase the speed of the lesson as players get their steps together.

6. Run forward and back forcing left.

Sample instructions: forward, forward, back, back, back, back, forward, forward, back, forward, back, back, forward, forward, etc.

7. Run forward and back, forcing right. Same sample instructions in step 6.

8. Once a player has the idea, tap dance between runs for the entire duration of the lesson. Tap the feet up and down when not running. Work on each step below for 1-4 minutes.

9. Run forward and back, forcing left and right.

Sample instructions: force left, forward, back, back, forward, force right, back, back, forward, forward, back, forward, back, force left, back, forward, forward, etc.

10. Run left and right, forcing left.

Sample instructions: left, left, right, right, right, left, right, left, left, right, right, right, etc.

11. Run left and right, forcing right. Use the sample instructions from step 10.

12. Run left and right, forcing left and right.

Sample instructions: force left, left, left, right, left, right, right, force right, left, left, right, force left, left, left, right, left, force right, etc.

13. Run left, right, forward, and back, forcing left and right. Make sure to tap dance between runs.

Sample instructions: force left, right, left, back, forward, back, right, force right, right, right, left, left, back, forward, back, back, right, left, etc.

14. Eventually you want to perform an all-out sprint for two steps.

15. The last part of this lesson, step 13, is the most important part. Repeat this many times.

Key Points

1. Take your time to get the steps together. Start as slow as needed.

2. Eventually you want to sprint all out for 2 steps in each direction.

3. Make sure to practice forcing left and right while moving left, right, forwards, and backwards.

How To Practice

Practice this as many times as needed till you can sprint full speed in each direction forcing either left or right.

77 Front

Player's Corner

Parts	1
Type	CORE
Players	2
Assist	YES
Ball	X
Court	🏀
Effort	2-3
Time	5

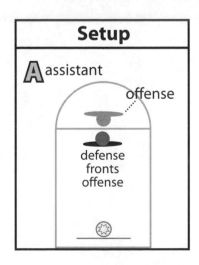

Setup

A assistant

offense

defense
fronts
offense

Briefs
The defense fronts an offensive player attempting to run into the lane area.

Why Do This
The defensive skill of staying in front, belly-to-belly, with the offense is called fronting. This lesson forces players to use jump-steps to stay in front of an offensive player without any additional instruction or experience. If you have difficulty with Lesson 75, Jump-Steps, do this first before trying it again. Defensive runs are also used in this lesson.

Directions

1. The offense sets up just outside the free-throw line facing the basket. The defense sets up facing the offense just inside the lane. *See the diagram Setup.*

2. The offense wants to get inside the lane and regularly charges into the lane. The defense keeps the offense out. *See the diagram Motion.*

3. The assistant watches to make sure players do things correctly without injury.

4. As the offense moves around the lane, the defense stays belly-to-belly with arms up ready to push the offense out. When the offense charges into the lane push the shoulders to keep him/her out. Don't push the stomach or face of the of-

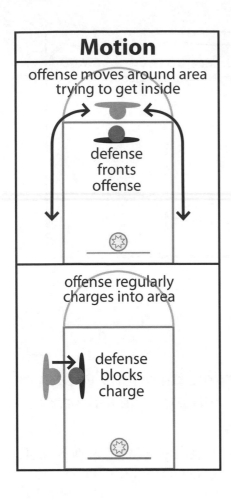

Motion

offense moves around area trying to get inside

defense fronts offense

offense regularly charges into area

defense blocks charge

fense. Don't push or grab from the side.

5. The offense should cooperate at first. Go half speed so the defense can get some practice. When the defense pushes your shoulders on an attempt to enter the lane area, don't continue pushing through the defense. Just take a step back and continue trying to enter the lane area.

6. The defense times the lesson, counting out loud, for 15-20 seconds before offense and defense switch.

7. The offense increases speed as the defense improves.

8. Repeat 3-5 times.

Key Points

1. Without any instruction, defenders will use jump-steps in this lesson.

2. This may be a better introduction to jump-steps than Lesson 75.

3. Make sure defenders push the shoulders of offense, not the face or stomach.

4. The offense moves fast enough to give the defense practice, but not so fast they he/she gets by.

How To Practice

Repeat this 1-3 times.

78 Go After Ball

Player's Corner

Parts	1	2
Type	CORE	CORE
Players	2	2
Assist	YES	YES
Ball	◯	◯
Court	X	X
Effort	3	3
Time	5	5

Setup/Motion Parts 1-2

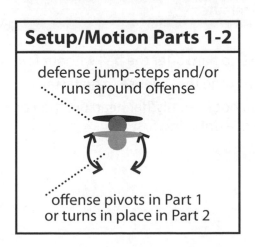

defense jump-steps and/or runs around offense

offense pivots in Part 1 or turns in place in Part 2

Brief
In Part 1, a defender goes after the ball of a pivoter.

In Part 2, a defender goes after the ball of a dribbler who only turns away.

Why Do This
Inexperienced defensive players often have the tendency to reach for the ball rather than move the feet. Reaching usually ends up with a foul call. This lesson forces a player to move their feet instead of reaching. This also teaches aggressive players not to foul. An assistant needs to urge the defense to go faster.

On the offensive side, this is a great drill for pivoting and for protecting the ball while dribbling.

Part 1 Go After Pivoter
Directions
1. The defense starts anywhere next to a pivoter who has a ball. *See the diagram Setup/Motion Parts 1-2.* The diagram shows the defense behind.

2. The pivoter must continue to pivot around both forward and back for 15 seconds. The pivoter times by counting out loud. Move the ball close to and then far from the body, to the left and to the right, up and down as well.

3. The defense goes after the ball, not by reaching, but by moving the feet. The defense literally runs around the pivoter for the ball. The defense tries to get in front of the pivoter.

4. The assistant must urge the defender to go all out. Otherwise, the defender will not make the required effort.

5. The offense just yells, "foul," on any touch. Do not stop for fouls, however, the defense stays on defense if there is a foul.

6. After 15 seconds, switch roles.

7. Continue for 2-5 minutes

Key Points

1. Defenders must go after the ball without fouling.

2. The assistant must urge the defense to go faster.

How To Practice

This needs to be repeated 2-5 times.

Part 2 Go After Dribbler
Directions

1. This is the same as the previous lesson except the offense is dribbling rather than pivoting.

2. The dribbler must dribble in place, not around the gym. You can turn around or swivel around, but no moving from place to place. Make sure to protect the ball. Regularly switch dribbling hands. Look up at the defense. *See the diagram Setup/Motion Parts 1-2.*

3. The defense must go after the ball for 15-20 seconds. No reaching allowed. Then switch roles unless there is a foul.

4. The assistant urges the defense to go faster.

5. Continue for 2-5 minutes.

Key Points

1. The defense must go hard after the ball without fouling.

2. The assistant must urge the defense to go faster.

3. If the dribbler can not keep his/her head up, then do not do this lesson. Practice dribbling first.

How To Practice

Repeat 2-5 times.

79 Mirror Drill

Player's Corner

Parts	1
Type	OPT
Players	2
Assist	NO
Ball	X
Court	X
Effort	2-3
Time	3

Setup

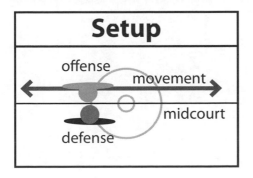

Brief

One player mirrors the movements of another player.

Why Do This

This is a move feet and hands drill that players usually enjoy. The leader (offense) needs to go slow enough so the follower (defense) can get practice.

Directions

1. Players set up facing each other in defensive position on either side of a line. Make sure to mark each end of the line so players know the range of motion allowed. The line can be 5 to 20 yards long. *See the diagram Setup.*

2. The leader moves back and forth along one side of the line. Initially go at half speed. If you move too fast the follower will not get practice. You can also move your arms, however remain facing the line and the other player at all times.

3. The defense must mirror all body, foot, and arm movements of the offense. It's okay if kids do silly things as long as they are moving at the right speed.

4. The offense counts to 10 while moving.

5. Repeat switching roles. Continue for 2-3 minutes. Speed up as the follower improves.

Key Points

1. The offense initially goes at half speed.

2. The offense must face the line or the other player during the drill.

How To Practice

This only needs to be done once or twice.

ON-BALL DEFENSE LESSONS

80 Forcing
81 Walk/Run Force
82 3-Yard Force

On-ball defense is how you cover a player with the ball. Each lesson is also helpful for off-ball defense because the same type of footwork is used. Lesson 80, Forcing, introduces the method used to cover the player with the ball. In Lesson 81, Walk/Run Force, a player works on forcing a moving player. In Lesson 82, 3-Yard Force, a player stays with an opponent going full speed.

80 Forcing

Player's Corner

Parts	1
Type	CORE
Players	1
Assist	YES
Ball	X
Court	X
Effort	1-2
Time	5-20

Briefs

Set up in the defensive forcing position at varying distances from the offense.

Why Do This

Forcing is the defensive technique used to cover the player with the ball. The idea is to force a player to go in a direction that he/she does not want to go. Righties like to dribble right, so the defense usually forces left. Lefties like to dribble left, so the defense usually forces right. With younger players, using the forcing technique can even stop a team from dribbling. Because of the footwork involved, forcing lessons help with all other defensive techniques including overplaying, fronting, and trapping.

Directions

1. The defense sets up one foot from a chair or an offensive player. The offense is stationary in this lesson. Do not move an inch. *See the diagram Forcing Setup.* An assistant watches and corrects the defense.

2. The defense sets up in defensive position, left foot forward, 1 foot away from the offense. The body is partially turned to the side at a 45-degree angle.

Forcing Setup

Defense Forcing Left

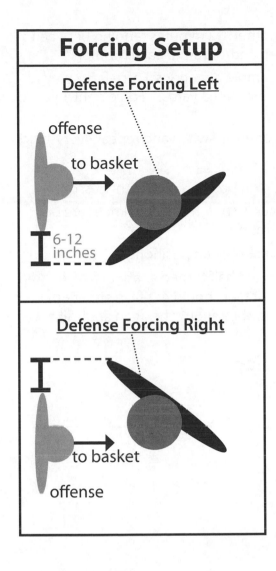

offense

to basket

6-12 inches

Defense Forcing Right

to basket

offense

Motion Forcing

Set up forcing left or right
1 foot to 3 yards away

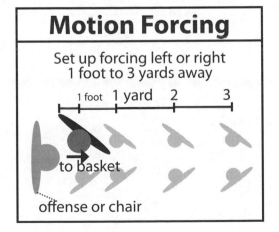

1 foot   1 yard   2   3

to basket

offense or chair

---

3. Move so that your left foot is 6-12 inches to the left of the offense. You are on the right side of the offense. *See the first part of the diagram Forcing Setup (Defense Forcing Left).*

4. The offensive player, if any, raises the right hand. If the offense goes right, they bump into you. If they go left, it is clear sailing. This is the force left position. Usually you force righties this way.

5. Setting up 6-12 inches to the side is overdoing it. In an actual game situation you may only be inches to one side.

•Do not work on hand positions yet for several reasons: **1)** the hand positions distract from the more important foot movement; **2)** hand positions are easy to teach once players have a clue how to play defense.

•The front arm, the one closest to the offense, is used for blocking the pass or shot. It is up, out, and forward. The back arm, the arm farther from the offense, is lower to the ground to defend against the dribble.

6. Now set up in the force right position with the right foot 6-12 inches to the right of the offense. The body is partially turned sideways. *See the second part of the diagram Forcing Setup (Defense Forcing Right).*

7. Jump back to the force left position, then force right again, then force left. An assistant should check your position before jumping to the next position.

8. For this part involving judging distance, start in the force left position 1 yard away from the defense. Judging distance is a critical skill because there is always an optimal distance to stay away from a defender. Covering either too close or too far will cause a problem. *See the diagram Motion Forcing.*

In general, the farther from the basket, the further you stay away from the defense. Close to the basket the defense always stays close to the offense. The coverage distance also varies with your ability to cover a particular defender. If you are faster, then you can stay closer. If you are slower, then you must play further off.

9. The assistant gives these sample directions for movement: move 2 yards away, three yards away, force right, two yards...One yard...One foot...

10. Continue until the player can accurately judge the distance.

11. Continue for another 1-2 minutes tapping between positions. Jump-step and/or run to each position.

12. Here are some sample directions: Force left 2 yards... Force right 1 foot...Force left 3 yards. ...Force right 1 yard... Force left 2 yards.

13. If a player is on offense, switch and repeat everything.

Key Points

1. Stay in the half-down position during this lesson.

2. Make sure the back is straight and the knees are bent, not the other way around.

3. Jump-step and run between positions.

4. You body and feet are half turned at about a 45 degree angle. On a court your feet should not face either down-court or the sidelines. They should be at an angle like your body.

How To Practice

Practice this 2-5 times.

81 Walk/Run Force

Player's Corner

Parts	1
Type	CORE
Players	2
Assist	NO
Ball	X
Court	X
Effort	2
Time	5-15

Setup

set up forcing left
stay 3 yards away

3 yards

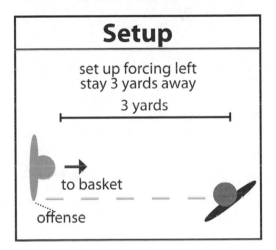

to basket

offense

Briefs

The defense maintains a constant distance from a moving offensive player.

Why Do This

A key to defending a player with the ball is to stay at a constant distance away. As the offense moves closer to the basket, this distance decreases. Three yards is used for most lessons, because at this distance the defense can easily recover from a mistake. Players readily shorten this distance when tighter coverage is called for.

The offense in these lessons does not have a ball, which makes it much easier to move. So defenders must work that much harder. Covering an actual dribbler will be easy after these lessons. Going full speed in Lesson 82 is the goal.

Directions

1. The defense sets up 3 yards from the offense, forcing left. We always practice forcing left first because most players are right handed. You want to make righties go to the left. Be ready to tap dance and maintain this 3-yard distance. *See the diagram Setup.*

2. The offense slowly walks forward and back for about 20-40 seconds. Faking a step forward or back is okay, but just walk. Make sure to walk in a straight line to make the lesson easier.

3. The defense tap dances and continues to maintain the 3-yard distance by jump-stepping. Take small quick jump-steps; do not stop tap dancing. Do not slide the feet.

4. The offense tells the defense if they are too close or too far. Yell "Too close" or "Too far" to defensive players not maintaining the distance.

5. After 1-3 minutes, offense and defense switch. Repeat.

6. Now repeat the entire lesson, steps 2-5, forcing right.

7. When players can perform this adequately, repeat steps 1-6 with the offense slowly jogging.

Key Points

1. The defense stays in defensive position with back up, knees bent.

2. Maintain the 3-yard distance by jump-stepping, no sliding the feet.

3. The offense must tell the defense when the 3-yard distance is not maintained.

How To Practice

Repeat this 5-15 times. Each time the offense should be able to move faster. It's okay for the offense to go slower if the defense cannot maintain the 3-yard distance.

82 3-Yard Force

Brief

The defense maintains the 3-yard distance on a player moving full-speed, full-court.

Why Do This

This is the goal of the defensive movement lessons. It is also a diagnostic tool which will probably tell you that you need a lot more work on defensive movement.

Directions

1. The offense and defense start at midcourt. The offense can run anywhere on the court: left, right, up, and back as well. Go full steam. Faking allowed. *See the diagram Setup.*

2. The defense sets up 3 yards away, forcing left; maintain this distance and relative position for the 15-second lesson.

• *See the diagram Maintain Position,* which shows a player who is maintaining a relative, 3-yard-distanced position at different locations on the court.

3. An assistant watches from the sidelines. Tell the defender if he/she is not maintaining the 3-yard distance forcing to the left.

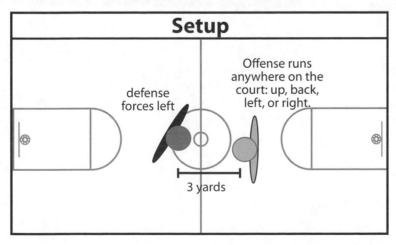

Setup

defense forces left

Offense runs anywhere on the court: up, back, left, or right.

3 yards

Maintain Position

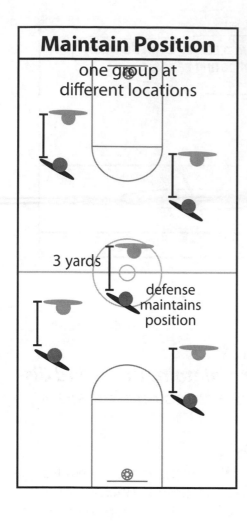

one group at different locations

3 yards

defense maintains position

4. The assistant times the lesson for 15-20 seconds.

5. Offense and defense switch roles and repeat.

6. Repeat steps 1-5 forcing right.

7. Most players will need a lot more work on previous lessons before they can adequately do this lesson. Not performing this lesson correctly should encourage players to work harder on previous lessons. Clearly demonstrating the need for more basic skills is usually a good strategy.

8. The assistant should attempt to notice the actual step where the offense loses the defense. Usually a player will jump-step instead of run or vice versa.

Key Points

1. As the offense moves, the defense maintains the 3-yard distance and the same relative position.

2. The assistant must tell the defense when he/she is too close, too far, too much left or right.

3. Most likely you will need to go back to previous lessons after you try this one.

How To Practice

This lesson is a test of a player's ability to play defense. If a player can stay with an offensive player who does not need to dribble, staying with a dribbler will be easy. A player can make a great effort, but rarely does a player adequately do this.

OFF-BALL DEFENSE LESSONS

See **About Off-Ball Defense** on the next page for more information about this section. Lesson 83, Overplay Basics, covers the method used for off-ball coverage. In Lesson 84, Move & Overplay, the defense covers a moving opponent. In Lesson 85, Step Around, a defender learns how to switch the side of coverage. In Lesson 86, Overplay Low Post, a defender covers a moving opponent in the post area. In Lesson 87, No-See Defense, the defense learns what to do when his/her coverage is lost. In Lesson 88, Overplay Cutter, the defense covers an opponent cutting across the lane.

About Off-Ball Defense

The quality of off-ball defense determines the effectiveness of a team's defense. When playing one-on-one, the offense usually wins. However, with four off-ball players helping-out with on-ball coverage, an offense can be shut down. For this same reason, off-ball defense is more difficult than on-ball defense. All defenders must stay with their offensive coverage, keep their eyes on the ball—which is elsewhere—and help-out if needed. There are also many off-ball coverage situations like covering a cutter in the lane or covering a player in the low post.

Overplaying is the defensive technique used to cover off-ball, offensive players. Since four out of five defensive players are off-the-ball at any time, overplaying is one of the most important defensive techniques to learn. Overplaying prevents the offense from catching a pass where they want—usually close to the basket. Properly overplaying also prevents cuts into the low post, or any other area. Because boxing out is easy from the overplay position, properly overplaying can help prevent offensive rebounds. As a team skill, overplaying enables ball-side help.

Overplaying is quite difficult because the defender must watch the ball while staying in contact with his/her coverage. When an overplayer takes his/her eyes off the ball, team defense suffers. These lessons stress the skill of keeping the eyes on the ball, so a defender can help out. Helping-out is a team skill not covered in these lessons. However, if an off-ball defender is capable of keeping his/her eyes on the ball, the next step, moving to help-out is easy. See **The Basketball Coach's Bible** for information on helping out and other team skills.

83 Overplay Basics

Player's Corner

Parts	1
Type	CORE
Players	1
Assist	YES
Ball	○
Court	🏀
Effort	1-2
Time	10-20

Briefs
One defender sets up in the overplay position on a stationary offensive player.

Why Do This
Overplaying prevents an offensive player from catching a pass. This lesson shows how to align the body to overplay a stationary off-ball offensive player.

Directions
1. The offense does not move an inch in this lesson, so a chair or stationary object can be used for the offense.

2. The defense sets up next to the offense aligned sideways to the ball. *See the diagrams Basic Overplay and Overplay Setup Steps 1-6.*

3. For proper body alignment, extend your arms straight out to the side. Now turn your body sideways so that one arm points to the ball. This gives you the proper alignment.

4. Move to the half-down position about 1 foot from the offense.

Basic Overplay

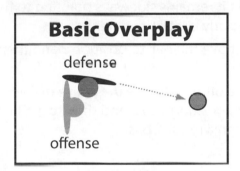

defense

offense

Overplay Setup

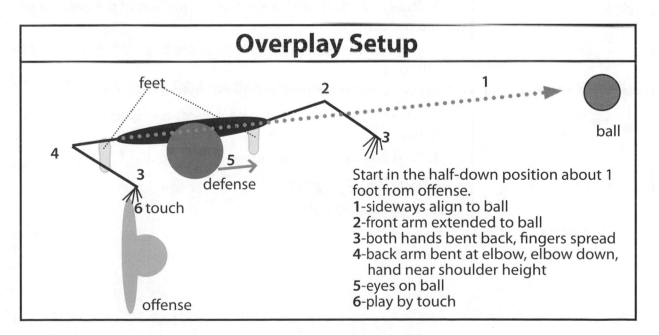

feet

defense

offense

ball

Start in the half-down position about 1 foot from offense.
1-sideways align to ball
2-front arm extended to ball
3-both hands bent back, fingers spread
4-back arm bent at elbow, elbow down, hand near shoulder height
5-eyes on ball
6-play by touch

5. The front foot, the foot closer to the ball, is 6-12 inches in front of the offense. The back foot is just behind the offense. The weight is on the front foot, because you are leaning forward to prevent the offense from receiving a pass.

6. Extend the front arm to the ball. Bend the hand back 90 degrees with fingers spread and extended. The hand is partially in front of the offense to deny the ball to the offense.

7. The back arm is bent in close and the elbow extended backward. The palm of the hand faces the defender, fingers spread apart. This hand and forearm are used to touch the offense.

8. Do not set up too close to the offense. If so, they can box you out of the play. Try to stay at least 1 foot away.

9. Keep the eyes on the ball. Play by touch.

10. The assistant needs to check the position of the defense. If okay, continue.

11. Start with the defense standing sideways next to the offense. *See the start ball position (1) in the diagram Overplay Right Side.*

12. As the assistant slowly moves the ball towards position *2*, reposition your body so that it remains sideways pointing to the ball. The assistant must regularly check the defense.

13. From position *2* slowly move the ball to position *3* and then back to *1*.

14. Now play defense on the other side. *See the diagram Overplay Left Side.* Move the ball from position *1* to *2* and then to *3*. Check the position of the defense on a regular basis.

Key Points

1. The assistant must check the body position of the defense on a regular basis.

2. The defender lines up sideways to the ball 1-2 feet ahead of the offense.

3. One arm is outstretched forward to block the pass.

4. The other arm is extended backwards barely touching the offense.

5. The defense keeps his/her eyes on the ball.

How To Practice

Repeat this only once.

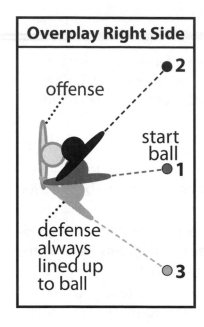

Overplay Right Side

offense

start ball

defense always lined up to ball

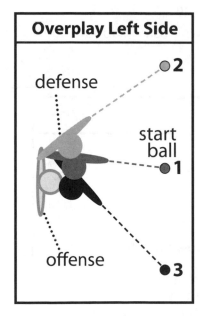

Overplay Left Side

defense

start ball

offense

84 Move & Overplay

Player's Corner

Parts	1	2
Type	CORE	CORE
Players	2	2
Assist	YES	YES
Ball	X	X
Court	X	X
Effort	2	2
Time	5 -15	5-15

Brief
In Part 1, the defense moves forward and backwards to overplay.

In Part 2, the defense moves left and right to overplay.

Why Do This
Overplaying is quite difficult because the defender must watch the ball while staying in contact with his/her coverage. When an overplayer takes his/her eyes off the ball, team defense suffers. This lesson stresses the skills of keeping the eyes on the ball and moving in the overplay position.

Part 1 Overplay Back & Forth
Directions
1. The offense sets up sideways to the ball. Place a ball, or another object to look at, 5 yards away. *See the diagram Setup/Motion Part 1A.*

2. The defense overplays, also lining up sideways to the ball.

3. Keep the back arm in contact with the offense to detect motion. Keep your eyes on the ball at all times.

4. When the offense starts walking forward and

Setup/Motion Part 1A

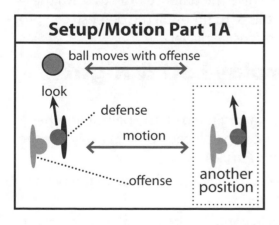

Stationary Ball

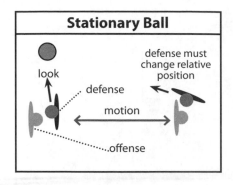

Setup/Motion Part 1B

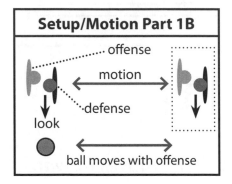

back, stay in this same relative position by jump-stepping forward and backward. Pretend that as the offense moves forward and back, the ball also moves forward and back. Otherwise, the defense (and offense) would need to continually change body position to line up to the ball. *See the diagram Stationary Ball.*

5. The offense can fake, but only slowly walks forward and backwards for 1-3 minutes. Correct the defense if he/she is not properly overplaying.

6. After 1 minute the defense tap dances for the entire lesson.

7. Switch roles and repeat steps 1-6.

8. Move the ball to the other side of the offense. The defense sets up on the right side of the offense looking in the other direction. *See the diagram Setup/Motion Part 1B.*

9. Repeat steps 1-7 making sure to tap dance all the time.

10. As the defense improves, the offense moves faster.

Key Points

1. The offense slowly walks up and back in one direction. No sideways motion.

2. Increase speed only when the defense improves.

3. Tell the defense when they are not properly overplaying or moving. Slow down to a speed where the defense can do it right.

4. The defense jump-steps forward and backward.

5. Play the offense by touch with the back hand and only look in the direction of the ball.

6. After the first minute the defense tap dances for the rest of the lesson.

How To Practice

This is very difficult, so give the defense time to learn the movements. Repeat this 3-10 times till the defense can properly cover a jogging offensive player.

Part 2 Overplay Left & Right
Directions

1. The offense sets up facing the ball. The ball, or another object in lieu of a ball, can be placed 10 yards away *See the diagram Setup/Motion Part 2A.*

2. The defense overplays, lining up sideways to the ball on the right side of the offense.

3. Keep the back arm in contact with the offense to detect

Setup/Motion Part 2A

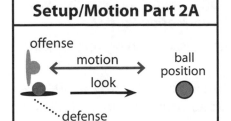

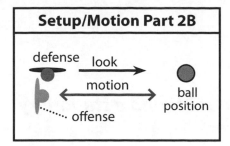

Setup/Motion Part 2B

defense   look →

motion ←→

ball position

offense

motion. Keep your eyes on the ball at all times.

4. When the offense starts walking forward and back, stay in this same relative position by jump-stepping left and right.

5. The offense can fake, but only walks forward and backwards for 1-3 minutes. Correct the defense if he/she is not properly overplaying.

6. The defense tap dances for the entire lesson.

7. Switch roles and repeat steps 1-6.

8. The defense now sets up on the left side of the offense turning the head left to see the ball. *See the diagram Setup/ Motion Part 2B.*

9. Repeat steps 1-7.

10. As the defense improves, the offense moves faster.

Key Points

1. The offense slowly walks only up and back in one direction. No sideways motion.

2. Increase speed only when the defense improves.

3. Tell the defense when they are not properly overplaying or moving. Slow down to a speed where the defense can do it right.

4. The defense jump-steps left and right.

5. Play the offense by touch with the back hand and only look in the direction of the ball.

6. The defense tap dances for the entire lesson.

How To Practice

Give the defense time to learn these movements. This is very difficult. Repeat this 3-10 times till the defense can properly cover a jogging offensive player.

85 Step Around

Player's Corner

Parts	1
Type	CORE
Players	2
Assist	YES
Ball	X
Court	🏀
Effort	2
Time	10-20

Setup

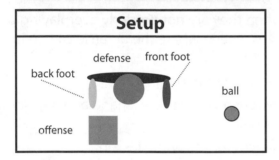

back foot · defense · front foot
ball
offense

Front Step-Around	**Back Step-Around**
a. 1st Step- Back Foot	**a.** 1st Step- Front Foot
b. Move In Front	**b.** Body Twisted Forward
c. 2nd Step- Front Foot	**c.** 2nd Step- Back Foot
d. New Position	**d.** New Position

Brief

A defender steps around a stationary low-post player.

Why Do This

When overplaying a post player and in other situations, the defense may need to quickly step around the offense to play defense on the other side. This lesson teaches a 2-step front route to the other side of the offense and also a 2-step back route, stepping behind the offense. Further from the basket it's usually better to step around behind. When covering a player close to the basket or when pressing, it is often better to step around via the front. In either case, it is important to step around quickly without taking extra steps, so the offense does not gain an advantage. *The diagram Why Step Around shows the need for this move.*

Directions

1. If a court is available use the setup in the diagram *Why Step-Around?* Otherwise setup anywhere. Since the offense does not move, a chair can be used for the offense. The defense sets up overplaying to the ball. *See the diagram Setup.*

2. There are two ways for a defender to step around the offense: a front route and a back route. First we will go in front. *See the diagram Front Step-Around.*

3. Bring the back foot forward across the body of the offense. (*a in diagram Front Step-Around*) Bring the back arm up high to prevent a lob pass. Contact the offense with the other arm. Make solid contact. Freeze in this position. (*b in the diagram*)

4. The eyes should be on the ball. Stay in touch with the offense with one arm.

5. Bring the other foot across by pivoting backwards on the forward foot to set up on the other side. Now you are overplaying from the other

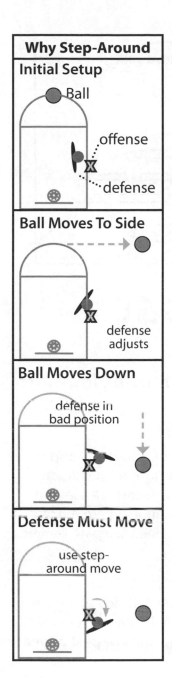

Why Step-Around

Initial Setup

Ball

offense

X

defense

Ball Moves To Side

defense adjusts

Ball Moves Down

defense in bad position

X

Defense Must Move

use step-around move

X

side. Hold this position. (*c and d in the diagram*)

6. Now we go back following the same directions. Bring the back foot forward across the body of the offense and back hand up high to prevent a pass. Contact the offense solidly with the other arm. Keep your eyes on the ball. Hold this position for a few seconds.

7. Bring the other foot to the other side of the offense by pivoting backwards on the forward foot.

8. Make sure you watch the ball. Do not turn your back to the ball at any time.

9. Repeat this 10-20 times till it is a smooth 2-step move with proper feet and arm movement.

10. Here are directions for the back step-around move staring from the overplay position. *See the diagram Back Step-Around.*

11. Take a long step with the front foot to the other side of the offense. This is a very awkward position. Twist your body forward so you can see the ball. (*a and b in the diagram Back Step Around*)

12. Quickly take a second step around, pivoting forward to the other side of the offensive player. (*c and d in the diagram Back Step Around*)

13. Go back to the other side via the back following the same directions.

14. Repeat 10-20 times.

15. Now start tap dancing and do the back move 4 times in a row, up and back twice.

16. Continue tap dancing and do the front move 4 times in a row, up and back twice.

17. Now use the front and back moves to completely step-around the defense twice moving in the same direction. Four moves are involved: front; back; front; back. Repeat the 4 moves going in the other direction.

18. If an assistant is available follow his/her directions from the overplay position, tap dancing between moves. Sample directions are: front, back, back, front, front, front, back, front, back, etc, until you can do this without problems.

Key Points

1. The front move involves arm movement and foot movement

2. Keep your eyes on the ball at all times during this lesson.

3. Both moves are two-step moves. Use only 2 steps.

4. Tap dance between moves.

How To Practice

Practice this 2-5 times or till you can do it smoothly without thinking.

86 Overplay Low Post

Player's Corner

Parts	1
Type	CORE
Players	2
Assist	YES
Ball	◯
Court	🏀
Effort	2-3
Time	10-25

Brief
A defender covers a moving low-post player.

Why Do This
Overplaying in the low post is especially important because the offense is close to the basket. Mistakes here lead to an easy score. This lesson covers the very difficult situation where the low post player cuts across the lane via a path behind the backboard.

Directions
1. An assistant sets up on the left side as a passer. An offensive player starts in the low post left side. The lone defender overplays the low post player. *See the diagram Setup.*

2. The low post player initially tries to get into lane by going in front of, or behind the defense. Slowly move up and back on the side of the lane. *See the diagram Motion.*

3. The defense sets up to overplay. Prevent a pass into the low-post area; make the offense come out for a pass. Prevent the offense from moving into the lane by jump-stepping to the spot first. When the offense tries to step into the lane, they should bang into you.

4. Play by touch. Keep your eye on the ball.

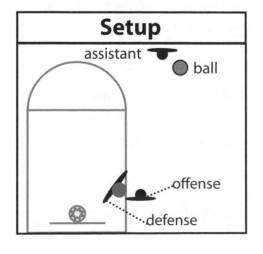

Setup

assistant · ball

offense

defense

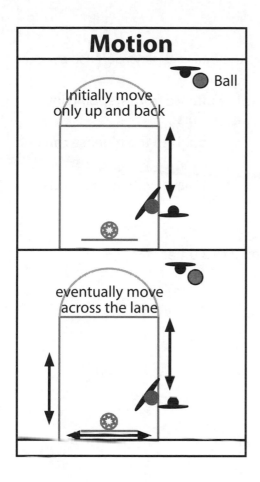

Motion

Initially move only up and back

Ball

eventually move across the lane

5. The passer, the assistant, attempts to pass to the low post. Use an overhead pass. It's okay to pass to the high post if no inside pass is available. After a successful pass, the catcher just passes the ball back and continues the lesson.

6. Continue for 10 seconds. The passer can count, then offense and defense switch positions.

7. Repeat steps 1-6 two to five times.

8. Repeat steps 1-7 setting up on the right side of the lane.

9. In the next part of the lesson, the offense crosses over to the other side of the lane. *See the diagram Motion.* Fake away from the lane, coordinate a fake-response pass with passer, then move toward the endline, behind the defense. Cut behind the basket to the other side.

10. The defense plays the cutter by touch. *See 1 & 2 in the diagram Overplaying Across The Lane.* As the offense cuts across the lane, open up to the ball by pivoting backward. (*2 & 3 in the diagram*) Stay in contact with the offense with the arms by reaching behind your body. Box them out as they cross the lane. Initially it's okay to play rough. Keep the eyes on the ball.

11. On the other side of the lane the defense pivots forward to overplay again. (*3 & 4 in the diagram*)

12. The offense moves up and back on this side of the lane (*4 & 5 in the diagram*) before cutting across to the original side.

13. Offense and defense switch positions. Repeat at least 5 times.

14. Initially the offense goes slow enough, so that the defense gets practice. As the defense improves, the offense moves faster.

Overplaying Across The Lane

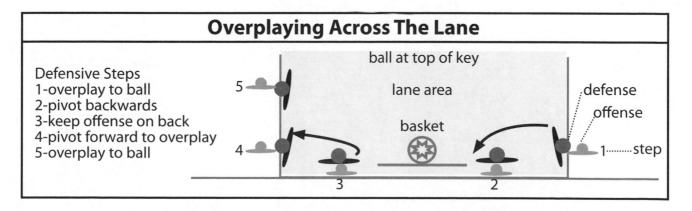

Defensive Steps
1-overplay to ball
2-pivot backwards
3-keep offense on back
4-pivot forward to overplay
5-overplay to ball

ball at top of key

lane area

basket

defense
offense

1········step

5

4

3

2

Key Points

1. The defense watches the ball and plays defense by touch.

2. The defense prevents the offense from stepping into the lane by getting to the spot first.

3. The offense moves slow enough so the defense can get practice.

4. The passer hits the low post player with a pass every once in a while.

How To Practice

Repeat the entire lesson 2 to 3 times.

87 No-See Defense

Brief
The defender stays in the middle of the lane area attempting to prevent a pass to the low-post area.

Why Do This
In a game it's not unusual for a defender to loose his/her coverage. The best way to recover is to immediately move to the middle of the lane. Then, locate the coverage at the first opportune moment—when a pass cannot be thrown into the lane. This lesson shows that a player in the middle of the lane can usually prevent a low post pass, if he/she does not turn around to look for the offense.

Directions
1. An assistant sets up near the free throw line with a ball. The other offensive player sets up in the low post on either side. The defense sets up in the middle of the lane facing the passer. *See the diagram Setup.*

2. The passer tries to hit the low-post player for a pass inside. Pass immediately if the defense turns around to look at the low-post player. The low-post player cuts from one side of the lane to the other. Make sure to count 3 seconds in the lane. *See the diagram Motion Lesson 5.*

Setup

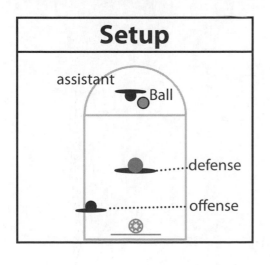

assistant
Ball
defense
offense

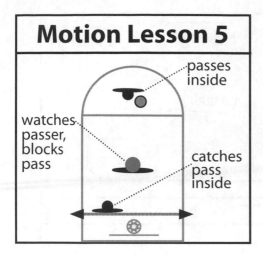

Motion Lesson 5

passes inside

watches passer, blocks pass

catches pass inside

3. The defense keeps his/her eyes on the ball, attempting to block the pass. You can move around, but stay close to the middle of the lane. Do not turn around to find the offense.

4. Run this lesson for 5 to 10 seconds or one pass. The passer can count out loud. Players switch positions after each pass.

5. Repeat 3-8 times.

Key Points

1. The defense does not turn around.

2. The offense moves back and forth across the lane.

How To Practice

This only needs to be practiced once. Don't just lob high passes over the head of a short defender. If players are not matched up equally, then adjust the lesson so the defense has some success if he/she plays correctly.

88 Overplay Cutter

Player's Corner

Parts	1
Type	CORE
Players	2
Assist	YES
Ball	○
Court	🏀
Effort	2-3
Time	5-15

Brief
The defender covers a cutter moving up and then diagonally across the lane.

Why Do This
Overplaying a cutter near the basket is one of the most difficult skills to learn. The defense needs to stay with the cutter, prevent the offense from getting good position, and watch the ball. In this lesson the defense plays a cutter running an figure eight pattern in the lane.

Directions
1. The offense starts in the low-post area. The defense overplays to the ball. The passer, the assistant, is near the top of the key. *See the diagrams Setup and Motion.*

2. The offense moves to the high post, *cut 1 in the diagram Motion*, then cuts from the high post on one side to the low post on the other, *cut 2*. Cut out again along the lane, *cut 3 in the diagram*. Then make another diagonal cut across the lane to the low post, *cut 4 in the diagram*.

3. Look for a pass when cutting.

4. The defense stays ahead of the cutter. The defensive positions, as the offense moves, are *in grey in the diagram Motion*.

> **On Cut 1** - Overplay using body position to prevent a move into the lane. Use the front arm extended and the body to prevent a catch near the lane area.
>
> **On Cut 2** - Intially stand in the path of the cutter. Make the offense go around you. After a few yards, overplay from the other side on the cut in. Maintain contact all across the lane while watching the ball.
>
> **On Cut 3** - Set up overplaying when the offense is in the low post. Overplay to prevent a pass near the lane or a cut into the lane. Block any attempt to cut into the lane by getting to the position first.

Setup

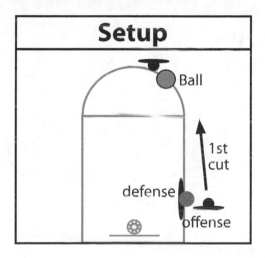

Motion

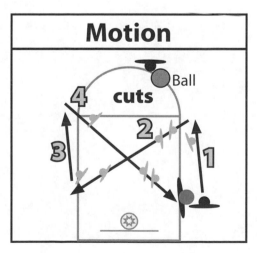

On Cut 4 - Continue to overplay on the cut. Block the path. Make the offense go around you. Overplay on the other side when the offense is just past the mid-lane area. Stop in the path of the cutter. Make contact. Keep eyes on the ball.

5. It's okay initially if the defense is a little rough and not perfect. There is no easy way to describe all the defensive movement. This is a difficult drill for the defense.

6. The offense plays harder as the defense learns how to cover the cutter.

7. Switch positions after each set of cuts.

8. Each player runs the 4 cut circuit 3-5 times.

Key Points

1. The defense watches the ball and plays the cutter by touch.

2. Prevent easy cuts by stepping in front of or beating the cutter to a spot.

3. If any defensive skills are missing, then go back and work on each one individually.

How To Practice

This only needs to be done once or twice.

DEFENSIVE SITUATIONS LESSONS

89 Covering The Shooter
90 Defense On Driver
91 Catch Up
92 Trapping Basics

Each defensive situation in this section is important. Many of these lessons are repeats of pressure shooting lessons with a focus on defense rather than shooting. Lesson 89, Covering The Shooter, works on the arm and body movement for optimum defense without fouling. Lesson 90, Defense On Driver, details how to force the driver from any court position. Lesson 91, Catch Up, shows how to cover a player running in for a basket. Lesson 92, Trapping Basics, teaches the basics of trapping, a technique important in full and half court presses.

89 Covering The Shooter

Player's Corner		
Parts	1	2
Type	CORE	CORE
Players	2	2
Assist	NO	NO
Ball	◯	◯
Court	🏀	🏀
Effort	3	3
Time	5	5

Briefs
In Part 1, the defense covers a shooter close to the basket.

In Part 2, the defense must run to the shooter under the basket before covering.

Why Do This
The key to effectively covering a shooter without fouling involves controlling the movement of the arms and the body. Any attempt to snuff the ball (down the throat of the offense) usually has adverse results. Often, a referee calls a foul when he/she sees flailing arms, even if there is no contact. Even if there is a successful block, the offense can recover the ball and score.

The primary objective of the defense is to alter the shot of the offense and then box out. The offense also gets practice shooting under pressure, like in several of the pressure-shooting lessons.

Part 1 Covering Shooter
Directions
1. The offense starts in the shooting position with the ball overhead, 1-2 feet from the basket. Shoot using the backboard. Don't worry about the shot being blocked. The defense is not allowed

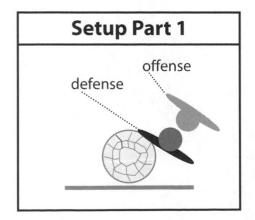

Setup Part 1

offense

defense

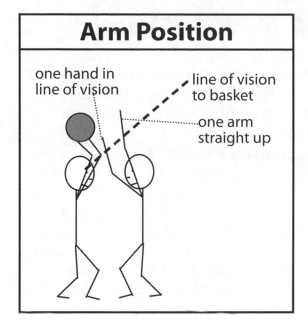

Arm Position

one hand in line of vision

line of vision to basket

one arm straight up

to block the shot. Make this shot. Call any touch a foul. *See the diagrams Setup Part 1 and Arm Position.*

2. The defense sets up directly in front of the offense. Play at 100%, no slacking off. The left arm and hand are fully extended upward, slightly to the right side of a right-handed shooter. Extend the right arm slightly to the left of a lefty.

3. Do not move this arm in any direction, side to side or back and forth. Especially, do not bring the arm downward to snuff the ball. Let the offense shoot the ball into your blocking hand. Altering the shot is just as good as a block. In this lesson, you are not going to block the shot, even if you have to slightly move your arm at the last moment.

4. The other hand should be about 6 inches or more from the shooter's face and in the shooter's line of sight to the basket, which is a little above the eyes. Attempt to obstruct the vision and distract the shooter. Wave your fingers; open and close your hand; any motion can distract the shooter.

5. Use your voice as well. Make funny noises. Yell "Fire; help; yikes, your laces are loose; your underwear is showing," or anything else that might distract the shooter. Do not make any abusive or derogatory statements concerning heritage.

6. After one player shoots, switch roles and repeat.

7. Repeat 5-10 times.

Key Points

1. The defense plays at 100%.

2. The defense puts out a great effort to block the shot, but does not block the shot.

3. The shooter calls any touch a foul.

How To Practice

Do this 3-10 times or till the defense can do it correctly.

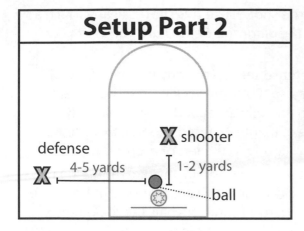

Setup Part 2

defense

X shooter

X 4-5 yards | 1-2 yards

ball

Part 2 Move To Shooter
Directions

1. The offense starts 1-2 yards from the basket. The ball is on the floor near the basket. The defense starts 4-5 yards from the basket. *See the diagram Setup Part 2.*

2. When the offense moves to pick up the ball, the defense runs to play defense. Set up in front of the offense. Put one hand straight up, the other in the line of vision. Make a strong effort to block the shot and impair the vision of the shooter like in the previous lesson. You must first get your body in place, then jump straight up to block the shot. Do not jump into the shooter. Again, do not block the shot.

3. The shooter must make the shot.

4. The defender gets the rebound and places the ball on the floor near the basket, before going to the shooting setup position. The shooter goes to the defensive setup position.

5. Repeat 5-10 times.

6. If you have covered boxing out, instruct the offense to go for the ball even if it goes in, and for the defense to box out.

Key Points

1. The defense plays at 100%.

2. The defense sets up in a position to block the shot with arms extended before jumping to block the shot.

3. The defense jumps straight up, not forward.

4. The defense must make a great effort to block the shot, but does not block the shot.

5. The shooter calls any touch a foul.

How To Practice

Do this 3-5 times or till the defense does it right.

90 Defense On Driver

Setup/Motion

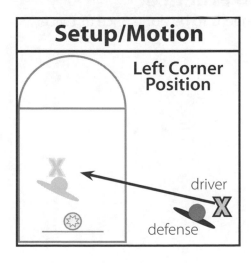

Left Corner Position

driver

defense

Briefs
The defense covers a driver to the basket.

Why Do This
The defense always wants to force an offensive player driving to the basket far away from the basket and toward other defenders. The basic forcing rules are:

(a) force a driver in the center of the court to the side;

(b) force a driver on the side or corner to the center.

In this lesson, the defender is put in the difficult situation of covering a driver who does not have to dribble for this lesson. Dribbling slows down the offense, so the defense will need to work harder to force a player who is not dribbling. This is also beneficial because defenders get practice looking at the driver, not the ball. Defenders watch the midsection of the driver, not reacting to any dribble or ball or body fake.

Directions
1. The offense starts in the far left corner, 10 yards from the basket. *See the diagram Setup/Motion.*

2. The offense sets up to drive to the basket with a ball. No dribbling at any time. You will sprint to the basket.

Force To Endline

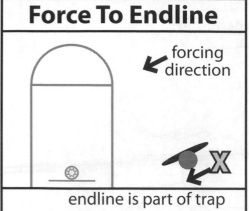

forcing direction

endline is part of trap

Forcing Directions

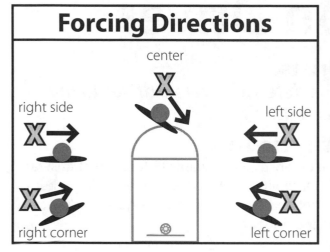

center

right side

left side

right corner

left corner

3. The defense quickly sets up, forcing to the center.

4. When the offense is ready, he/she sprints to the basket. The defense forces to the center and continues to force the driver till both are one yard past the basket. *See the final positions in grey in the diagram Setup/Motion.*

•Another way to set up involves trapping the driver on the endline. This usually does not work well, because a driver only needs 6 inches on the endline side to step by. *See the diagram Force To Endline.*

5. After the drive, offense and defense switch positions.

6. Repeat 3-5 times.

7. After the first few times, the offense just runs to the start position and drives to the basket without waiting for the defense. The defense must set up quickly before the offense.

8. Repeat steps 1-7 starting at the left side position and forcing again to the center. *See the diagram Forcing Directions, which shows all the starting positions.*

9. Repeat steps 1-7 again starting at the center, forcing to the left, and then starting at the right side and right corner positions.

Key Points

1. After the first few times the offense just sets up and goes.

2. The defense must setup before the offense.

3. The defense forces to the center and continues to force till both players are past the basket.

How To Practice

This only needs to be done once or twice.

91 Catch Up

Player's Corner

Parts	1
Type	CORE
Players	2
Assist	YES
Ball	○
Court	🏀
Effort	3
Time	5

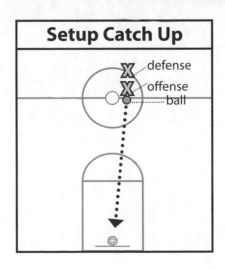

Setup Catch Up

defense
offense
ball

Briefs
The defense tries to catch up to player driving to the basket.

Why Do This
This is a very important hustle drill for the defense. It also teaches not to foul while attempting to stop a player driving to the basket. The last part of the lesson involving the sprint back is great for teaching the transition and defensive readiness. This lesson is a repeat of Lesson 41 which focused on the offense. Make sure to do that lesson first. Focus on the defense in this lesson.

Directions
1. The offense has 5 seconds to take off to the basket from midcourt. Don't wait for the defense. Dribble in for a layup. Make sure to make the layup. The last step must be up or slow. It's even okay to stop and shoot a 1-foot shot. Make the shot. Get the rebound.

2. The defense sets up behind the offense. As soon as the offense moves, the defense attempts to catch up. To catch up you must run 3 feet ahead of the dribbler before stepping in front.

3. You may not reach in from the side or attempt to block the shot unless you run ahead. However, you can just yell and wave your arms. Make sure

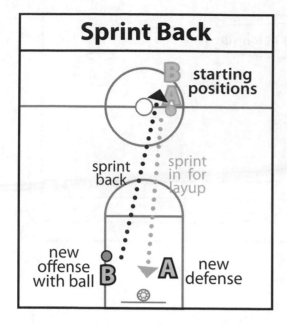

Sprint Back

starting positions

sprint back

sprint in for layup

new offense with ball

new defense

to box out and get the rebound whether or not the shot is made.

4. If the defender does catch up, he/she just forces the offense away from the basket to one side or the other. The offense stops and takes a short shot.

5. Switch roles after each shot.

6. Repeat 5-10 times.

7. To make this more demanding for the defense and more fun, allow the shooter to set up and go without waitng for the defense. *See the diagram Sprint Back.*

In the diagram, A is the initial shooter who just sprinted to the basket; B is the initial defender. When B gets the ball under the boards, he/she sprints back to midcourt without waiting for A. It's okay to dribble.

Set up and go, sprint in for a layup when ready. Do not wait for A, if A is slow to setup. This forces the new defender to sprint back to midcourt with the new shooter.

Key Points

1. The offense does not wait for the defense to be ready. Just take off.

2. The defense must run 3 feet past the offense before playing defense.

3. Do not reach in from the side. It's okay to wave arms or distract the offense.

4. The defense boxes out, even if the shot goes in. The offense always goes for the rebound.

How To Practice

Repeat this 2-5 times.

92 Trapping Basics

Setup For Trap

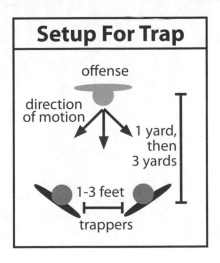

Briefs
Two players trap a slow-moving offensive player.

Why Do This
Trapping uses two defenders to prevent a player from dribbling. Tying up the dribbler, forcing a bad pass, or slowing down the offense are good results.

Trapping is a good strategy against teams that do not pass well. Trapping can be used as a half-court or full-court strategy usually for only part of the game, because eventually the offense will adjust. One problem with the full-court trap is that if the ball goes by the trappers, the defense is vulnerable for an easy shot.

Not allowing the dribbler to actually dribble in these lessons makes things much more difficult and beneficial for the trappers.

Directions
1. The defense initially sets up 1 yard away from the offense, the assistant. One defender forces right, the other forces left. The inside foot of each defender is slightly inside the feet of the offense. Defenders vary the distance between themselves from 1-3 feet to prevent the offense from running through the gap between them. After setting up properly, the trappers move to a distance of 3

yards from the offense. *See the diagram Setup For Trap.*

2. The offense attempts to walk by, through, or around the defense. No running.

3. The defense tap dances and moves with the offense, staying in the same relative position. Defenders must co-ordinate efforts. Block the offense if they try to go through or around. Push the shoulder(s) if the offense gets close. Again, the defense is just reactive; position yourself properly waiting for the offense to run into you.

4. The assistant times the lesson for 15 seconds. Point out defensive problems.

5. Repeat with the defensive players switching positions from force left to force right.

6. Repeat steps 1-5 at least three times.

7. When the defense forces properly, the assistant increases the speed of movement.

Key Points

1. As the offense moves, the defense jump-steps keeping the offense trapped in the same relative position.

2. The faster the assistant can move, the better the lesson.

How To Practice

With the assistant moving slowly this only needs to be practiced 1-3 times. With an assistant going full speed, practice this as much as needed. However, it's better to spend most of your defensive time on defensive movement lessons like Lessons 74-83. This is just an application of a skill already learned.

Part 3
Appendices

A. Table Of Lessons

B. Cool Down

PART 3: APPENDICES

Appendix A: Table Of Lessons

Table Explanation
All table features are discussed in more detail in other sections and are also part of each lesson.

Lesson Number/Name
The lessons are numbered from 1 to 92. Each lesson also has a name.

Lesson Groups
The dark shaded rows going completely across the chart are the groups. The lessons are divided into 23 groups or topics which are not numbered.

Parts
Number of parts to each lesson. This effects all other information because each part has its own characteristics.

Type
There are 3 types of lessons. Core is *core or C*. Advanced is *adv or A*. Optional is *opt or O*. If all the parts for a lesson are the same, then the full or abbreviated word will be used. For lessons with parts that differ, only the first letters will be given. For example, COA means that Part 1 is core, Part 2 is optional, and Part 3 is advanced. If all parts are *core*, then the word *core* will be used.

Players
The minimum number of players needed to perform a lesson. All lessons are designed for either one or two players. For lessons with parts that vary, each part will be given a number. For example, 121, means that Part 1 involves one player, Part 2 two players and Part 3 one player. If all parts are the same, then only one number will be used.

Assist
Indicates if an assistant is needed for the lesson using **yes** or **no**. If parts vary then Y means yes, N means no. For example, YNN means Part 1 needs an assistant, but Parts 2 & 3 do not. If all parts are the same, then only one word will be used.

Ball
Yes means that a ball is needed for this lesson. *No* means that a ball is not needed. YNY means that Part 1 needs a ball, Part 2 does not, and Part 3 does. If all parts are the same, only one word is used.

Court
Yes means you need a court for this lesson or lesson part. *No* means that you don't. YNY means that Part 1 requires a court, Part 2 does not, and Part 3 does. If all parts are the same, only one word is used.

Effort Level
1 = little physical activity, technique-level lesson

2 = moderate activity, practice-level

3 = maximum physical effort involved, game-level

1-2, 3, 1 means that Part 1 involves an effort level of 1-2, Part 2 is 3, and Part 3 is 1. If all parts are the same, only one number is used.

Time
The time gives you an idea of the time in minutes needed to complete all parts of the entire lesson. The first time may take much longer than the 5th time. Older players may need less time than younger ones.

Appendix A

Lesson Number/Name	Parts	Type	Players	Assist	Ball	Court	Effort	Time
Ball Handling Lessons								
1 Touch	1	core	1	yes	yes	no	1	3
2 Hands Ready	1	core	1	no	yes	no	1	3
3 Grab Ball	4	core	2	no	yes	no	2-3	20
4 Go For Ball	3	core	2	yes	yes	no	3	9
5 Prevent Tie Ups/Fouls	3	COA	2	no	yes	no	3	9-15
Pivoting Lessons								
6 Start Pivoting	2	core	1	no	no	no	1,1-2	6-10
7 Jab-Step	2	core	1	no	yes	no	1-2	6-10
8 Ball Fake	2	core	1	no	yes	no	1-2	6-10
9 Crossover Step	2	core	1	no	yes	no	1-2	6-10
10 Pivot Routines	3	core	1	no	yes	no	1-2	15-20
11 Pivot With Defense	2	A	2	YN	yes	no	3	10
Wrist Work Lessons								
12 Loosen & Flick	3	core	1	no	no	no	1	15
13 Shoot Pass Dribble	3	core	1	no	no	no	1	15
Dribbling Lessons								
14 Dribble Basics	3	core	1	no	NNY	no	1	15
15 Dribble Twist	4	CCCO	2221	no	yes	no	2	20
16 Dribble Move	4	no	2	no	yes	no	2	20
17 Protect Ball	2	CO	2	no	yes	no	3	10-20
Layups Lessons								
18 No-Step Layup	2	core	1	yes	yes	NY	1,1-2	10
19 One-Step Layup	2	core	1	no	yes	yes	2	10
20 Speed Layup	1	core	1	yes	yes	yes	3	5
Continuous Motion Lessons								
21 Dribble Circuit	1	opt	1	no	yes	yes	2	5-20
22 Pass Circuit	1	opt	2	no	yes	yes	2	5-20
23 Weave Circuit	1	core	2	no	yes	yes	2	5-20

Lesson Number/Name	Parts	Type	Players	Assist	Ball	Court	Effort	Time
Shot Technique Lessons								
24 Touch Two	1	core	1	no	yes	no	1	3
25 Wrist Work	3	core	1	no	no	no	1	3
26 Body Alignment	1	core	1	yes	yes	no	1	5-15
27 Extension	3	core	1	NNY	yes	NNY	121	9-15
28 1-Foot Shot	3	CCO	1	no	yes	yes	122	15
Moves Lessons								
29 Jab Fake Moves	2	opt	1	yes	yes	yes	2	10-20
30 Pivot Moves	2	opt	1	no	yes	yes	2	10-20
31 Ball Fake Moves	2	adv	1	no	yes	yes	2	10-20
Hook Shot Lessons								
32 Regular Hook	1	adv	1	yes	yes	yes	1-2	5-20
33 Step Hook	2	adv	1	no	yes	yes	1-2	10-20
34 Jump Hook	2	AO	1	YN	yes	yes	1-2	10-30
35 Underneath Hooks	1	adv	1	no	yes	yes	2	5-25
Practice Shooting Lessons								
36 Driving To The Basket	4	core	1	no	yes	yes	2	20
37 Near To Far	1	core	1	no	yes	yes	2	5-15
38 Practice Shoot	3	CCO	1	no	yes	yes	2	15-45
Pressure Shot Lessons								
39 Quick Shot	3	CCO	122	yes	yes	yes	3	15
40 Run Shoot	3	CCO	122	yes	yes	yes	3	15
41 Catch Up	1	core	2	yes	yes	yes	3	5
42 Defense In Face	1	core	2	yes	yes	yes	3	5
43 Fouled Shooting	1	core	1	yes	yes	yes	3	5
Free Throws Lessons								
44 Free-Throw Technique	1	core	1	no	yes	no	2	5-15
45 Free-Throw Shot	3	CCO	1	nyy	yes	yes	2	15

Lesson Number/Name	Parts	Type	Players	Assist	Ball	Court	Effort	Time
Passing Lessons								
46 Passing Technique	3	core	112	no	YNY	no	112	15
47 Overhead Pass	1	core	2	no	yes	no	2	5-10
48 Fake Pass	1	core	2	yes	yes	no	2	5-15
49 Side Pass	1	core	2	no	yes	no	2	5-15
50 Bounce Pass	1	core	2	no	yes	no	2	5-15
51 Back Pass	1	core	2	no	yes	no	2	5-15
52 Baseball Pass	1	core	2	yes	yes	no	2	10
Catch Cut Lessons								
53 Basic Catching	2	core	1	no	NY	no	1	10-40
54 Catching on the Move	2	core	1	yes	yes	no	2	10-15
55 Catching Bad Passes	1	core	1	yes	yes	no	2-3	5
56 Flash To Ball	2	core	1	NY	yes	yes	1,1-2	10-20
57 Loose Ball Drill	2	core	2	yes	yes	NY	3	10
TLC Skills Lessons								
58 Cut Fake Technique	4	core	1	yes	yes	no	2	15
59 Timing	3	core	2	yes	yes	NNY	2	15-30
60 Communication	2	core	2	yes	yes	no	2	6-10
61 Pass Off Dribble	2	opt	2	no	yes	yes	2	10-20
Play Transition Lessons								
62 Play 1	2	opt	2	yes	yes	yes	2	10-30
63 Play 2	1	opt	2	no	yes	yes	2	5-15
64 Play 3	1	opt	2	no	yes	yes	2	5-15
65 In & Out Pattern	1	opt	2	no	yes	yes	2	5-15
Rebound Box Out Lessons								
66 Rebound Grab	1	core	2	no	yes	no	2	5
67 Watch The Ball	1	core	1	yes	yes	yes	2	3-5
68 Ready Position	1	core	1	yes	no	no	2	3
69 Positioning	1	core	2	yes	yes	yes	3	5
70 Block and Box	2	core	2	no	no	no	1-3	10
71 Box Out	2	core	2	yes	yes	yes	2-3	10-30

Lesson Number/Name	Parts	Type	Players	Assist	Ball	Court	Effort	Time
Screening Lessons								
72 Setting A Screen	1	adv	2	no	no	yes	2	5-10
73 Using A Screen	2	adv	2	no	NY	yes	2	10-25
Defense Basics Lessons								
74 Defensive Position	1	core	1	yes	no	no	2	5-10
75 Jump-Steps	1	core	1	yes	no	no	2	5-10
76 Defensive Runs	1	core	1	yes	no	no	1-3	5-20
77 Front	1	core	2	yes	no	yes	2-3	5
78 Go After Ball	2	core	2	yes	yes	no	3	10
79 Mirror	1	opt	2	no	no	no	2-3	3
On-Ball Defense Lessons								
80 Forcing	1	core	1	yes	no	no	1-2	5-20
81 Walk/Run Force	1	core	2	no	no	no	2	5-15
82 3-Yard Force	1	core	2	yes	no	no	3	5
Off-Ball Defense Lessons								
83 Overplay Basics	1	core	1	yes	yes	yes	1-2	10-20
84 Move & Overplay	2	core	2	yes	no	no	2	10-30
85 Step Around	1	core	2	yes	no	yes	2	10-20
86 Overplay Low Post	1	core	2	yes	yes	yes	2-3	10-25
87 No-See Defense	1	core	2	yes	yes	yes	3	5
88 Overplay Cutter	1	core	2	yes	yes	no	2-3	5-15
Defensive Situations Lessons								
89 Covering The Shooter	2	core	2	no	yes	yes	3	10
90 Defense On Driver	1	core	2	no	yes	yes	3	10
91 Catch Up	1	core	2	yes	yes	yes	3	5
92 Trapping Basics	1	opt	2	yes	no	no	2	5-15

PART 3: APPENDICES

Appendix B: Cool Down

This is a cool down with a few strengthening exercises. Perform the exercises gently, using steady pressure–no jerky or forced movements that can cause injury. The goal is to gradually extend the range of muscle movement. Inhale during the first part of an exercise, like a sit-up, and exhale when lowering to the original position. Joe Fareira, a veteran track coach from the Philadelphia area, assisted me in developing this cool down.

Two sets of muscle groups are mentioned often in the exercises. The hamstrings are located at the back of the thigh. The quadriceps are located at the front outside of each thigh.

# Name	Directions	Diagram
1 Hurdler's Stretch	Start this common runners' stretch sitting on the floor with both feet straight out in front of you, knees straight. Bend the right thigh back so that it makes an L with the other foot. This may be very difficult, so instruct players to go only as far as comfortable. Bend the calf toward the body. See the Diagram. Bend forward at the waist as far as possible. Hold the ankle or the farthest part on the leg that can be reached for 10 seconds. This stretches the hamstrings. Lay backward as far as possible from this same position for 10 seconds to stretch the quadriceps. Repeat this with the right leg forward.	
2 Feet overhead	Lie down with the back on the floor. Bring the legs straight up together and back over the head. Try to touch the floor with your toes. Hold this position for 10 seconds. See diagram. Lower the legs slowly to the floor. This exercise strengthens the lower back.	
3 Sit-Ups	Do 10 sit-ups slowly with the legs bent. Inhale as you count to 4 on the roll up and exhale counting to 4 as you roll down. Have a partner hold the feet down if there is nothing to put their feet under. This strengthens the mid-section and lower back.	
4 Back-Ups	Lie on the stomach, arms behind the back. Bring the chest and head upwards. Inhale, counting to 4 on the way up, and then exhale, counting again to 4 on the way down. Do 5 slowly. This strengthens the stomach area.	
5 Back stretch	Lie on stomach. Bend calves up and extend arms behind back to grab feet. Pull for 10 seconds. Repeat. This stretches the back, arms and other parts of the body.	

# Name	Directions	Diagram
6 Twister	Standing up with hands behind head, slowly rotate downward to the left. At the halfway point the head is between the legs as close to the ground as possible. Continue rotating upward to the right to the original position. Keep the legs in one position while rotating; if your legs are straight, keep them straight, if bent, keep them bent. Count to 6 or 8 on each rotation. Repeat, rotating in the opposite direction. Do 3 times.	
7 Toe Touches (3)	(1) With the feet together, bend from the waist and touch your toes. Hold for 10 seconds. (2) Repeat this with the feet far apart. This time hold the left foot with both hands for 10 seconds. Repeat, holding the right foot. (3) For a third stretch, crisscross the feet first one way, then the other. The back foot is stretched in this exercise. These stretch all muscles up to the hip.	together straddled crossed
8 Push up	Start on the knees and walk with the hands to a push up position. Do a push up and walk back. Repeat 3 times	
9 Windmills	From a standing position rotate both arms forward (clockwise), making a circle with the hands. Repeat 10 times. Rotate the arms 10 times in the opposite direction.	
10 Head Rotations	Rotate the head from left to down to right to back. Count to 6 on each rotation. Repeat 3 times. This exercise relieves tension.	
11 Hamstring Stretch	Place the heel of one foot forward on a raised object 3 feet off the ground. Lean forward, keeping the leg straight. Grab ankle and hold for 5-10 seconds. Repeat, raising the other foot. Use a partner to hold the foot if no objects are around. Repeat again.	
12 Quadriceps Stretch	Stand near a wall or object you can touch for balance. Raise one foot behind and grab it with the same side arm. Lift gently. Hold for 5-10 seconds and then repeat, using the other foot and arm. Repeat again.	

# Name	Directions	Diagram
13 Wall Leans (3)	(1) With feet 1 yard from the wall, lean toward the wall, keeping the heels on the floor and the legs straight. Hold for 5-10 seconds. This stretches the Achilles tendon and the calf. (2) Repeat this with your toes on a 3-inch-high piece of wood or other object. You want the heels to be lower than the toes. Hold for 10 seconds. (3) Now step forward with one foot and raise the other off the ground. Hold for 10 seconds and repeat with the other foot. This also stretches the Achilles tendon and the calf.	

PART 3: APPENDICES

INDEX

M

major section group 57
managers 133
Maravich, Pete 101
misconceptions 25—26
  drills 25
missed shots 191, 195
moves 43, 79, 91
  faking 159—163
  scoring 157—166, 167—178
myths 26—28. *See also* **misconceptions**

N

nose shooters. *See* **shooters: nose shooters**
novices 43, 168, 192. *See also* **inexperienced players**

O

off-ball
  defense 309—324
off-ball defense 52
offense
  half-court 47
  off-ball players 242
  pressure 48
offensive skills 26, 39—43, 245
  keys 53
older players. *See* **experienced players**
on-ball defense 52
one-foot shot 137, 153
opposite hand 158, 160, 168, 178
opposite hand layup 42, 125, 134
opposite pivot foot 168
Overbrook High School 18—19
overplay 46

P

pass
  chest 54
pass-response fake 244, 251. *See* **faking**
passing 42, 226
  behind the back 137
  chest pass 101, 213, 251
  hand-off 137
  hook pass 137
  overhead pass 218—221
  side back pass 224—225
  technique 214—216
  touch 215—216
  types 137
  using arms 101
  while dribbling 251—252
  wrists 105, 106—107, 215—216

pass fake 166
pass follow 33
Philadelphia SPHAAs 18
picking. *See* **screening**
pick & roll. *See* **screen & roll**
pivoting 37, 78, 79—100, 158, 228
  favorite-foot 80
  game level 98—100
  left & right foot 229
  routines 94—96
pivot fake 164
pivot point 82
positional play 23
Practice Planning Guide. *See also* **planning practice**
press 227
pressure
  defense 48
  full-court 48
  offense 48
pros 24, 125, 150, 158, 168. *See also* **experienced players**
protecting the ball
  dribbling 122—124
pump fake 165

Q

quadriceps 343
quick release 168

R

reading the defense 38. *See also* **looking**
ready position
  hands 68
  rebounding 68
rebounding 43, 65, 74, 267—280
  keys 54
  ready position 68
referees 326
repetition 28, 50, 179, 209
  plays 254

S

scoring moves. *See* **moves: scoring**
screening 46
screen & roll 286
shooting 42. *See also* **free throw**
  arming the ball 101, 208
  backspin 144
  body alignment 147—149
  experienced players 154
  extension 150—152, 153
  fadaways 154
  free throws 205—212

We have 14 DVDs that detail almost every lesson in the book. Purchase them individually or buy the sets below.

Videos are DVD-R. Each video has 30 additional minutes of previews. Discounts available for sets.

1. Fundamentals I - Covers all individual skills in order in the bible. 48 min

2. Fundamentals II - Covers all team skills in the bible including plays. 42 min

3. Planning Practice I - Goes through a planned practice giving options. 41 min

4. Planning Practice II - Forty ways to get more out of practice and players. 41 min

5. Shooting I - Techniques that yield rapid and permanent improvement. 35 minutes

6. Shooting II - The basic shots as well as moves and sensible ways to practice. 47 min

7. Shooting III - Players learn to shoot as well in a game as they do in practice. 43 min

8. Dribbling - Anyone can be a good dribbler. These methods show how. 36 min

9. Defense I - Teaches defense keys and basics for first graders or pros. 39 min

10. Defense II - Off ball defense, help out, picks, box out,+ many defensive situations. 41 min

11. Defense III - Effective coordinated team defense in every situation. 42 min

12. Offense I - Offense starts with the skills in this video including passing, catching, faking, and pivoting. 51 min

13. Offense II - TLC- The complex skills of timing, looking, and communication, TLC, make an offense successful. 49 min

14. Offense III - Team offense includes plays, patterns of movement, transitions, out-of-bound plays and offense against a press. 50 min

Call 800-979-8642 or visit **mrbasketball.net** for more information.

Video Sets
The Shooting/Dribbling Set: 5-8
The key to shooting is shooting technique, not aim. That's why zillions of repetitions yield little results. Video 5 shows how to develop and maintain shooting technique. Video 6 shows how to practice without destroying technique as well as presents a special free throw technique. Video 7 deals with shooting under game-like pressure. Video 8 makes any player a good dribbler.

The Defense Set: 9-11
The key to defense is defensive footwork and conditioning. Video 9 deals with the two major defensive steps, defensive position, and on-ball coverage. Video 10 deals with off-ball coverage which is the key to team defense. Several 2-on-1, 2-on-2, and 1-on-2 situations are also covered including the trap. Video 11 deals with team defense including person-to-person, zone, and half and full-court traps.

The Offense Set: 12-14
The key to offense is reacting to the defense, not rehearsed plays. An effective offense can be taught in 15 minutes to players with offensive skills. Video 12 deals with passing, catching, cutting, and faking skills. Video 13 covers TLC (timing, looking, & communication) skills. Video 14 covers basic and advanced team offensive patterns.

The Starter Set: 5,8,9,12
The starter set gets you started on every key skill. The set includes these videos: Shooting 1, DVD 1; Dribbling, DVD 8; Defense 1, DVD 9; and Offense 1, DVD 12.

The Basic Set: 1-4
The basic set shows a little of everything, but videos 5-14 more fully explain each drill. Video 1 covers each individual skill. Video 2 covers all team skills. Video 3 works through a practice using the planning guide. Video 4 presents 40 ways to get more out of each practice.